Motor City Nightmare:

Going Gonzo With

TED NUGENT

Martin Popoff

First published as Epic Ted Nugent in Canada in 2012
This revised edition published 2017 by Wymer Publishing
Bedford, England
www.wymerpublishing.co.uk
Tel: 01234 326691
Wymer Publishing is a trading name of Wymer (UK) Ltd

ISBN 978-1-908724-59-5

Edited by Jerry Bloom.

Every effort has been made to trace the copyright holders of the
photographs in this book but some were unreachable. We would
be grateful if the photographers concerned would contact us.

Front and back cover images © Richard Galbraith.

Printed and bound by
Clays, Bungay, England

A catalogue record for this book is available from the British Library.

Cover design by Eduardo Rodriguez & Andy Francis.

Motor City Nightmare:

Going Gonzo With

TED NUGENT

Martin Popoff

WP
WYMER
PUBLISHING
Bedford, England

Contents

Preface

Welcome to the 2017 edition of my tome on Deadly Tedly. Now, I'm still not there yet, mostly by choice, this idea of finding and shaping the story in these rock biogs that I do, something I learned from working on the Rush movie and 11 episodes of *Metal Evolution*. No, my plan remains to marble in my own thoughts, in measured doses, in the right place through a linear take and tale, in with a whole heap of the story coming from the guys involved, largely unedited or tightened. This is because I trust you to enjoy an academic, complete examination the way I do and not require too urgently to be "entertained."

But man, something of a story emerged from this fond stroll through Ted's world, and that's this weird recurring situation where Ted swears up and down how black and soulful and rhythm and blues his music is. And yet me and everybody I know (granted, angry metalheads all) consider his rhythm sections completely, as he says of metal others, "Caucasian," and his best songs and the riffs that built them, pretty darn heavy metal, or for you young 'uns, proto metal, heavy metal for their day.

It's all very weird, with Ted also not lining up with his diehard fans in the figuring which productions are weak and which are strong, on top of which of his songs are the classics, and how *Bound And Gagged* and *Fred Bear* and *Lovejacker* and all this Foghat rock... not his finest moments. Ted, please, I beg of you, *Fred Bear*... I understand it's all about the sentiment and the story, but the music is barely even there, barely written.

Not raggin' on Ted, it's just that I wish he'd cop to how metal his magic moments are, and pretty squared-off, rigidly 4/4, not that funky or greasy. I mean, sure, he is expected to like *Cat Scratch Fever* and the freedom (don't get me started) that it's afforded him, but that is white rock, maybe a little feint toward boogie in the verse, but pure non-funk come chorus time. No?

Am I dwelling? Well, my chip persists because of all this putting down of *State Of Shock* and *Scream Dream*, when, dammit all if they aren't practically my most beloved and valued from the catalogue. That is until *Craveman*, *Love Grenade* and *Shut Up & Jam!* which are so damn potent, it's why I wrote this thick tree of a tome to include them and didn't resign myself to focusing on a longer, harder look at the '70s, or conversely just the Epic records, which tick over into 1981.

Blah blah blah, many of you know this story, but here's actually the best place to relate it. As I told Mark Cicchini, who helped me invaluably by kindly supplying his research archive to plunder and dig under, I wanted to write this book because Ted makes me happy. By the way, that first long talk with Mark about Ted... he's a buddy for life now 'cos of that and I ain't even met him in person yet. I was almost crying with our shared Ted-ness. But yeah, this music of his, no matter what the era, it puts a smile on my face, cheers me up, more so lifts me up, because of the example of living that bleeds through the man's well-meaning rantings and ravings. Why it does that, beyond the life force flyin' through the lyrics, is that I then recall the handful of interviews and meetings I've had with him and more importantly—and here comes the reminiscing—the fact that my first concert ever in a big city was Ted, Be Bop Deluxe and Rex, on the *Free For All* tour in Spokane, Washington.

Story is, my dad took me, my brother and two of my buddies, John Polidano and Bobby Davidson, to the show. We were 13 and a little wary (but mostly stoked) by the funny-smelling smoke in the air, the crazy teenage hoodlums everywhere, people throwing up - the cavernous darkness of the B-city hockey barn in which these Canucks did not belong. Memories include the big red self-titled Rex album display in the local hippie record store the day before. I bought the album there, I believe, not having it ahead of time (already had Free For All), and when I got it home, was pleased to hear that it was essentially a cross between a Kiss, Aerosmith and Ted. Years later, I've written up the story of both their albums (before Rex became Rex Smith) in my *Ye Olde Metal* book series. Drummer Mike Ratti very kindly sent his two custom-designed bass drum heads, which are on the wall in my office. All I remember of them live was Rex in a red jumpsuit doing flips on stage, and that the music was solid American '70s hard rock. Be Bop Deluxe... vaguely remember the suits but not much more.

I connected with a soul brother in Ben Upham who shot that show. What's more, it turns out he worked at the very Eucalyptus Records that was part of our magic circuit when we got to Spokane to buy records (raised in Trail, two hours and 15 minutes straight north into Canada). Eucalyptus was one of those funky, hippie *chains* like a Peaches, this one on Division being bright and airy, and like the indie stores, prone to these big splashy displays when an album would come out. As usual, I must name-check along with Eucalyptus, Strawberry Jams and Magic Mushrooms, which is where the Rex display was lovingly crafted (I believe there was a *Free For All* display as well).

Ben and I recently reminisced. He doesn't remember much of the show other than how impressed he was with Be Bop Deluxe, and some shenanigans him and his buds got up to on a hill after the show, as midnight greeted his birthday kinda high. As I told him, the one thing I remember most is, early on a twinned pyro blast, timed with Ted jumping off the riser and his white light bulb autograph logo turning on for the first time behind the band. For a split second I worried about blindness and deafness. There, that's about the whole story.

Did you know Ted can be pretty outspoken on things outside of music? I thought you did. Well, there ain't much of that in this book. One reason is for logic's sake I had to stick somewhat to topic, to story, and all his political stuff and hunting and gun stuff and freedom-fighting is way off that topic. As I say somewhere in here, rock 'n' roll is about the least outdoors pursuit thing there is, and so Ted, quite fascinatingly, is *really* an outdoors guy in the rest of his life.

Also, however, I really wanted this to be a book that was somewhere around at least 90% music, because Ted himself has written about the other stuff, which you can also learn about in interviews and Ted's own journalistic writings. One of the challenges we joke about amongst us rock fans who get to talk to our heroes occasionally, when you're talking to Ted, like most big stars, the clock is ticking. It's pretty much up to you what road you wanna go down with him. Just be prepared to hang up the phone and realize you didn't get anything on the other roads, because the one you took each other down was your half hour ride right there.

Before I forget, just in case you haven't figured it out, I wanted to re-state why this book focuses on Ted's years with Epic Records. I wanted to present some level of narrative thrust, of story. So, breaking it down, the trunk of the book is every album Ted recorded for Epic Records, presented in stand-alone chapters. The Amboy Dukes get a big chapter and at the end, I speak through the eerie yet near perfect geometry of the fact that everything for Atlantic is/was a downer—that's one chapter, the bad news. Then the final two chapters envelope the happy ending, the Deadly Tedinator triumphs of *Craveman* and *Love Grenade*, the former issued on Spitfire, the latter on Eagle, which are related companies, and then *Shut Up & Jam!* on Frontiers.

Okay, last thought, and more a reiteration. I love it when my rock heroes see the light, return from having screwed up so bad, and made what can be debated in earnest as the best records of their whole damn career. Bands in that camp for me right now—and not all have pooched it as bad as Ted sort of did from *Nugent* through *Spirit Of The Wild*... Deep Purple, Uriah Heep, Motörhead, Cheap Trick, ZZ Top, Van Halen even Rush. But Ted? Man, I shoulda called this book, "GI Joe, lookin' for a firefight!" because that's a white-hot magic second or two that righteously represents so many, heavy, grinding, groovy hard rocking moments all over Ted's last three records. What kills me is that the next line is, "Everywhere I go I try and make things right." That's Ted and you gotta love him for it. Hell, that's anybody that is so political—on the left or on the right. They have a hobby that is ultimately altruistic, except none of them can orate the hell out of a position the way Ted can, hard as nails, but kinda with a wink of an eye that says that what you've just heard is a gorgeously hurried and harried piece of piss and poetry, 'cos who has time for talking when there's so much doing to be done?

Martin Popoff
martinp@inforamp.net | www.martinpopoff.com

The Amboy Dukes
"Ted was beyond hope"

The Whackmaster, The Tedinator, Deadly Tedly… the man that would become a super-hero for guns and what to do with them began life much like any wholesome Midwest kid stung by the bee of garage rock. Dad, namely Warren Henry Nugent, was an army staff sergeant, and the family was Catholic. Neither of those social contours meant much to Ted, outside of guns and grounding, and both would chafe hard against the persona Ted would build for himself in the late '60s as guitar-howlin' hippie, granted hippie with a strange hippie-denigrating streak.

Born in Detroit on 13th December 1948, Ted grew up with dad, mother Marion, a couple of brothers and a sister before the family moved to Palatine, Illinois when Ted was 16. Here fired up his third and most famous under-rated garage band The Amboy Dukes while living in the Chicago area. Before The Amboy Dukes, however, when the family was still in Detroit, was The Royal High Boys (named for a greaser shirt style called the High Boy) and most significantly Ted's second band, The Lourds with Ted getting a taste of the spotlight at 14 with the latter while sharing the stage at Cobo Hall with the Beau Brummells, Martha And The Vandellas and The Supremes. When school was over for the day and The Lourds took over, Ted found himself with an outfit that "played the nastiest Beatles and a lot of Stones. That was it for me. Kick in the mouth rhythm 'n' blues. I dug the way those English cats took our music and tore it apart."

"Being such a young age, if somebody slaps a football in your hand, you'd probably go out and play football," muses Ted, beginning us on our tale at the tender Tedly age of seven. "They put a guitar in my hand and I jumped on that. But I don't think that really has a bearing on why it continued.

I mean, once I saw Elvis on TV, Ted was beyond hope. Then the Stones and the Beatles were on TV and it was beyond pity. I had no hope whatsoever. I took a few lessons and was upset with the discipline involved, so I quit. I took a total of maybe two years of lessons, taught me the names of the strings, how to hold my plectrum and the basic boogie-woogie chords."

Once in Chicago, and having transitioned to the Amboy Dukes, the band found themselves playing their first gigs at The Cellar in Arlington Heights where Ted was enrolled at St. Viator High School. The Cellar, an actual below-ground venue and later a warehouse, was in operation from 1964 to 1970. Besides Ted and his Rolling Stones-lookalike crew, the venue featured as house band Shadows Of Knight (to distinguish from the more famous English Shadows), as well as H.P. Lovecraft, The Huns, The Other Half and Little Boy Blues, providing a hotbed of a scene in which Ted energetically would learn to compete.

Too cool for school was Ted, who bristles at his short tenure at St. Viator. "They're the ones that taught me how to deal with the ultimate bullshit. It was dehumanizing. There was one format, one well-defined outline for everybody. An inch of skin around the ears, your pants can't be less than 14 inches at the bottom. I'm trying to conceive of how this is important. What's this thing of skin going to do for me? Baggy pants—you do not steal cars in baggy pants? Give me a break! So it was a great lesson."

After recounting to *Circus'* Robert Duncan all manner of nightmare scenarios at his Catholic high school, Ted provided some detailed background explanation with respect to the transition from The Lourds in Detroit to the Amboy Dukes in Illinois.

"This all happened when I had just moved to Chicago, and when I'd moved there, I'd just gone through a catastrophic adventure of my life. Which consisted of having the hottest band in the whole Detroit area, who were ready to break nationally, and having my folks make me move to Chicago. I'd just turned 16 and I destroyed $30,000 worth of moving vans. Then I decided to do my parents bidding. I shaved my hair off and I decided I'd do whatever they wanted, but I was gonna rock and I was gonna roll. If they wanted me to stay home, I'd live at home; I'd go to the school of their choice; I'd wear my hair the way they wanted; I'd wear the clothes they wanted me to wear, as these were all big conflicts in my life: my hair, my clothes, my hours, my style. I went, 'I'll do all these things, but mom, dad, I will own guitars, and I will be practicing, I will have a rock 'n' roll band, and when I graduate from school—Bye! You will not see son number two ever again. Unless you change. 'Cause I ain't changing. But now I'll do your bidding.' From that moment on I lived in my bedroom and I practiced with a vengeance."

Ted would not let his parents forget their strictures. "Oh absolutely. When I graduated and I split, the next time they saw me, I was driving a limousine, new suits, *Journey To The Center Of The Mind* on the charts, and I went, 'Yeah, mom and dad, you were wrong. Let me hear it. I want an apology and I want you to say, I was wrong. Let me hear it.' They cried, the whole shot. I didn't cry. I went, 'Thank you.' And I said, 'I love you. You're my parents. I've always love you. But I'm a-goin' this a-way.' My dad was still against it and he said, 'But you can't cut your hair?' I went, 'Quit!'"

Offering some elaboration on the moving van story, Ted told journalist Drew Abrams, "If you wanna go right back to conception, I started playing when I was just about nine or so. I had a band when I was as young as 11. Whenever it was a sock hop or some Bar Mitzvah, I played it. Then when I was 14, I had a band called The Lourds and we were literally creating new assholes hither and yon for people. I was the youngest guy in the band and I had bleached blonde hair combed down like a Beach Boy. We were sellin' out concerts right and left. I was watchin' the fuckin' Stones on Ed Sullivan and saying, 'Yeah, I'm gonna be on your show, you prick!' All of a sudden my parents moved to Chicago. The night before I moved the whole band went to the Allied Moving Van parking lot. We destroyed $30,000 worth of trucks but we got caught and they got new trucks and we moved to Chicago anyhow. So they made me shave my head. I owed my dad about three grand in insurance money for destroying those trucks so I went to work in a steel plant to pay off my debt. I went to an all-boys Catholic school. I taught guitar. This was right when the Shadows Of Knight were the big thing in the North Chicago area, and Billy Lee And The Rivieras were just changing their name to Mitch Ryder And The Detroit Wheels. I was goin' 'C'mon, Detroiters, show them fuckers what rock is what!' *Jenny Take A Ride* came out and my heart was goin' 'Whom, whom!' and I was diggin' it!"

"Finally, I found the right musicians to start the band of escapism, the band to take me beyondo, extremo, escapo, wayo outo and I called it The Amboy Dukes, because there was an Amboy Dukes in Detroit back when I had been in Detroit who had disbanded. I didn't know what the name meant or anything but I liked the sound of it, so I used it in Chicago. Immediately I took the first three Stones albums and we learned all the Stones' songs, all the Yardbirds' songs and we went in and with in a year we had completely taken over the club circuit—took it over!"

So to clarify and expand with respect to the transition, The Royal High Boys feature a very young Mr. Nugent at around 12 to 13 years old along with drummer Tom Noel, first as a duo, the band then adding second guitarist John Finley. The Lourds takes us from Ted as a 13-year-old through about 15, still in Detroit, in '61 through '64, the year in which the band whacked out 60 other Detroit bands in a battle of the bands, playing covers of *High Heeled Sneakers* and *Shake A Tail Feather*, Ted jumping up on the judges table to perform his guitar solo. Winning this contest is what leads to the life-changing Cobo Hall slot in 1965, although the band's earliest gigs were at Benedictine High School and the Walled Lake Casino. The Lourds had a couple of lineups, closing out their run consisting of Ted, John Finley, Pete Primm, Jim Butler and vocalist John Drake.

The move to Chicago happens in the summer of 1965, when Ted is 16. Ted's name-usurped version of The Amboy Dukes begins life in Chicago right then, the first lineup consisting of guitarists Gary Hicks and Ted, bassist Dick Treat, drummer Gail Uptadale, and vocalist Bob Lehnert, who is soon to be replaced by a returning John Drake. Inside of two years, just after his graduation from high school, Ted's moves back to Detroit on his own, or to clarify, without his family, but with The Amboy Dukes, who eventually set up in a band house.

"I was already starting to mount the amplifiers up and we were getting' kicked out of places for bein' too loud which was great," continues Ted. "Then all of a sudden the Shadows got *Gloria*, and they left the area and we became the top dogs, but we were way too high energy for the Chicago area, way too! They wanted R&B. I was fuckin' jackin' my guitar off, screamin', playin' with my teeth, throwin' it up in the air, smackin' it and these kids were petrified. They didn't know what to think of all this. So I took me back to Detroit after graduating from this all-boys Catholic academy and we took over Detroit! Took it over! The MC5, the SRC, the Rationals, oh, we took it right out from under them! I mean, Baby Please Don't Go, guitars screamin', fuckin' amps howlin' like never before! Forget it! The Who had nothing on us as far as destroyin' stuff! We'd reach out into the first row, bring people on stage, smack 'em and send 'em back! I mean, we were just doin' everything! Just goin'! I made sure we had more amps, we were louder; I mean, I didn't care about taste, there was no room for taste, no one in my band was allowed to be tasteful, man – you had to be ridiculous! There was no control; it was just out and out blatant destructo rock!"

"I went after my success with a vengeance," Ted told *Rolling Stone*. "I wanted to prove to my parents that what I had in mind was good, proper and right. My father was over-strict. He was strict to the point of silliness. 'Because I said so' is not a reason. Silly things, like how to eat your dinner: beans first, then meat, potatoes, salad. One glass of milk all day. In the morning there were special juice glasses and only one glass of juice. Now what the fuck is that supposed to mean? Sure we were on a budget. But that's insipid. He was in the phone company and then he had a salesman's business, travelled a lot. I'm sure he did all these things because he loved us and he was out there in our best interest. He was from the old school of discipline for discipline's sake, which I disagree with totally. He was a staff sergeant at the age of 19 in the army, and he maintained that approach throughout our lives."

"I drank like a pig in junior high, just to be obnoxious," reveals Ted, sure to raise some eyebrows given his decades-deep sermons on the evils of the sauce. "That's when I invented the Flyin' Lip Lock—it's an old Detroit dance—and also the Big D Barbecue Bone Lick. That's when we'd go to the sock hops and we'd just chug an entire fifth of Jack Daniels or Old Grand Dad or Southern Comfort or something and we'd just get—I was only 14— we would just get wounded. I would go flyin' across the fuckin' floors, chompin' on chicks' ankles. The ones who would cooperate, we'd give 'em the ankle rotation, where the chicks would get on your nose, they'd hold their ankles, and you'd spin 'em around. When smoke comes out of their anuses, you know you've accomplished something!"

"I smoked a lot of dope with the MC5 in 1967, and everybody would be flopping around like gaffed bonitos on a sunlit beach and I would feel nothing. Then I realized I didn't need to drink this stuff that gives me a horrible stomachache and smells like rhino cum to make me get wild. I mean, that stuff just gives you a fog. And I have no need for fog."

The Amboy Dukes—and even Ted Nugent as solo act—lived and breathed on a yin-yang dynamic similar to that of both Kiss and the Alice Cooper group. Kiss had Gene and Paul to hold it together as counterbalance to the trouble boy rock 'n' roll spirit of Ace and Peter. Alice's band—in particular Glen Buxton and next in line Neal Smith—were drug and drink party mavens up for anything, while Alice and Dennis led level-headed. Ted? Well, early on, he had the likes of KJ Knight and most roaringly, the legendary Rusty Day to deal with. Later, there was Derek St. Holmes who provided the outlaw aspect seemingly so crucial to the crafting of wild rock 'n' roll. It is telling that the band moniker The Amboy Dukes is derived from the name of a fictional street gang from Brooklyn, as told in Irving Shulman's 1947 novel of the same name. Every gang has its leader, its foot soldiers, and a whole lotta shakin' goin on.

But the original Amboy Dukes, before it got too crazy, slaked their rebellious rock 'n' roll spirit from no more than the hard-charging attitude of Detroit itself, always fueled by the competitive spirit of the band's de facto leader, Ted, the epitome of "If you want something done right, you gotta do it yourself"—or more succinctly put, "backstraps!" As the story goes, the move back to Detroit happened the very night Ted graduated from high school, the young Nuge driving off, arriving and then sleeping on a park bench for the first handful of nights.

"Well, I didn't consider it anything but a band, just a rock 'n' roll band," notes Nugent, quickly summing up the weird dichotomy of Ted sitting at the centre of what quickly became a psych band, that solitude represented around their lone hit, 1968's *Journey To The Center Of The Mind*. "On our Ford Econoline van back then, it said The Amboy Dukes Show, just like the Motown Revue or the James Brown Show, you know what I mean? We considered ourselves R&B guys, strictly R&B guys. We played all the old

Stax, Volt hits, *Soul Man*, *Hold On! I'm Comin'*, *Skinny Legs*. We played Motown songs, we played James Brown songs, the Stones, Bo Diddley, Chuck Berry. So we considered ourselves an R&B band. But horrifically and quite pathetically, some of the members, most notably Steve Farmer, got so suicidal into the drug use and abuse that his idea for *Journey To The Center Of The Mind* was a polar opposite of mine. Mine was an intellectual, sincere review of your overall cause and effect of life. What do you do and how are you spending your time? How are you taking care of your sacred temple? How are you taking care of other people? His was about taking LSD and seeing colours. You know, pretty pathetic. But the lyrics, also quite amazingly hold up to my vision of reviewing your overall life."

It's something we've heard many times from Ted, but one of the man's most inspiring rants is the one, in all its variations, that explains further his musical inspirations taken to heart as a kid in the mid-'60s.

"The music has a life of its own, and I'm merely just a facilitator. I think God loves me more than he may love you (laughs), because he gives me this unbelievable American dream of adventure and dynamo and emotion and excitement. There's so much stimuli in my life, and just any music going on… even today we open up the show with *Journey To The Center Of The Mind*, which was written in 1967. I went on about this guitar lick onstage every night, and one of the guys mentioned, you know, I said in the dressing room that I first learned this guitar lick in 1958, and the basic lick is Joe Williams, *Baby Please Don't Go*, and of course the Amboy Dukes recorded that in 1967. So on stage, I tell the people that I've been playing this for 50 fucking years! I'm a big fan of defiance. I love Rosa Parks and all the middle fingers on fire. I think in this culture war that we're waging – and I can explain the details of the yin and yang of that culture war, who stands on which line in the sand—but all my music is knee-jerk, spontaneous, and a direct result, even after all these years, of me craving that spark, that original primal scream of Joe Williams and that lick, and Howlin' Wolf, Muddy Waters, Lightning Hopkins, Bo Diddley, Chuck Berry, Little Richard, Jerry Lee Lewis, of course, just compounded with the ferocity from James Brown, Wilson Pickett, Sam and Dave, the Motown Funk Brothers, Booker T, just all of these unbelievably emoting and sincere black artists, whose music was just desperately sincere, both in the funny *Wang Dang Doodle* songs, as in my *Wang Dang Sweet Poontang* and *Wango Tango*."

"The Amboy Dukes, Dave Palmer and Greg Arama? 15 and 16 years old," continues Ted, reflecting on the great rhythm sections he's had with him from day one, again, adding Motown to the psyche of his band from Motor City. "Listen to them play on *Journey To The Center Of The Mind*. That is gravity defying for young white guys. Just mesmerizing in their gifts. They're my rhythm section in 196-fuckin'-7. Even Dave Palmer and Bill White on *Baby Please Don't Go*, in early 1967, on the first Amboy Dukes album; listen to the rhythm throttle. That is the genuflection at the altar of James Brown and the Famous Flames. We all honed in on that Motown Funk Brothers authenticity and the authority, and it's always been about the music."

Even Ted's choice of the iconic hollow-body Gibson Byrdland as his trademark guitar derives from a reverence for roots. Although he says he's spent time with a few different guitars, he's since standardized on a dependable duality. "Onstage now I'm using my Byrdlands half the time and the Les Paul the other half. So my sound is about Chuck Berry meets Duane Eddy meets certainly Hendrix and Beck and Clapton and Page and Billy Gibbons and Eddie Van Halen. But again it comes from the Bo Diddley, Chuck Berry, Lonnie Mack world. Even The Ventures and people like that. Probably the most defining moment was watching Jimmy McCarty, of Billy Lee And The Rivieras in 1960, which became Mitch Ryder And The Detroit Wheels, and he used the Gibson Byrdland. So I guess I don't have to explain that anymore. He had a Gibson Byrdland and a Fender twin reverb amp. I just thought it was the most intense, rich, fat, grinding monster animal guitar sound I'd ever heard."

As alluded to, the garage rock persona of the young Amboy Dukes quickly took on a wilder psych component as they moved toward their self-titled debut album in 1967, coupled with the move to Detroit, which had a much harder rocking take on hippie music than that of the flower powered left coast.

"I am so moved and proud that I can tell you why Detroit has always and so early on played a pivotal director of American music, and worldwide music, obviously," begins Ted, unstoppable on the topic of Detroit and its raging rock 'n' roll infernos in the late '60s. "Much has been said about the industrial element to that uppity defiant rock 'n' roll. That's inaccurate. Yes, we had an assembly line monotony, and the Herculean work ethic of my fellow Detroiters is well-documented. The epicentre of productivity, of global, unprecedented quality, class, vehicles and merchandise. Literally Detroit won World War II, figuratively and literally. But the reason that MC5 were the MC5 and that I am what I am and that Jack White is what he is, and that Eminem is what he is and that Kid Rock is what he is, and Grand Funk and Bob Seger and Brownsville Station and Dick Wagner and The Frost and the SRC and the Stooges, the reason we are what we are, believe me when I tell you—Mitch Ryder And The Detroit Wheels taught us. Many of the artists I just mentioned may not know it or admit it, but I was able to be there when Billy Lee And The Rivieras headlined the Walled Lake Casino in '62, and my band, The Lourds, opened up for them, along with Gene Pitney and Martha And The Vandellas. How's that? I was there, man. And I sponged Martha And The Vandella's rhythm and philosophy. I sponged the aura of a professional Gene Pitney pop artist performing to an audience of young people."

"I became one with the wind of Jimmy McCarty on that Gibson Byrdland through a Fender amp," continues Ted. "Remember, Billy Lee And The Rivieras became Mitch Ryder And The Detroit Wheels. When *Jenny Take A Ride* came out, I'm going to say '64 or '65, they had such a musical authority, Mitch Ryder, Billy Levise was so tuned into his black inspirations, he was black. He hit every note with a fire and a passion that was unprecedented, except by the Little Richards and the Jerry Lee Lewises, maybe even more so. What Earl Elliott did on that... boy, I want to say the name of it... the Rickenbacker bass. Earl Elliott on bass guitar wearing a black silk glove, by the way, and Johnny Badanjek, Johnny Bee, a virtual rhythm orgy unto himself on drums. Joe Kubert on rhythm guitar, Gibson 335, Jimmy McCarty on Gibson Byrdland guitar through a Fender amp, what they created was such class, unprecedented tightness of structure and musical communication between them, that it rearranged our psyches, inspired by the greats of Bo Diddley and Chuck Berry—can't say their names often enough. And the Beatles, The Yardbirds and the Stones that were now coming up and bringing black American music to the globe."

"But Billy Lee And The Rivieras were light years ahead of their age. They were just teenagers, but they understood that they had to play tight; they had to practice, make every movement musically interesting and fascinating and intense. Every song was a peak. I wish you could have witnessed it. Just play the intro to *Jenny Take A Ride* and listen to the way that Johnny Badanjek brings the band in on his drums. You can't not dance to it. So my point is that all of us garage bands, all of us kids, got a dose of Billy Lee And The Rivieras, before they became known as Mitch Ryder. Nobody plays like that. When Johnny comes in with that bass drum, nobody plays like that. And when he came in and played that with me on my 6,000th concert, one of the greatest joys a guitar player can ever experience. Just magic stuff."

Driving the point home, Ted elaborates that, "The only word that really delivers what Mitch Ryder And The Detroit Wheels taught us was musical authority. Mitch Ryder broke six tambourines per song. Not per night, per song. Every song culminated in a pinnacle of inescapable outrage propelled by Johnny Badanjek, primarily, and Earl Elliott on bass that taught every band in Detroit, okay, we can't play like pussies any more. We can't play like white boys any more. We all watched Billy And The Rivieras at Club 1270 and all the little teen clubs and all the little dance parties and all the little fraternity and sorority pool parties and stuff. They were just everywhere. They played every night. And what they taught all of us, and what I perpetuated and continued was that (sings); it's like Johnny Badanjek was a human tambourine and maracas and cowbell and just an orgy of every grinding, unifying rhythm. You have to watch this guy play, even as old as we are, when he unleashed his rhythmical fury on my 6000th concert in 2009, and we played *Jenny Take A Ride*, as the guitar player, even though I'd had the world's greatest drummers in the world. You stop and think of my drummers. Carmine Appice, Tommy Aldridge, Tommy Clufetos, Cliff Davies - my buddy from Heart, Denny Carmassi. I mean look at Mick Brown, my drummers, the greatest drummers that have ever lived have propelled my music, so when I hear a guy like Johnny Badanjek, who's gotta be in his 60s, it harkens me back to that day in 1962 or whatever it was that taught me that every song is the most important song of your life."

"Every song. Not every concert, not just your hits. So when the MC5 and The Up and The Rationals and The SRC and Bob Seger and… I mean I could go on and on, certainly MC5 and certainly Brownsville Station and certainly Grand Funk Railroad, to this very day Jack White and Kid Rock and even Eminem, they realize that you've got this song as your statement. What are you gonna do with it? You don't just perform it, you eat it. You deliver it. You hump it. You pound it home. And that's why my career is unstoppable, because people know when they see a Ted Nugent concert, every minute of every concert, every lick in every song is going to be the absolute animal best conceivable from this trio of musicians that believe in their music and will make you believe immediately. So that set a bar in Detroit that forced every band to never settle for okay or good. If you were a good band in Detroit, you wouldn't make it a week. You have to be incredible."

Steve Lyman, guitarist for one of the great Detroit bands, SRC, most definitely noticed Ted Nugent's intensity and ambition. "He was very competitive at the time. We played a small teen club that was on Allen Park, just west of Detroit, and the opening band for us was Ted Nugent And The Amboy Dukes, probably at the time just called the Amboy Dukes. I'd previously never heard of them. Which happened a lot back then, where local groups that were making a major effort to do something on their own were so busy doing their own thing, that unless they happened to play a gig with another group, they were hardly aware of who else was doing what. My memories of Ted, starting at that time and even after that, was that he was a good guitar player, but he was so much of a show-off that it actually bordered on the level of obnoxiousness, to me (laughs). Ted used to come by our house in Ann Arbor once in a while, after we got to know each other. Mostly to chit chat with the other guitarist in our band, Gary Quackenbush, comparing their thoughts on what guitars are the best. It was mostly technical stuff."

Grand Funk's Don Brewer seconds Ted's quickly growing reputation as slightly forceful of personality. "The first time I met Ted it was actually at a show we were opening for Led Zeppelin at The Olympia. Ted showed up, and as Ted always does, he'd come busting into the dressing room and make himself known, make himself at home. With his boisterous, 'Hi, I'm Ted and I'm gonna take over!' So he takes over the room—that was the first time I met him. I still feel the same way about Ted. It's like... wow! Wow!"

"Crazy, loudmouth, aggressive, nice guy, but he'll do crazy things," offers Carmine Appice, adding a third bit of evidence to Ted's audaciousness. "We played with Hendrix. Vanilla Fudge, Hendrix, and just The Amboy Dukes. Actually, my manager managed him for a while, and told him he should be Ted Nugent And The Amboy Dukes, and eventually turned them into Ted Nugent. So we were really close. Ted was like... for instance, he would open up for Vanilla Fudge, and then Vanilla Fudge went on, and then Hendrix came on, and he had the balls to go up and play with his teeth. I said, 'Man, what are ya doing? You know Hendrix is known for that.' He said, 'Yeah, but a lot of people don't know that Hendrix did it first, and then if they see me doing it first night, then they'll think he's copying me.' He's a wild man."

"But the interesting thing about Ted," continues Steve Lyman, "is back in the days when all the drug experimentation was going on, people smoking marijuana or whatever, I never knew him to dabble in any of that. He would make a point of that, and I guess, presently, where he is adamantly anti-drug. I sincerely believe that's where he stood back then. Which for me is kind of ironic, because a lot of the public that was, let's say, getting into his music, in terms of being inspired by his music, were people who were getting stoned all the time and he had nothing to do with that. I think he got almost militant within his own band, where anybody in his band who was getting into that, he would go ahead and fire them. In retrospect, there's probably a good point to that. You can go down the list and see how many bands were ruined by people getting lost in substance abuse."

But Ted already had the chops to back it up. Notes Dick Wagner, one of the scene's top axemen at the time with his band The Frost, "We were definitely one of the most popular bands. We were the ones doing rock 'n' roll with like melody and harmonies; very sophisticated for the time. I was fortunate to be one of the two guitar players in town that was really getting recognition and the other was Ted Nugent. Ted was a huge inspiration. So blatantly open about his beliefs and his way of life, and his way of presenting music. I think he was an influence on a lot of guitar players as I was too. His place in the history of rock 'n' roll is not for me to determine, but obviously he played a big role. The Amboy Dukes are one of the forerunners. I mean Nugent and that first single, *Journey To The Center Of The Mind*, that definitely happening."

It wasn't just the local artists that helped harden their fellow Detroit bands one upon the other. The Grande Ballroom and little brother Eastown Theater brought the big names through town at a breath-taking pace, The Who in particular making an impression on Ted and his gang of howling feedbackers.

"Keith Moon—talk about uninhibited maniac primal scream garage band drums personified," explains Ted. "Get the hell out of here. I mean I was just in the studio yesterday, and I literally told my drummer Jon Kutz, I said Keith Moon! I want Keith Moon on this section right here! I want you to piss people off! I want you to break shit! I want you to go wild, but never lose the groove. That, in essence, was The Who's most powerful imprint. Propelled by this maniacal clang-a-thon by Entwistle and Moon, but never losing the groove. Remember I talked about the early primal scream experimental, uninhibitedness of youthful garageness, those guys had it but they never lost the musicality. Keith Moon, earth-moving virtuoso. John Entwistle, earth-moving virtuoso who created a rhythm punch that established a new energy dynamic bar for all of us to attain. And then with Daltrey and this incredible song-smithing, Pete Townsend clang-a-thon guitar chord basher. Remember, I didn't just hear The Who or see The Who. The Who hired the Amboy Dukes to open up for them at the Southfield High School prom in 1969 (ed. actually November 22, 1967). I played the high school gymnasium, the Southfield high school gymnasium with my band the Amboy Dukes, opened up for The Who in '69 because they knew that we had the loudest, baddest PA system in the world, I think."

"And to witness them up close and personal like that, and to meet Pete and John and Keith and Roger, even though that was more of a personal indulgent moment, but the fascination and the reverence I had for those guys was a result, a direct result, of their musical prowess and their musical vitality. Again it was that, certainly influenced by the black rhythm and blues masters, but catapulted into heretofore uncharted musical outrage territories of that clang factor. Nobody bashed guitar chords like Pete, nobody beat the living shit out of the drums in such a maniacal display of basically a drum solo through the whole fucking song, and no one filled the rhythm guitar and the grinding pulse of the song like Entwistle with his incredible dexterity. Listen to the *My Generation* bass solo. What was that, '63? '64? I don't remember what it was. But it was way early and it was just unprecedented, so The Who overall – and this is a powerful statement – were equally, on many levels, as influential as the Stones and the Beatles. That's how powerful that songwriting and musicianship was."

Owner of the Grande Ballroom, Russ Gibb, recalls The Cream at his place as one of the seminal inspirational gigs in town. But he was a regular booker of all the local acts as well, including The Amboy Dukes. "The funny part about Ted," recalls Gibb, "was that when he first came to the club, he was on the radio, and his mother had to bring him. His mother would sit in the… and I was afraid we were going to be busted. The police were already swarming around the place. I didn't understand quite what was going on. But his mother would sit in my office with me while he performed. He was just a young guy, an interesting kid. He sometimes presents himself that he has always been sort of a straight shooter, and he fooled around a little bit when he was young. Last time I saw him, I was kidding him about that. I said, 'I see you're trying to make your image cleaner these days, but let's face it, you were involved in rock 'n' rolling as all of us were.' So that was… no, Ted was an interesting guy, and he's still an interesting guy. He's his own person. I admire anybody who is willing to jump on the bandwagon for what they believe, if that's what they believe. God bless them, go for it."

The fact that Russ and his partner Tom Wright were so supportive of locals was key in making Detroit bands better. Indeed, this is something you hear from all of them, and really, the proof is in the energy and showmanship of The Stooges, MC5, Alice Cooper and really, the Amboy Dukes from the start, especially Ted.

Says Gibb, "Yes, well, that's because having been a schoolteacher, I had a great affinity for… because in the early days, we didn't have any big name bands. It was a local band because I could get them cheap! They would play just for the opportunity. MC5 became the house band because they could go there 24 hours a day when we weren't working and they could use it as a rehearsal space. We let most bands use it as a rehearsal place anytime they wanted to. It's always a pain for new bands, finding a place to practice and get their act together. Whereas we would say, 'Hey, it's a building here, we have a crew living here, and if you can use it, use it but don't abuse it.' Most of them didn't. They were great about helping the Grande, and they built its reputation."

"And the crowds were part and parcel of it," adds Gibb, referring to the legendary intensity of the Detroit concert-goer. "It was not a closed society. You could come down to the Grande, three o'clock on a Saturday afternoon or on a Tuesday afternoon, and some band might be rehearsing, and you would have a little coterie of friends who were there listening, and becoming part and parcel of your message and your music, so it was wide open. That was encouraged around here. Because when you work in a shop, there's a brotherhood that you don't forget. Again, you have to remember, there was a rhythm to this town. It was an auto town. I think that Detroit was unto itself, an amazing place for music. We were a factory town. Many of the folks, myself included, worked on the line at one time in our career, and you get on the line, and there's a mechanical rhythm that knocks your fucking pants off. So there was always this sort of hard driving sound in the background of a great giant machine plugging away."

Plugging away, it actually didn't take long for the Amboy Dukes to sign a deal with Mainstream Records and issue their first and second albums in quick succession, the self-titled in November of '67, followed by *Journey To The Centre Of The Mind* in April of '68.

Right place right time, says Amboy Dukes vocalist John Drake. "What I think was happening, a lot of the record companies at the time... let's just take Cleveland for an example. Cleveland was a type of town where The Raspberries came from and groups like that, with Jimmy Ienner as their producer. Capitol made a big sweep through; into a lot of States they did this. Michigan just hadn't been hit yet with the talent. I think when Elektra came through with the MC5 and Stooges, we were going to sign with Columbia at the time. But we had a manager and he hooked us up with a small label. He said you really don't want to get in a rut with the big label and get swept under like so many groups. So we signed with a small label and then we were distributed by Atlantic, which made it a lot easier. You can really keep an eye on business, and you're not worried about, well how come this one group is way ahead of us, and we're down here with that record? But I just think it was Detroit's turn at the time."

"I had met Ted when he was probably 14 or 15, something like that," continues Drake, offering the back story. "He was a neighbour of mine back in Detroit. I was in a band and we were looking for a guitar player. John, in our band, said, 'I know a guy named Ted Nugent that doesn't live far from here; maybe he'd fit in.' Well at the time Ted was—we were so young—Ted was still taking guitar lessons. He, you know, could plankiddy-plank on the guitar and I said, 'Whoa, you're hired.' I said that sounds good. Better than anything else I could find at the time. As a group with him in it, we got progressively better. He was the type of guy and I was too, where an eight hour rehearsal every single day didn't bother me. We were just at it constantly. If we weren't playing we were rehearsing. It just never stopped with us. Ted just got better and better."

"Pretty soon after we started going out on the road, he had really pulled some wild stuff out there," laughs Drake. "I mean there was a band one time we worked with from Toronto called Grant Smith and the Power. Grant Smith was a powerhouse band out of Toronto. I was actually scared of this band. I'd heard them before, and I'd go man, 'Oh man, I'd hate to go up against them.' Well we did, in Windsor. This was an all-white soul band, two drummers, all this stuff, you know, real powerhouse deal, horn section. Grant Smith was a great singer and a great showman. I looked at him and I go, 'Man oh man, what am I gonna do? What are we gonna do? There're six of us, there's got to be 12 of them.' These boys out of Toronto put on one heck of a show. Still we were headlining the show anyway. I mean these Canadians came out to see us, although Grant Smith brought a lot of people with them. He had a lot of fans at the time; he had records out at the time too. What could we do?"

"Well Ted... during the middle of *Baby Please Don't Go*, jumped off the stage, took off his guitar and was twirling it around his head. What we thought was a brick wall wasn't. It looked like a brick wall but it had like a brick covering over it kinda, and so Ted thought he was going to throw the guitar into the brick wall and everything. We were just gonna kick the equipment over like The Who. We're gonna have to make some attention here with this big powerhouse band. So Ted took the guitar, only it went through the wall! There was this big gaping hole into the furnace room, right? You could see the furnace back there and the fan blowing away. So Ted ran down the aisle, ran all the way up, jumped back on stage; dove through the hole in the wall, into the furnace room where there's nothing but dirt back there and furnaces. He's blazing away on the guitar in the furnace room, and we ended the song there. The crowd went insane and just shut Grant Smith and the Power right down. I went whoa!"

"We had all kinds of things," chuckles Drake. "In those days if you were good enough you'd put drum solos in and things of that nature. I think it's the way we dressed a lot of times. As a matter of fact, I went to a Halloween party the other night and I wore a coat or a jacket out of 1968 that I had worn on a Jimi Hendrix tour. People were looking at that but the clothes were really flash. That was one of the things that we had learned. After that it kind of settled down. Then the glam bands started coming out and the clothes came back out sort of speak."

Drake says that the leadership dynamic was much different in the early days, than it would become for Ted as a solo act. "Yes, well, Ted wasn't running the band in those days—I was. It wasn't like he was the big leader of everything. He was a member of the band like I was. It was pretty democratic. I had done a stint in the army, okay? Ted kept writing to me, 'Well I'm putting a new band together' and this and that. So when I got out I was only in Detroit for three days and then moved in with his family in Chicago. I was working for his dad who fired me. I said, 'Listen, I'm going back to Detroit. We have to set something up; what we need is a band house.' So we found the house and everything, moved the Chicago band in. We were working before any records came out, we were working, and we could support ourselves. It was only a five-man band at the time, and then three of them got really homesick for Chicago. They were just kids. Their parents came and picked them up or whatever, and they took a hike. Ted and I told them good riddance if they can't take it, and then we fired the other one. We fired the drummer; he went back to Chicago. So then I knew all the musicians in Detroit and I hand-picked them, like Greg Arama from Rusty's band. I mean we had a contract coming up and we were definitely going to stay working now. So I hand-picked all the guys and we just whipped them into shape. We really got well rehearsed and started getting... We were doing good when Ted and I were in a band called The Lourds. We were packing places all over the joint."

"I don't think Ted so much avoided the draft," recalls John, giving Ted a pass despite Nugent's own admission of shame and regret at not having gone. "I think he was in school at the time. Ted is probably two years younger than me; but with that difference I think what happened with Ted is that... I had just gone into the American army. What happened was they came out with what's known as a lottery. My lottery number turned out to be 354. If I could have missed it by two or three weeks, I would have never had to have gone anyway. I think he had a high lotto number. I don't think it's anything he did outrageous, but there was a guy that I knew..."

This is where we get the crazy story about "Ted" going through a whole routine to get out of the draft. The story we all have heard, well, John insists that it happened to a future Amboy Dukes drummer...

"No, you know who that was? It was a guy named KJ Knight. Now KJ Knight used to be in a band called KJ Knight And The Knightriders, a local band. His name was Ken; I use to call him Kenny but he went by the name of KJ. He wound up being one of Ted's drummers. So KJ goes, 'Well I'm getting drafted, but they will never take me.' I go, really? Trust me I had already been in and out of that stuff, okay? I go, 'They'll take you alright, Kenny.' He goes, 'Nah they won't take me.' So what he did... he had to go down and take a physical, as you have to do in the American army at that time. What he did is... I think it was in two weeks or a month, he didn't take a shower; he fried up a bunch of bacon and wiped all the grease all over his body. He did not change his underwear, did not do anything for two weeks to a month! Did not wash his hair, went in there smelling like a rose, and they told him immediately get out. They said, 'You're not even fit for the army, you're not.' They knew if they got him in, he'd really go crazy! That guy's name was KJ Knight."

Nonetheless Ted does admit pulling a few stunts to avoid the call-up, calling his half-dodge one of his biggest regrets, and the act of a dumb kid who might even have been a little scared, definitely not heroic enough to give up rock 'n' roll for fighting communism.

Creem writer Jaan Uhelski had a few words to say on the interesting dynamic and kinship between John Drake and The Nuge. Aside from deeming Ted a "royal asshole in an Indian costume," she didn't see him as particularly wild. "I think he was more personally crazy. But no, he wasn't much crazier than anybody else. But there was a lead singer John Drake, or John Brake, depending on what era you get him, and they had the same personality. They were both tall, aggressive; shit-stirring kind of guys. So I think the competition between the two of them, you know, just egged Ted on. I don't remember him being flamboyant in The Amboy Dukes. They dressed in kind of proto-English mod clothes, like brocades and fancy things. That's the funny thing, there's the stripped-down Ted and then you look at the poofter Ted. Early on there's like a strange disconnect. But he was a band member so he couldn't go out and steal the spotlight, because there were four other guys in the band who were doing the exact same thing. I never understood why they couldn't make it because they really had almost everything that they needed. They had the songs, they had the looks, they had the big personalities; they had a record contract."

While acknowledging the influence and presence of Dick Wagner on the Detroit scene, John Drake indicates that, "Ted had his own guitar hero out of Detroit and the guy's name was George Cole. He was an unheard of, but he used to work with Rusty Day who replaced me and then eventually wound up in Cactus. Rusty was a drummer in a band called Rusty Day And The Midnighters, and George was his guitar player. Ted just idolized this guy. I mean, George was older. I think Ted was probably 18 years old and George may have been 26 or 27. Well, George could play rock 'n' roll and just pick up any record; if you want it to sound like Chucky Berry he'll lift it note-for-note with the sound on it. He was perfect! So Ted used to corner him and ask him all kinds of questions and pick up all kinds of tricks from George. There were a lot of guys that never made it out of there that were just phenomenal. A lot of good ones came out of Detroit."

For all of Nugent's talk of rhythm and blues in all its flavours, Drake says that, "He really wasn't like a soul guy. Many times I've been to Toronto, people were really into soul music there. But Ted—and I'm not knocking Ted; he's a very close friend of mine—but he wanted to be that real soulful guy but just wasn't born with it. He just wasn't born with the soulful stuff. I mean when you hear his solo guitar… I've heard a lot of soul guitar players and he just doesn't happen to be one of them. But he's hell of a guitarist, don't get me wrong. When you're growing up, it depends on your influences. I was attracted to soul music; that was my thing."

"As a matter of fact what we would do… our keyboard player, Andy Solomon, was from Philadelphia. Before every show, The Amboy Dukes had a four-part vocal that they… you know, four of us sang out of the six. So what we would do, we'd never warm up backstage. We used to do like a band rehearsal, then after that we would do a vocal rehearsal. The vocalists would rehearse. So it wasn't all together. You want the vocals real tight on this, so you really had two rehearsals on it. What we would always do before a gig is that we would never do our own material. We would do doo-wop music out of the '50s. Like ahhh-doom-boppa-doom-boopa-doom-boopa-doom-hey. So we knew all these songs out of the '50s and that's what we liked to do. We found by hitting the really high notes and everything that it really loosened the vocals up prior to going up on stage doing our own music. So when we'd do that, boy we were ready to go."

"I know exactly what they were," continues John, on what Ted's contemporary influences might have been, if not based in soul music. "There was Jeff Beck; he loved Beck. When we were living in the Gorham Hotel in New York, our neighbour upstairs was Jimmy Page. Jimi Hendrix was my neighbour, Page, Sly And The Family Stone; Yardbirds. We were all… my favourite guy was Keith Relf, the lead singer of the Yardbirds. We used to go down to the bar at the Gorham Hotel and I would talk to Keith, and the weird thing about it was, we never talked music. We'd talk about the politics in London, we'd talk about soccer, which I knew nothing about. We would go on like that and he'd ask about Americans and things like that."

Ted didn't neglect to take the opportunity of swapping tips with Jimmy Page. After all, they were more or less on equal footing in the late '60s. "Yes, he'd talk with Jimmy, but then Hendrix… I don't think Ted really liked Hendrix all that much. Although as kids we copied him; like a lot of bands we'd do *Purple Haze* and *Foxy Lady* and all this stuff. He was an influence on our band, certainly Jimi was, but Jimi Hendrix was another soul guy. He came out of Little Richard's band and he had been in other bands, you know soul bands, the Isley Brothers too. Ted didn't like Jimi for the simple fact that he knew Jimi was a druggy. Ted, believe me, he loathed drugs. Believe me! This is Mr. Anti Drug himself. I don't like it because you're not going to function well on it. You're just not gonna, and you would hear all these horror stories about, oh these people do this, and they do that. Well if that were the truth—and I knew at the time people would talk about these people I knew—you couldn't do tours like they did if you were all drugged up all the time. It would be impossible."

With regard to the Amboy Dukes' early trips to record tracks, "Detroit never quite had the studios," explains Drake. "You had Motown, but you had Motown groups who signed to Motown. Really why would a white group record there? They had an off-shoot studio called Golden World, which I had done my earliest recordings at when I was 16, 17 years old. There was always that chip on the shoulder—how come New York has this, LA's got that, we don't have this and that? So all our stuff was recorded in New York; that's where we had to go. We were doing the demos in Chicago at the time, coming from Detroit and all that was sent to New York until we finally got invited into New York, to the Capitol studios for the first album. I mean I was just stunned by what they had as opposed to what we had. There was an envy thing for sure."

"So yes, these Chicago demos would be sent to New York and we probably did four or five of them, then we got some attention there, and they said we'll bring the band in. Well these cheapskates...okay, bring the band in, but now we've got to take a train. We had to load all this equipment onto a train, you're on the way to New York, now you're cutting through part of Canada, the train hits a car broadside. The train stops up in Canada, and I'm going what the hell is going on? So I went outside of the train and man, these people really got nailed bad by this train. Finally the train gets to Grand Central Station in New York. It took us probably 12 taxicabs to get to the studio with our equipment. We're lugging everything in the cabs! So now we finally set up in Capitol studios in New York. All we had to offer them was our demos, probably four that we had sent to them, maybe 27 originals and one unoriginal song called *Baby Please Don't Go*. So they listened to our music, they don't like this and they don't like that. This is like our big shot of the day. And so Ted cuts loose on *Baby Please Don't Go*. I mean he ripped it! The guy in the studios said, go get so and so from down the hall, from another record company and he said you gotta see this guy. Ted had just gone nuts in the studio, which was a good thing. I think that's what really landed our first contract."

"I like the first one," begins Drake, asked for his impression of the two albums he made with the band. "It was called *The Amboy Dukes*, and it featured *Baby Please Don't Go* on it. Now that was written by a guy named Joe Williams out of Chicago who was an old black guy, stand-up bass player in a jazz band. Van Morrison had done that but it was a flipside of his big hit *Gloria*. We had picked up on it and we had decided to, you know, we liked this song. We'd been messing with it for years anyways, out of our former group, The Lourds. Ted really started working with the song and really put some nice feedback on it. Then we tried it out live and man oh man, it was like woooo!"

Indeed, the band's ol' rock 'n' roll cover was a minor hit for good reason, Ted really letting fly, demonstrating both subtlety and pure aggression, pioneering the use of feedback, and in general, demonstrating an extensive enough guitar vocabulary for the day to be considered, for the few who heard the song, somewhat of a guitar hero.

"Elsewhere, me and Steve Farmer were writing a lot of stuff," continues Drake. "You've got to remember, on that first album there were a lot of cover tunes. We did *I Feel Free* by Cream, *Let's Go Get Stoned*, Ray Charles. It was getting airplay; it was doing fine. I mean we did okay. Let me put it like this—it was enough to pay the bills out at our band house. I was lucky with that. Finally we were getting some money. Sound-wise, I think we were kind of on our own. I never tried to pattern myself after a band. When I did *Let's Go Get Stoned*, that was definitely a Ray Charles song. I liked Ray Charles at the time but I also liked The Cream, so we put a Cream song on there. Some of the other songs, it was just like Steve Farmer would write them and I just thought they were god-awful. That was just filler stuff to me."

"We got signed to a three record deal off of that first time we had gone to New York," continues Drake. "They had advanced us—which sounds like a lot of money; doesn't sound like much today, but it was a lot then—I think it was about $250,000 for three albums. I know it sounds like a lot but out of that 250 you don't keep that money. You gotta pay for your own sessions and you have to pay the band and you have to pay for a lot of things—you've got a high overhead."

How did this Mainstream company afford all that?

"Well Mainstream were recording big hit records back in the 1950s. At that time on the same label, they had Janis Joplin. So they were starting to get really kinda hip with the thing. The offices were fantastic! And our producer; the guy's name was Bob Shad (ed. also founder of the company, in 1964). He was recording in New York. This was a musician's musician. He's recording the New York Philharmonic Orchestra, I mean this guy… oh he was recording a lot of big film soundtracks at the time too, like *The Blue Max* with George Peppard."

Then things got a little heavier for the second album, *Journey To The Center Of The Mind*, as witnessed on Ted's riff and guitar break within the title track and other Deep Purple Mk. 1-ish manoeuvres along the way, Ted playing Ritchie and Andy Solomon doing Jon Lord, three months before Purple would even have a record out.

"I think it's because of all the music that was coming out at the time," offers Drake. "You could hear Amboy Dukes but you could also hear a lot of other groups like Hendrix and Steppenwolf. These groups were really laying it down and we just wanted to keep up. That's what was selling and that's what we liked to do, and we had a lot of fun with it too. It was easy for us to write this stuff too. We considered the band a hard rock act although some of our writing doesn't reflect that. I think when our first record came out, *Baby Please Don't Go*. I really wanted to stay along those lines. *Journey To The Center Of The Mind* came out, and it was a hard rocker and I wanted to stay right there. Then music started to change. The next one that came out was *You Talk Sunshine, I Breathe Fire*. That didn't do a lot for us. I just really wanted to stay along the lines of the *Baby Please Don't Go* thing. I thought we had been much, much better off with that whole idea."

All the while, The Amboy Dukes were participating in the great Detroit tradition of honing their chops in a band house. "That was phenomenal!" laughs Drake. "It was way out in the woods where you couldn't hear anything for miles. We were buried in the woods and Ted just loved it. Ted would get up before rehearsal and he'd go hunting in the morning. Andy Solomon and I, our keyboard player, you know we'd get up to have cornflakes or something, and we had a table... it was up on the second floor, and we'd open the curtains; and you could see the roof right there. It was like a flat roof looking out and that's all you see is woods around you. And what do we see? One morning I open it up and I see ten dead squirrels with arrows in them. I got up and I said, 'God, Andy shut the shades man!' I go, 'He's at it again!' Oh yeah he's out there hunting away first thing in the morning."

Drake still owns the place. "Yes, and I had Edgar Winter over there, I've had—you name it—oh, Small Faces; we jammed with them all night long one night. We had Ian McLagan not too long ago in Chicago, and he remembers coming to the house with Ron Wood and all these guys. We just sat up and jammed all night long. Then the next night we went down to Olympia Stadium in Detroit where they were playing. Three Dog Night was the headlining band after Rod Stewart and The Faces and everybody walked out. They really came to see Stewart and the Faces. Those were great guys. Plus Alice Cooper—I've known all those guys for a long time. With Alice, he came over and we threw a big, big party. We had everything from champagne to this and that. This was really when he really started. I said Alice, 'I've been talking to some people...' I said, 'You've got the No.1 record coming out next week. It's going to be a stone-cold smash. That's all there is to it.' Sure enough it came true for him. You know, he really put himself on the map."

As the band transitions to the second album, the career gets a shot in the arm with *Journey To The Center Of The Mind* becoming a minor chart sensation. "Well what happened was, the band was sitting upstairs at the band house," says Drake, of the psychedelic nugget's birthing. "We were having lunch or dinner or whatever. I mean we were all living together. It was after one of those eight-hour grueling Nugent rehearsals. We're sitting up there and chatting. We had guitars all over the place and all kinds of instruments.

We're watching TV and then Ted said, 'I'll bet you the next commercial that comes on TV, I don't care what it is, whatever the music is, I'll play it note-for-note.' I said really? I said, 'Okay you're that good, huh?' And he goes, I am. So here's your guitar, hand him a guitar. Only a commercial didn't come on. Do you know what came on? *Bonanza* and he goes, Dun-didda-din-din-din-da-da-din-din-dah-nah! *Journey To The Center Of The Mind* is, Da-dun-da-dun-dada-da-dah. So it came from *Bonanza*. Yeah! He just switched it around, wow!"

So all of a sudden, The Amboy Dukes have a hippie anthem on their hands. "If you want to know the truth, we didn't care about hippies," says Drake. "We were not going to be some hippie band like The Dead; it wasn't anything like that. It's like, God how can I put it? I don't think I had a lot of respect for hippies. I mean they'd show up and you just thought, please go take a shower, go do something. I didn't care for them myself. Whatever their politics were... but did I like the Vietnam War? Hell no, at that time. No I didn't like it. But I didn't care for hippies, I mean they would show up; that was just part of the scene. I don't care. The hippies were cool; they bought records and that's really I cared about that."

"A lot more money was put into it for one thing," says Drake, comparing the first album to the second. "We had advanced to a studio called A&R in New York. Now this is the place where The Young Rascals had done their stuff, which we toured with them. Frankie Valli, The Four Seasons; God so many hit records came from A&R in New York. "Journey" probably took... remember, you can't work at it constantly because you're going out on the road, and then you're coming back, so all that time was involved too. I'd say we probably had the next one out in probably five, six months. Because you had release dates and it has to be out there. You're always pressed for another hit record. These companies would press you. It's like you're coming off of that single, and it's 'What have you got new?' 'Well we haven't written anything yet.' 'Well you better start writing.' There's always that pressure but there's so many other things going on around you. All of a sudden, you hope you come up with an idea or you're always mucking around with something. So there's always going to be some music there, but is it going to click the way you want it?"

As explained in the liner essay to the second album, a whole side of the thing was meant to be digested as a concept, a half-concept album as it were, in the fine tradition of Rush.

"*Journey To The Center Of The Mind*, in my opinion, which I found interesting, would have actually been the very first rock opera before Tommy," notes Drake. "Because the one side played all the way through. There are no skips in it. You put the needle down and it was... how can I put it? Like a dream sequence. You're just kicking back. It got some great reviews and it sold an awful lot of albums. The single sold tons too. We did really, really well with that."

"And then the *Migration* thing came along, which I thought was a disaster. But we were working on a third album in-between that, that was called *The Gods Live In The Cities And The Men Live In The Skies*. The other album we were writing was called *The Gods Live In The Cities And The Men Live In The Skies*. But off of that, before Rusty came onto the scene and the *Migration* thing was done, we had released a song that was going on the album that wasn't even written. We were in the middle of it, but they needed a single and that particular one was *You Talk Sunshine, I Breathe Fire*—that came off of that. If the album had been completed, that would have been one of the things off of *The Gods Live In The Cities And The Men Live In The Skies*."

This track, a competent, almost modern rocker, shows up as a bonus track to the "Journey" album. John Drake is the lead singer on it and it's the last song on which he is vocalist, save for some uncredited back-ups that make it on to *Migration*.

"Yes, that's the last single I did with them, but I had done other singles with The Amboy Dukes that would never appear on albums; I think one of them is called *Aftermath*, which we put a sitar on. I had charted Billboards six times. Sometimes not really high but if you get in the Top 100 that means you're in the top 100 bands in the States, and you're still doing good with it."

Weirdly, in the process of Drake being replaced by Rusty "Russell Edward Davidson" Day, what happened was that Drake was there for the recording of *Migration*, did his vocals, and then got them wiped off. Still, he is audible in places because he's part of the back-up vocals. Then of course, you're in a situation where Day had to mimic the removed leads.

"Yeah I was on it with Rusty. All they did was take my voice off of it. You can hear me in the background as I'm doing back-up. A lot of times singers will do a lead vocal, and then they'll get together with the back-up singers and then lay some back-ups down. So my back-ups are still there. Just in my opinion, and I loved Rusty, don't get me wrong. It just seemed really unusual to me, very unusual. I was like, wow this guy's like... it's not his fault, but God, he's stealing my stuff here. What's going on?"

"Lots of stories about Rusty," adds Drake. "God rest his soul. Rusty was a guy who after I had left the Amboy Dukes, Ted hired him as the lead singer. It was because Greg Arama used to work with him, our bass player. I told Ted, I said, 'You're picking a bad guy when you pick Rusty.' I said, 'I'd really be looking for another singer if I were you.' I had already done the album Rusty was on. That thing was finished. They just took my voice off and put Rusty's on. That's all there was to that on the third album. With the drugs and everything, Ted fired him. Rusty just couldn't stand Ted; Ted couldn't stand Rusty. Ted knew he made a mistake, I wasn't about to come back and all this other stuff. Later, Rusty got murdered down in Florida on a drug deal. It was bad. Did I like Rusty personally? Yes, he was personable, sure. But he was a lot better off in Cactus with Jim McCarty and those guys."

So John Drake leaves, one of many proposed pop stars passing through the revolving door of this band, The Amboy Dukes stumbling through the '60s and low '70s with its guitarist slowly and methodically emerging as the only actual star among them.

"Yes, the last one for me was *Migration*, so that would have been 1969. The problem with that was, we were doing our first work in early '67, and that's when Rusty Day came onto the scene. Ted and I were having all kinds of problems. It was like a power struggle thing. I didn't want any of that. I don't know what the hell he was looking for, or what he was thinking. He never knew Rusty Day like I knew him, and I knew Rusty for years. But Ted had a driving force like nothing will ever stop me; I don't care what it is. No matter what I have to do, nothing will stop me. How bad do you want something? You can get anything you want if you want it bad enough. I've always believed that. I believed that Ted and I would get back together again. I believed he was going to have another big hit record out soon."

As regards Rusty, "Not only was he dealing dope but he was just a doper. The whole thing… I mean I don't want to say bad things about dead people, but this guy was bad news all the way down the line. He was dealing dope down in Florida with a friend of mine, Garth McRae. I'd see Garth in Detroit and I'd go, 'Garth, where did you get the new car? Man you must be doing phenomenally!' He says, 'Yeah, I'm a stockbroker in Chicago.' Well, he was living in Chicago but that wasn't his deal. This guy was making all kinds of drug deals up in Canada. I'd seen him come back, and one night I'm sitting in a bar with him, and he opened up this suitcase and it was filled with all Canadian money. I'm going, 'Where did you get all the cash?' There's always that exchange difference. The bar would take it. He's buying drinks for everybody and you'd just do the exchange on the money and stuff like that."

"So he moved down to Florida. He moved in with Rusty, and I guess from what I understand they were ripping people off and taking a lot of money. Garth took God knows how much money out of Chicago from one of the bike gangs here. He moved in with Rusty and they started looking for him. They put these hit guys on him. It took them awhile to find out where they went, but when they found him, they killed Rusty, they killed Rusty's son and killed Garth."

"The story I heard from John our rhythm guitar player, who just passed away, was telling me, he was telling Rusty, 'You better stop this stuff. There's some bad people out there looking for ya.' Stop the stealing and taking the money and he wouldn't deliver the goods, and one day they caught up with him and just killed them all in his house. Garth was hiding in the closet under a pile of clothes. When they found him, they made an example out of him too. Yeah, you see this stuff gets nuts after awhile. When I first started to do rock 'n' roll, I thought gee whiz this is fun and I'm getting paid for it. I liked to battle with the bands, that type of thing, when I'm a kid. But as it advances into it, and when the years starts flying by, then you see what this business is all about. You learn to stay away from this and stay away from that."

"The man was always at rehearsal – he always had an attitude – but he did his job," says Cactus' Tim Bogert, remembering Rusty. "He did what he was supposed to do. If you liked him he was amazing, if you didn't like… and there was no gray area. You either liked him a lot or you thought he sucked. This guy can't sing, baaahhhrrr. And other people thought, oh this guy's really cool. He was the lyricist. Yeah, whatever popped out of his head. The jam tunes that we wrote, one of us would come up with a riff, Jimmy or I, and we'd be yelling out chord changes, and Rusty would just be able to spew a song out off the top of his head and remember it. That's the hard part, and suddenly we have a song. We would write all the time like that. Rusty knew a thousand blues tunes, yeah. He probably knows every word. Howlin' Wolf and John Lee Hooker and Muddy Waters, I mean we could go into a medley of twenty tunes. We would do it on an encore sometimes where we would go into all sorts of stuff. Rusty would start singing a thing, we knew all the correct lines to those tunes, so we'd just go and do it and fire on. It was wonderful, the most fun I've ever had in a band. Rusty was amazing. Interesting man. Hard living man who literally really practiced what he preached. He wasn't a weekend warrior, he was a real guy. It killed him. So I mean he was real. I admired that about him. I was so afraid of him because he was a hard fella. But yeah, he sure was something. I think he was one of the most amazing front men I've ever worked with."

"Rusty was a wild man," adds Carmine Appice, band mate of Rusty, Tim and Jim McCarty in Cactus. "I mean, you can listen to his lyrics and get a good vibe of what Rusty was about (laughs). He was into freedom, he was into power to the people; he was into legalizing drugs. He was a very aggressive kind of guy. He used to carry knives around with him. Sometimes he'd even have a pistol, illegally. And he was easily riled up by police at a gig who were trying to do security. He would always tell the audience to revolt against them and sometimes he got arrested because of it. But he was a real sweetheart deep inside, but he was not afraid to take a chance, and as we know, that's how he died."

"I've got a funny story about Rusty," continues Carmine. "When we went to England, and Rusty was a drummer, and so was Jim McCarty at one point, they were both fans of Ginger Baker. We were hanging out at the Speakeasy, and Rusty is a very rough kind of guy. He carried guns, knives, he dealt drugs all the time; even when he was in the band to his friends. He went up to Ginger Baker and said, 'Hey, Ginger, I'm Rusty Day, I play with Cactus, with Carmen Appice and Tim Bogert, Vanilla Fudge, and I'm a real fan of your playing.' Ginger turned around and said, 'Why don't you talk to yourself?' (laughs). We said oh my God, when Rusty told us that, we thought Ginger better watch his ass, because Rusty will stab him. Then on the same tour, we ended up doing a festival with Ginger Baker's Air Force, Cactus, Sly And The Family Stone, all the groups of the day, and we landed at an airport, and had to take a bus somewhere to go to a festival, and two people got left behind. It was Ginger and Rusty, and they ended up coming to the festival in a Mini Cooper with the driver, just the two of them. We're all contemplating that they were going to arrive, and they were both going to be dead (laughs). But yes, after Cactus, he got killed in a drug deal. He was getting into it very heavily. He always carried guns and knives. If you listen to the lyrics, he's always talking rebellion and fuck the police and he was always like a rabble rouser."

With Ted being so anti-drug, and by all accounts of the two of them at each other's throats, I wondered what Rusty had ever said to the Cactus guys about his previous band. "He loved Ted Nugent. He loved Ted. Rusty didn't push his concepts on you if you weren't into it. Rusty was actually a good dude. He had a really interesting crazy voice, great melodies and great lyrics, crazy; crazy lyrics. Like we would start playing and he would just start singing, lyrically. That's how a lot of our songs came about."

Given Detroit Wheels and Cactus guitar great Jim McCarty's assessment of Rusty, one could see why Ted would be so impressed with him, or impressed enough with him to put up with the drug side of it. "Rusty had an encyclopedic knowledge song-wise," recalls Jim. "He had a thousand songs from all those years playing the bars in Detroit. If you started a groove, he could start pulling lyrics out. If they weren't his own lyrics, he could pull lyrics out of countless R&B songs that he knew. If you listen to the live CD that they released last year, that's a pretty good example of what Rusty did. We ran through about half a dozen tunes, and it was just like a free-form jam at that point."

"Rusty was a character," continues Jim. "Like I say, if you had a thousand songs in your catalogue, he would be there, and he was a very solid front man. I don't know if I consider him a great singer or not, but he knew how to work the crowd. He knew how to grab a crowd, whether you liked it or not (laughs). But Rusty lived a hard life; he lived his life full-tilt. That's what cost him his life. There was no half way with him, and then he was murdered, shot. They came into his house. He was down in Florida and he was doing business with some people he shouldn't have been doing business with, I guess. It wasn't any surprise how he ended up, but the real tragedy was Jocko, who was about 12 or 13 at the time, and visiting from Detroit; they murdered him too. About two or three other guys that were visiting. Everybody got killed. Really terrible."

"Rusty Day was a very close friend of mine," offers a perhaps not so forthcoming John Sinclair, celebrated manager of the MC5. "I was his manager for a while. He was a great guy, great singer, and a great performer, came to very tragic end. He was a hippie. I don't know, he might've had some involvement in the exchanging of substances for money, but I didn't have any first-hand experience of that."

"But everyone always hated Ted Nugent," continues Sinclair. "He's an asshole. Like he is today. He was the same guy when he was 18. He didn't get high (laughs) and everybody else did. He was a suburban kid, and an egomaniac on the guitar. He had that song *Journey To The Center Of The Mind*. He alleges that he didn't know what the other guys in the band were talking about (laughs)."

Barring the sordid Rusty Day saga, John Drake's memories of lead singing with the Amboy Dukes is, in the balance, overwhelmingly positive, due to all the touring the band managed in a brief, intense period of time. "There's so many; I'm trying to think. We did shows with The Who, Jimi Hendrix of course; I've worked with Lou Reed when he was in the Velvet Underground."

But alas, no dates outside of North America. "No, and you want to know why that always made me mad? I mean, we played all over Canada of course, but that was still North America. It was all because the agency that we had was Premier Talent, which was probably the biggest in the country at the time that you could get. We had the right agency but they always felt for what we were doing… you know, the excuse was the money was not right. They weren't offering enough money, and we're not going to send you until the money's right. So I said, 'So when is the money going to be right?' I said,

'We need the exposure. I mean we got a No.1 record in London, a No.1 record in Hawaii, we got a No.1...' you know what I mean? These are huge records! I said, 'Let's get it on, let's go, let's take it, it's out there! Let us do the first tour over in Europe and then believe me, we'll do just fine on the second one. We're not going to lose any money so call it a break even tour the first time, so what. Let's go back the second time and then watch. You know, you'll see what we do the second time around.' These guys, these agencies are so tight. It was just like, 'The money's not right.' Everything was about money! When you get up on a certain level, it kind of takes the fun out of it. Then you start realizing yourself, well, we were successful enough to realize that we weren't really all that successful. Although Ted had been quite successful. You start realizing that and it takes a lot more. I mean our tours, and I'm telling the truth, we'd go out six months at a time—that's a haul. You go out to work a record, today, what do these bands do? They may pick 15 cities or something? A dozen cities where they know they are going to clean up. Well in those days you're going to do a lot more than 15. Half the time I didn't know where I was at. I had to ask my roadman; I go, 'What town is this?'"

Citing the usual cautionary tale, Drake reflects that, "Once you really go down the road of rock 'n' roll, you don't know how people are going to react. I mean, rock 'n' roll is like a drug; it's a very powerful drug. You better be able to know how to handle it and the success that comes with it. 'Cause some people just totally lose it. All of a sudden you have a lot of money, you're a kid with a lot of money. You're like a five-year-old, and they turn you loose in a candy shop and say, 'Eat all you want. Eat yourself to death.' Some of them do it! I mean I'm talking about the rock 'n' rollers."

"We did a gig one time at The Fillmore East and we were backstage in rehearsal. The Chamber Brothers were headlining that show, there was the original Blood, Sweat, and Tears, the Staple Singers, and The Amboy Dukes were on the show. So Bill Graham believed—and I don't know why he believed this—but he believed that if these rockers get into the booze and stuff, it really makes for a really great show. So I'd been in rehearsal just sipping a few beers. When I get to the show and we're backstage—we get down early for rehearsal and everything like that—I'm looking around and I go, man, look, they've got whiskey back here; they have everything! It's like a kid in a candy shop and it's all free! So I started dipping into it and I'm not really a liquor drinker. So I did a little too much of it, okay? I get out on stage and The Fillmore East in those days, the stage was high and it was an old auditorium. They used to have an orchestra pit down there. We're doing three nights there. So I was up there singing this song and I really started getting tipsy because I hadn't eaten all day. I can feel the microphone stand bending because I'm trying to hold myself up without going head first into the orchestra pit. I go, 'Oh my God, what am I doing?' We finish the show, and I thought, at that time I said, 'What the hell am I doing? I could've killed myself!' I went home and got a good night's rest back at the hotel. Didn't touch anything for the next two days."

"If you don't get a standing ovation there, you're screwed," continues John. "So the next day *Variety* hits the stands and they said the lead singer of The Amboy Dukes looked like an escapee from an Elvis Presley trainee centre. I go, 'You bastards! How dare you!' But I thought I must have done something really bad that I don't know about."

John confirms the stories that Ted barely touches booze, mainly because for whatever reason, it gets him drunk pretty easily. "Yeah it's true. Some people if they drink beer or whatever, they have a tolerance for it. It's possible that he does not have the tolerance. I remember once in awhile, you know, come to the ranch out here in Michigan and we'll sip a few beers and go fishing and stuff like that. I think he would do something like that once in awhile, but never the drugs. No, never. Man, he is like stone-cold crazy against that stuff."

"He always was anti-drug, and I don't think he's ever taken a drug in his life," affirms journalist Jaan Uhelski. "I think he only started drinking in his later years. Last time I interviewed him, he told me he was drinking margaritas in the hot tub at Sammy Hagar's, that kind of thing. No, he was stringently and proudly anti-drug. I think the hunter thing he may have done that, but he didn't talk about it. I mean that was so utterly uncool back in the '60s to even talk about anything like that. I mean that really didn't come until later, until he got the measure of fame and the focus on him, and then he started revealing those parts of himself. I just remembered him as more of a city kid rather than this country guy."

"I snorted Coke once in '67," divulged Ted in '77, to *Music Express*. "Mild-mannered high but nowhere near as good as a good piece of ass or a good turkey dinner. I saw all these imbeciles dropping off like flies with all these drugs. I just had to see an accident one time to realize that you don't drive into the bridge."

Post *Migration*, The Amboy Dukes continued their sideways drift with the utterly bizarre (and bizarrely titled) *Marriage On The Rocks/Rock Bottom*, issued January 15, 1971. Said Ted, "That was a good album, some real tasty guitar work which people don't usually give me credit for. I can play excellent acoustic as well as the heaviest electric—just listen to the title track."

The band now consisted of four of the six guys from the last record, following the neat deletion of both vocalist Rusty Day and rhythm guitarist (and until now, chief writer), Steve Farmer. Lead vocals were handled by keyboardist Andy Solomon with Ted singing as well. This fourth record saw the band migrate to Polydor, but with such a deconstructed set of songs, the Dukes were lucky to squeak out a No.191 placement on the Billboard charts.

Following this album, explains new drummer KJ Knight, replacement for Dave Palmer, was *Survival Of The Fittest*. "The first time I played with the Amboy Dukes, we had a deal with Polydor Records. The first record released on Polydor was *Marriage On The Rocks/Rock Bottom*, which really wasn't a commercial success. Then I joined the band and we toured the album, and we recorded the album *Survival Of The Fittest*, at the Eastown Theatre, the summer of 1970. I think the album charted around No.123 and sold about 50,000 copies in its first year of release. The second time I joined the band, the members of the group were John Angelos and Rob Grange, who stayed with Ted during his really successful years. But we didn't have a record deal. We just kind of travelled around the country playing, you know, not promoting anything, and I would say that, that was like a downtime for the band; we were lost. We were just out there trying to keep our name in the public. I think Ted was still searching for the right combination of musicians and the right music."

The album was indeed recorded at The Eastown, little brother to the Grande Ballroom, on 31st and 1st August 1970. KJ is the new drummer, but there's also a new bassist in Rob Ruzga. Vocal duties are handled by Andy,

Ted and KJ.

"I would have to say that we were high energy rock 'n' roll," ventures KJ, trying to peg the sound of this floundering band, now all of a sudden more hippie-fried than the psychedelic bands left and brave enough to enter the new decade. "That seemed to be the way all the bands were back then—MC5, Stooges—and we were all inspired by Mitch Ryder And The Detroit Wheels for sure. Mitch was definitely the godfather of Detroit rock 'n' roll. But we were definitely what you would call a high energy rock 'n' roll band. We weren't really psych (laughs). I mean, Ted was always really conservative. I don't think he ever saw himself as a hippie. He was very much anti-drugs, so I would say that we weren't a hippie type of band or a head band. I wouldn't say we were anything like that. Ted's influences were the Rolling Stones and definitely Jim McCarty of the Detroit Wheels; those were his main influences. The Detroit Wheels came out on the Detroit scene in around '63 or '64, and they had some phenomenal hits, like *Jenny Take A Ride*. And that was a group that we all saw. They were like the pioneers, and matter of fact, earlier, Mitch had a group called Billy Lee And The Rivieras that played on the local scene as well."

After admitting he never asked the guys why the album he now had to tour had two titles, KJ additionally remarks with a laugh, "I'll tell you what, when I first joined the band, I had to learn some of the songs from that particular album and one was *The Inexhaustible Quest For The Cosmic Cabbage*, which was like a ten-minute piece of avant garde music. I swear to God, I could never memorize the whole thing. Halfway through the song I would just fake it and play anything."

With respect to *Survival Of The Fittest*, Knight's one recorded document with the Dukes, he explains that, "The idea was we were going to do half the album in the studio. We were going to do four cuts, which were *Survival*, *Rattle My Snake*, *Mr. Jones' Hanging Party*, and *Slidin' On*. We were going to do those in the studio, and then we were going to do a long version of *Prodigal Man*, where everybody soloed, and we were going to do live. But it turned out we were going to do the whole album live. Eastown was selected because it was in the east and a fan-favourite venue. Very similar to the Grande, really. The Ballroom had fantastic acoustics, and it was more known;

and a favourite place for the MC5 to play. As a matter of fact, that place was around even before rock 'n' roll. My dad, Don Mills, who was a drummer, he played big band and played the Grande Ballroom in the '50s. As far as the Eastown, like I say, it was a theater, another place that had great acoustics, just a fantastic place to play."

For two records running now, Ted Nugent had come out as the chief songwriter for The Amboy Dukes. Notes KJ, "I think *Mr. Jones' Hanging Party* was Ted's first song that he ever wrote that was an anti-drug song, and it probably had to do with the fact that poor Greg Arama, our bass player who we loved so much, became addicted to heroin. Eventually because of this, Ted had to let him go, and I think the song was inspired by poor Greg's downward spiral. Ted just wrote songs about things that inspired him, and obviously at that time he was beginning to become very involved with his hunting and all of those things, so I think some of the lyrics were inspired by his love for the outdoors."

"Greg Arama came to New York and played in my band Ursa Major," notes Dick Wagner, on the acquisition of Arama. "He was originally from there. Greg had a unique personality, let's put it that way. Totally dedicated to his bass; I mean he never put it down. He was playing his bass 24 hours a day. Very cantankerous and not easy to get along with because he was so strange. Matter of fact after he left the band, he wrote a letter to me and he signed it, 'Rock 'n' roll or death.' A month later he committed suicide. I think he was trying to get back in the band. It was just beyond because we just couldn't get along. It was constant fighting and constant negativism. So I couldn't work with him anymore. But he plays great on that Ursa Major album. So he was definitely a major force in the sound, but a major negative influence in the band. He was always wanting to fight and stuff. I never got into that side of it because I wouldn't let that happen. It became like... a universal thought that Greg had to go. It was too bad because he was great and who knows what was going on in that mind? Man, he was out there."

As evidenced on the *Survival Of The Fittest* album cover, Ted dressed as a combination of cowboys, Indians and hippies, but as importantly, the cover featured Ted alone, no other band dudes. "At that particular time," explains Knight, "because there'd been so many changes with the Amboy

Dukes, I think at this particular point, Ted was doing everything anyway. He was in charge of booking the group, he would drive the limo, he would organize everything, it really was his band. As a matter of fact, on the back cover of that album, there's a collage that was done by Andy Solomon's mother, Mavis - a really nice piece of artwork. But she used a photo of former Amboy Dukes. The photo was actually Ted, Greg Arama, Andy Solomon and Dave Palmer, the drummer that I replaced, and not only are there no pictures of me and Rob Ruzga, the band's bass player, it was only pictures of former players."

Ted was doing a lot to keep things afloat, but the band essentially had no manager. "No, well, let's see, our road manager was Phil Nicholson, who is a really cool dude. But at the time I played with them, there was no actual band manager. I would say that Phil Basile from Breakout Management, who helped Ted get his record deal with Polydor Records would be the closest thing to a band manager. But I think he was more on the scene, and had a contract with Ted just based on the fact that he had helped get the record deal. But he did not individually manage the members of the band. we were booked by Diversified Management, DMA, a company that was run by Dave Leon, and so he was like our booking agent, kind of like a manager in a way. But we didn't really have a manager."

Phil Nicholson, credited as Recording Supervisor, is one person that would take on a position of authority within Ted's back office (*Saint Philips Friend* on the second album is named for him), tour managing the band for years, significantly through its golden run in the '80s. Of his boss, he says that, "Ted's a character in the mould of Erroll Flynn. Not quite as devious, but as far as being a real individual and going about things the way he sees them. There are things people consider extremes, but he's one of the few people I know who can be very articulate of exactly what he wants to do. No matter how people look at him—'madman' and all that—he's probably one of the clearest-thinking guys I've ever met. I have never run across a person I respect as much, and that has nothing to do with our situation. There's a difference between confidence and ego, and Ted's full of confidence."

"Everybody can hate him now," joked Ted, in conversation with *Creem's* Debbie Burr back in 1970, when he handed at least some of the responsibility over to road manager Phil. "But at one time, when there was shit to be given out, I was the one to do it. Now if it doesn't have six strings, I don't want it. Before, I was really the leader of the group. I was the Brian Wilson of the Amboy Dukes. When someone had a complaint like, 'We don't like Rusty on stage; he's always high and sings flat,' they came and told me and I had to tell Rusty. It's the group's group. No Amboy Duke has ever decided to leave. It's always been decided for him. I don't know what you've heard ... something like, 'Nugent sucks.' Well, I don't care; maybe I suck, but they were fired!"

"In Steve Farmer's case," continues Ted, "he can't play guitar and he can't sing on stage. He sings like a bitch in the studio and is a fine writer, but he has no place on stage. I tried to teach him some licks and get him to play really well. It turned out that his dynamite writing and great studio vocals just weren't enough to keep up with the group. In other words, whenever the Amboy Dukes go into the studio or need a writer, Steve's always there. I'd like to think that, but he can't play guitar and there's just no room for friendship on stage. I'm still best of friends with Steve, John Drake and Rick Lober, too, for that matter. Drake and I played together for six years. Rick was really mentally uptight with us because I wouldn't let him smoke dope on stage or at practice. We decided that neither one of us could stand it."

As for the ousting of Rusty Day... "Rusty hates my guts. It's great," adds Nugent. "It's true. Rusty threatened to cut my arms with a razor. That was after I hit him in the head with a pipe. But he was in the back of the limo and couldn't reach me. That was coming back from the Fillmore. You can't pinpoint the conflict with Rusty. If you were Ted Nugent he'd hate you. It must be the combination of the letters." Of course drugs were at the heart of it, and "drugs suck!" spat Ted. "I never used drugs. I take gelatin capsules. 'Oh, drugs are cool.' Numerous friends of mine have had good experiences ... two died. My drugs are my land up north and my big car to rip people's heads apart and the engine that goes 170 and all are products of my guitar. Drugs are for the druggist, but I don't see any use for them."

"It had to do with the people I played with for six years," continues Ted, asked about the $500 fine he imposed on his band, lest they be caught chasing a high. "When I wanted them to do a new lick or a funny part, they couldn't get it into their heads 'cause they were flipping out. Which is fine, but it should come after the music. The music should induce it. But, you know, they were just hemorrhaging right there on the floor. But nobody ever had the $500, so I forgot it."

Ted goes on to express good riddance to his past manager. "There was a cat named Bob Henkins who somehow got out of the used car business with his father and into the rock world. He dug people, but he had no communication with either music or people. He got hold of the Amboy Dukes and screwed us out of shape. He got hold of The Frost, The Scarlet Letter (ed. by 1970, re-named Savage Grace) and Ellie Pop and tried to screw them, but they all shook him. I knew him way back when he was a partner with John Rhys about five years ago when I had The Lourds in Detroit. Then, anybody could have come up to any kid who played guitar, say 'recording studio' and right away they're his victim. I thought he was the king man who was going to do it for me. So, when I got it together in Chicago, I called him to come and hear us. Bob came and liked the sound, and told us about the real king of the music industry, Mr. Bob Shad, Mainstream Records, Mr. Gentleman himself, the cat who had his hands on Cannonball Adderly and Wes Montgomery... you name 'em. He had his hands on them all right, but as soon as they saw what went down, they split. Henkins talked us into recording for Shad, telling us how perfect he was and we bought it, 'cause we had nothing else to go by. We recorded and really got fucked."

"*Journey To The Center Of The Mind* would have made it on Shitsville Incorporated," adds Ted. "It was No.10 in the nation without a bit of promotion. They finally promoted it after it fell off a spot. We were super burned on everything. We saw writing royalties, they can't shake that, but nothing on the recording or performance royalties. No one made anything from Mainstream except Steve Farmer and I for writing. *Migration* sold like a bitch, but it's been over such a long period of time it never made the charts. It had a regional breakout in every state in the nation, but Mainstream claims it sold nothing. Phil Basile manages us now. He's also got Vanilla Fudge and Dusty Springfield, and does the tour direction for Beck, Ten Years After and Led Zeppelin. We were on tour with the Fudge and he dug us then, but didn't want to work with Henkins. When we fired Henkins, we played his club in

New York, The Action House. He saw what was going down with Henkins and is going to mend it."

"It's planet-cosmos," says Ted in closing, asked to sum up *Marriage On The Rocks/Rock Bottom*. "It's not really a very far-out thing, especially for the people here in Michigan 'cause we've got our own thing here, you know the festivals and revivals. It's about the marriage of love and man and woman and music. Music is the wedding band. It really is. The new album is to *Migration* what *Migration* was to *Journey To The Center Of The Mind*. "Journey" was an orange fart. *Migration* was the orange, with the fart removed. "Marriage" is a whole new colour with no farts blown."

"One of the reasons why I left the band was I wasn't making any money," explains Knight. "I was only paid 175 bucks a week the first time I played with them. We were out there pretty much just promoting Nugent. I'll tell you what, it didn't really matter who was on stage with Ted Nugent. People were coming to see him play. So I think that's why. But another thing was, back then, a lot of guys self-destructed because of drugs. But yeah, Ted was the ultimate showman. I mean, back in the day, he would get on top of a two-stacked-high Fender amp and jump off the amps and land standing on his feet. Before his solo, he would go backstage and change into like a loin cloth and come swinging out from a rope tied to the rafters, back on stage. His brother, Johnny, who is one of the road crew would take a Styrofoam wig head, and place it on top of the amp, squirt some lighter fluid on it and set it on fire. Ted would have his bow and arrow onstage and he would shoot the flaming head off. Ted was a fantastic shot, and he would hit it, and the crowd would go crazy! He had terrific energy, fantastic showman, and that rubbed off on the rest of us too."

"He's definitely a very competitive individual, and probably the most self-confident individual I've ever known," continues Knight. "We always went out there every night with the attitude that we were going to blow everybody away. But we did not do very good sales-wise. I mean, Ted did not write Top 40 commercial material. Our albums were definitely underground albums that were played on the FM stations. The reason, I believe, that Ted gained the popularity that he did is that we played out so often. And we put on a great live performance. I mean, we played sometimes

200, 250 dates a year."

But again, never outside of North America. "We played in Canada and we played a lot in the United States, although we didn't play much on the West Coast. We were very, very popular in Florida. We played the Hollywood Sportatorium, and we played Pirate's World in Miami. We frequently toured with Alice Cooper, Brownsville Station, and an all-girl band called Cradle, which featured Suzi Quatro, the gorgeous Nancy Quatro and Patti Quatro. So we became good friends with Alice Cooper, and Cub Koda and Mike Lutz from Brownsville Station, and Cradle."

"The most memorable gig was when we play the Montreal Forum in 1970," continues Knight, "and the reason this gig was so special is that Nugent bought me a new set of drums that was on order with Al Nalli Music. We decided at the end of the set, when we were playing our last chord, we would thrash on for like ten minutes on the final chord, and I would dismantle my old drums and throw pieces of the set to the audience for souvenirs, kind of like Keith Moon. But what happened was, when we hit the final chord, I picked up my high-hat and started twirling it around over my head, and hit Greg Arama right in the forehead. Blood was streaming down his face, but he kept on playing, so I kind of in a frenzy started whipping my drums out in the audience and they were hitting people and people were getting hurt. Nugent turned around, set his guitar against his amp and took a running headfirst leap right out into the middle of the crowd. Then our roadie came out and took my bass drum with the mounted toms and the sharp spurs, and tossed it out into the crowd. When we were done playing, there were several people injured and they had to take three people to hospital. As it turned out, no one was actually hurt but that was a really wild night. Back at that time too, Woodstock had come, so the outdoor festivals became a big deal. So we played a lot of huge outdoor festivals during that time, including the Erie Canal Soda Pop Festival, which took place in Illinois in '72. I think there were 300,000 people at that venue. Probably the largest crowd we ever performed in front of."

Turns out that KJ had a connection with Rusty Day as well. "Yes, well, Rusty and I were tremendous friends. The first time I met Rusty was when he played at my father's teenage nightclub in Garden City, Michigan, the

Club Shangri-La. Rusty and I started hanging out together, probably in 1967, when I was about 17 years old. We used to go to the Blind Pig, downtown Detroit, and our favourite place to hang was the Chess Mate Coffee House. That's where we heard a fantastic drummer named Steve Muruga Booker, who became my mentor. He was a jazz drummer who was known for his marathon drum solos. But Rusty was a huge influence on my life, and Rusty and I played together in a few bands. We had a band called The Day And Night Dealers Blues Band, and of course, Rusty was also a very big drug dealer, and one of the biggest drug dealers in Detroit, as well as being a fantastic entertainer, vocalist and celebrity. But what happened was, eventually Rusty moved to Florida, where he was murdered, as a result of a drug deal that went bad. I saw Rusty four days prior to his murder. But Rusty was a great friend and we played in several bands together and we had a lot of experiences together."

"He made a lot more money dealing drugs than he ever did playing music," laughs Knight. "But the thing was, when Rusty was playing with Ted Nugent, their personalities clashed, because Ted was vehemently against the use of drugs, although that *Migration* album they played on together was a great album, they weren't together very long, because they couldn't get along because of their opposing views regarding drugs."

Was there also friction because Rusty was making money and nobody else was?

"I don't think Rusty made that known. So I don't know if there was any friction along those lines. At that point, Rusty was just coming up as a drug dealer. It's not that he was making huge money. Later on in his life he started dealing more heavily. But I mean, you know, I don't think he did much dealing during the time he played with Cactus, because that was an extremely popular band and they were always touring. But once he got out of Cactus, then Rusty went on to play in Detroit, which was an offspring of the Detroit Wheels. As time went on, he got less involved with the music and more involved with the drug dealing. When Rusty was murdered, 3rd June 1982, I had seen him four days before. At the time that Rusty was murdered, he wasn't really playing much music at all, but as a drug dealer he was doing very well."

As drugs would kill Rusty, drugs were also at the heart of Detroit's decline as a ground zero for hard-charging rock 'n' roll in the late '70s. The Stooges and the MC5 both collapsed due to drugs, and with Rusty and Greg Arama, the Amboy Dukes were somewhat hobbled by them as well. Further parallels proffered, The Amboy Dukes would enter the aforementioned period of drift, not emerging on record again until 1974 with the robust *Call Of The Wild*. This period of malaise through '71, '72, into '73 was also matched by Detroit's decline as a manufacturing powerhouse, ignited, at least symbolically, by the race riots of 1967.

"I will try not to cry, as I share with you the curse of self-imposed dependency," begins orator-in-chief, Ted Nugent. "The ruination and suicide of Detroit as a city is paralleled by the horror story of self-inflicted suicide of certain musical enterprises in that city. There is not a distinction between the ultra-leftist Communist-inspired political representation in Detroit. If you follow the gimme demands of the mayors of Detroit not demanding productivity from its citizens, but literally rewarding slovenliness and demanding taxpayers create safety nets to the point where there was no drive, no rewards for being the best that you could be... now there was actually rewards for being the worst that you can be. Burn down your city and don't feel guilty—we'll build you a new one. So let me get this right. So effort isn't necessary any more? Somebody else will cover me?"

"The same social cultural suicide that has turned Detroit into an embarrassing moonscape is the same self-inflicted societal and cultural suicide of drug abuse of the greatest musicians that have ever lived. You will never sit across from a person who more dearly reveres what Wayne Kramer and the guys in the MC5 represented. But as I said to Wayne eye to eye, I will say to you now. If you knowingly and intentionally infest your sacred temple with poisons that will compromise your spirits so that you can tune out and drop out, you mean you're actually going to take this gift of life, indulge in poisons too that you don't have to be aware of this gift of life around you? This is a desirable procedure?"

"Poisoning your sacred temple so you can't play your guitar as good as you could? This is a desirable path you're taking horrifically? Tragically and heartbreakingly that's what happened. The MC5, I told you as we were eating some good antelope sausage here, I'm pretty good with descriptive articulation. When I describe something to you, you don't ask what it is I'm describing. You can close your eyes and see what I'm describing. I am helpless to find words to adequately describe the power, musical authority and unprecedented positive energy of the MC5 at their peak. It was... I'm emotional about this. It was stupefying. I thought I was a bad motherfucker on the guitar. I thought the Amboy Dukes were bad motherfuckers, had that James Brown, Wilson Pickett, Sam & Dave shake going on. Staxx, Volt, Motown, man, we had the grind, the groove, we were black guys, man. Then I saw the MC5. The Amboy Dukes... when I witnessed the MC5 coming back from Chicago – I had moved to Chicago from Detroit in '64-ish, and I came back upon graduating in '67 – I wasn't aware of the MC5. The first night I saw them, you know what I did? I made the Amboy Dukes practice four times as often. Four times as focused, and four times as dedicated."

"Because what Mitch Ryder And The Detroit Wheels established for me in my youth, as a bar of excellent, the MC5 created a new elevated bar of intensity, and you know the most important word of music? Your music and your career will be based on one word more than any: Believability. When you witnessed the MC5, you couldn't not believe them. It was as authentic as the kiss to a loved one in their coffin. It was as authentic as the first embrace of your newborn child. It was powerful beyond description, and then they got stoned and turned into fucking idiots who couldn't play, couldn't sing, couldn't dance, and couldn't accomplish anything. So if you do drugs, you're a fucking idiot. Drive safely."

In closing, Ted places his band inside of this era that was now dead or certainly dying. "I think the Ramones would tell you that the reason they covered *Journey To The Center Of The Mind* was because the Amboy Dukes were the quintessential garage band. We had all the flailing kerrang outrage, but we revered the music element, the musicality of our performances, so that once again I cannot emphasize the word tightness. I emphasize tightness because musical... you know The Clash were cute, and I don't mean to offend the Clash fans out there, but they weren't tight enough for us. They weren't tight enough for me. They weren't sensual enough for me. I know they had hit records and they had a great following, and they were considered to be this defiant, uppity rebel-type of music, but I'd already lived with the MC5, so I'm sorry, the Clash didn't even qualify as far as I was concerned. I'd been to the mountaintop. Certainly the Amboy Dukes were the mountaintop and the MC5 were the mountaintop and The Who were the mountaintop, and all of those bands I just mentioned really played good. Really had great chops, and I believe were motivated by the music of a statement of rebellion and defiance, where I think The Clash—and I don't mean to pick on The Clash—but I think their thing was a pose of rebellion and defiance. Music was secondary to them. But The Who, with the MC5 and Amboy Dukes, music was first and foremost and primary."

"It was more of a decline when you started looking at the riots in 1967," adds Ted's singer John Drake, seconding Ted's disappointment with the winding wane of good things for the motor city. "There was really this beginning of the end for Detroit. It just slowly went downhill from there. It never recovered, and I think that hurt the bands a lot. There weren't as many places to play for them anymore. I mean for the non-touring bands and things of this nature, that didn't help anything. The Grande at that time ran until about '74, '75. Something like that, I forget. The Grande, man that was one dangerous neighbourhood then. They beat Leslie West up like you wouldn't believe. This was just before a show. It was the neighbourhood! The punks in the hood got a hold of him. He didn't know anything about the neighbourhood. They were a west coast band and he just thinks, 'Oh we're doing another gig in this ballroom and stuff,' and man they beat him. They broke his ribs and he said, 'I swear to God, I'll never be back here as long as I live.' It was just a rough neighbourhood and why it declined? It's simple—people didn't have jobs anymore and all the motor companies were moving out. It had always been a one-horse town. I mean, you had your choice. You could do music or you're affiliated with one of the car companies. Now take your choice. I was not about to be affiliated with that stuff. I just couldn't bring myself to sit there and work eight to ten hours in a factory every day. General Motors, Ford, Chrysler... all of it left. You know, these cars are built in every other place now but there. I think they build Mustangs or something, Lincolns. But really that's about it. There's not a lot of cars being built in Detroit anymore."

So as discussed, the Amboy Dukes, crazy psych band as they were, were officially past due date once 1970 rolled into '71 and '72. Lineup changes kept happening and it was looking like Ted's career was going into the dumper, let alone that and those of the other near-anonymous players passing through the ranks.

One important addition during these lost years, going on to great fame with Ted as solo artist, would be bassist Rob "De La" Grange, who saw the revolving door first hand. Rob had been a mainstay on the Flint, Michigan scene, and when Ted found himself in need of a bassist, he personally called upon Rob to audition.

Notes Rob, "When I was in the Amboy Dukes with Ted—and I really have to be on his side about this—we would have singers in the band that were drunk all the time, didn't show up for gigs. You would go to pick them up at their mum's house and he was still sleeping from just going to bed, and we really had a low tolerance for rock guys who thought they were rock stars before they even had a hit album (laughs). If you look at the history of Ted Nugent, he's had so many people go through his band, and the primary reason that a lot of them didn't work out was because they were always high. So even in the '70s, he didn't tolerate it. He basically said listen man, I don't want to deal with all the tardiness, the guys can't show up, they don't practice, they're either too high or too drunk all the time. I don't want anything to do with it. When you're in that lifestyle, you see so many people, too high, too drunk, can't function, or they die. So you go, I don't want anything to do with that. No, when I played with him, he did not drink, he did not smoke, didn't smoke marijuana, didn't do any drugs, anything like that. It's just, he didn't care for it and you have to respect that."

KJ Knight, who overlapped with Rob Grange in the band in the early '70s, figures that Ted kept on with Rob so long into the '70s, "because Rob Grange played like Greg Arama, the original bass player, and Ted loved that about Rob. Rob was a really great guy and very dedicated, and he was very dependable."

Recording through June and July of '73, the band, now called Ted Nugent & The Amboy Dukes, went on to issue a new record by the end of July. The new label was the small DiscReet imprint, but the record represented a giant leap forward for the band, *Call Of The Wild* featuring competent although not exemplary hard rock songs much more indicative of the times.

Parallels with the Alice Cooper band arise yet again. Deep back to the early history of Alice Cooper, the band was signed to Frank Zappa's label. Frank took a liking to the freaks, which the Alice Cooper guys most definitely were for the duration of the psych weirdness all over *Pretties For You* and *Easy Action*. Fights with manager Herbie Cohen were always part of the mix for both Alice and Frank, not to mention Alice's management, Shep Gordon and Joey Greenberg. Flash forward and another freak band (albeit like Alice circa *Love It To Death*, moving away from a hippie vibe), The Amboy Dukes wind up on a Frank Zappa imprint, and in the small print on the back of *Call Of The Wild*, there's the name Herbie Cohen again, credited as "DiscReet Business."

Ted's band at this point was a trio (a format Ted would relish later in life), consisting of Ted and his bassist Mr. Grange, along with Vic Mastrianni on drums. Gabe Magno gets a thanks for some keyboard and flute work, while Andy Jezowski gets the same for additional vocal work.

Enter manager Lew Futterman, soon to play a large role in taking the Motor City Madman stratospheric.

"Let me go back to the beginning of the relationship because it's sort of interesting," relates Lew. "I had really never been involved in heavy metal prior to my involvement with Ted. I started out in the music business promoting jazz and folk concerts at colleges back in the very early days of the college concert business. This would have been in the very early '60s, so '61, '62. I got involved then in a lot of progressive rock situations. Went from promoting to managing to, lo and behold, producing records, and I had a certain level of success with more progressive areas of rock and also some blues. I was instrumental in resurrecting Jimmy Witherspoon's career, and I was both his manager and producer. Anyway, I had a group from England called If and they became college concert favourites in America, and I worked primarily with local agencies around the country in booking them."

"And the people who booked Ted out of Detroit at the time—this is after he spun off of the Amboy Dukes and went out on his own—they kept saying to me, 'Oh Lew, we've got this artist. Remember the Amboy Dukes? *Journey To The Center Of The Mind*? Ted Nugent? Well he's a great performing artist and hasn't had an album out on his own, but just a great performing artist, works all the time and has a big following despite not having an album out. You gotta come see him.' Finally I agreed. I was going off to the Midem, the big music event in the south of France and I needed some stuff to peddle. I ran down to Atlanta in early January, and lo and behold the first big snowstorm in Atlanta in 20 years that day. We had eight or ten inches of snow on the ground in Atlanta in January, a Monday night, and Ted was playing in one of those cavernous old clubs that used to exist back in those days. This would have been probably about '72, '73. Anyway, there were a thousand people in this club on a snowy Monday night in Atlanta. Ted did a great show; the people screaming and yelling loved him, and I left there saying you know what? Anybody who can draw a thousand people in a snowstorm on a Monday night in January has to have some magic to him. And the idea is we gotta find a way of bottling the magic."

"So I took his demo that was just sort of a muddy mess," continues Futterman. "But it had enough of interest on it, both on Ted's songs and in his playing. Of course his history with the Amboy Dukes meant that I was able to get a deal for him with Bizarre Records. Bizarre as in crazy. Frank Zappa's old label. I got him a deal and they were distributed by Warner Bros. We spent two years with them trying to get Ted's magic on record and the records sold okay. They sold 50, 60, 70,000 copies. Enough to sort of cover their cost and so on, but we didn't get the magic, really. Bizarre was the overall company and DiscReet was the imprint. The contract was bizarre but... you gotta remember this is a long time ago. My brain is mashed potatoes. We did the two albums, they were okay, they had some good songs on them. They were sort of decent reflections of what they did in person. They didn't have the kind of shape to them that really was needed."

The two albums Lew is referring to are *Call Of The Wild* and its follow-up *Tooth, Fang & Claw*, both issued in 1974. Featuring the same lineup, both records are on DiscReet and are always viewed as a paired set by watchers of Ted. *Call Of The Wild* contains no tracks that lived on into Ted's solo career, however the grinding *Pony Express*, honky tonkin' Elf-ish party rocker *Ain't It The Truth* and proto-metal album closer *Cannon Balls*, with a bit of spit and polish, could have held their own on Ted's self-titled solo album soon to turn heads in 1975.

The new direction and new sound came about somewhat through the inspiration of a solo hunting trip on which Ted cleared his head of all post shackles, The Nuge emerging with a new sense of purpose.

"I've spoken about how I'm the master of escaping the music," Ted told me in 2014. "Well, back then I wasn't so much. I was young and completely out of control. I graduated from high school in '67, playing 300+ dates a year, and we backed it down to like 250 (laughs). I didn't do a whole lot of extensive hunting. I was still in the learning process in the outdoor world, even though I've been hunting since I was born. But I didn't know much. So when I went hunting, I didn't play the guitar much. I mean literally, when I got off the road, and I went hunting for two weeks, I probably didn't even touch the guitar. Well, since about '73, when I took my escape from the road to the Uncompahgre National Forest in Colorado and confirmed myself, I made sure that I didn't just have a little window of primal scream exaltation, but rather extensive fall hunting trips. So I wasn't rushed, so I could be more aware of my surroundings and my duty to be a conscientious, reasoning predator, kill cleanly, aim small, miss small, and absorb the spirituality of that revival power of nature. So I learned to go into both worlds. And even then when I started racing off-road with Parnelli Jones and Mickey Thompson, I learned to plunge 100% of my being into the given endeavour. So those new songs, very many of them... I mean, just the title *Tooth, Fang & Claw* and *Call Of The Wild*, those were hunting influences."

Hence the feast shot on the back of *Tooth, Fang & Claw*. "Yes, the back of the record was us at a big banquet table with pheasants and deer hawks and *Tooth, Fang & Claw*, that is nature. It's interesting you ask me that, because I've never thought of that juxtaposition, in that I was writing songs about the wild, but I was writing them on the road. Whereas now, I'm writing songs like *Shut Up & Jam!* and *Fear Itself*, and I'm writin' 'em when I'm off the road hunting! These new songs are more about society and things other than hunting—yet I'm writing them during the hunting season."

"Ted Nugent's no jumped-up Johnny-come-lately," read a rare early UK review for *Call Of The Wild*. "He's been around for ten years now, most of them in obscurity. He couldn't have come a moment sooner. The time is now right again for raw, aggressive guitarists—and Ted's the best of the bunch. He plays his guitar like it was a gun, spattering out notes instead of bullets. He's also a speed king, rarely playing a slow number; and the faster the song, the better Ted likes it. To add to all that, Nugent is one of rock's great showman, recently offering to take on all comers in a Guitar Battle. You bet he won't find many takers."

Rolling Stone's Alan Niester made a good point in recognizing that The Nuge was Detroit's last man standing an' grandstanding. "Nugent was one of the original purveyors of wall-to-wall blitzkrieg guitar and *Call Of The Wild* is nearly a trip backward into turn-of-the-decade Detroit when melody, subtlety and musicianship took city-wide back seats to noise, power and vitality. Nugent is the chief surviving proponent of the city's kick-out-the-jams philosophy and hasn't mellowed a bit. A forerunner of everyone from Jimi Hendrix to the Iron Butterfly, Nugent has outlasted most of them by simply standing still. He sounds as good as ever."

On to *Tooth, Fang & Claw*, and indeed two compositions stayed in Ted's live set through the transition, namely *Hibernation* and *Great White Buffalo* even if both lack much modernity, sounding dated even within the oddly southern-rocking bunch of songs on the two DiscReet records.

"I remember it like it was yesterday," recalls Ted, asked about the penning of *Great White Buffalo* decades after the fact. "We were in the studio tuning up and jamming for the *Tooth, Fang & Claw* record in upstate NY with Lew Futterman producing, when as usual I started slamming out this driving, grinding rhythmical guitar theme-line lick. That was yet another magical moment like the original musical burst of so many of my songs. I was tuning up my blonde Byrdland, and that pattern leaped forth with a force to reckon with. Killer bass player, Rob 'De La' Grange, stopped me and asked what the hell that was, and I said, 'I don't know, just jackin' around, tuning up'."

"He told me to play it again, but I failed to play the lick the same as I had just done moments before and he kept badgering me to re-discover the lick. I didn't. But after recording some other songs, I again went to tune up my Gibson and the lick burst forth again. Rob yelled 'That's it! That's it!' So eventually I stumbled onto the lick again and we immediately recorded it as

I shouted out the arrangement like a stream of consciousness. I played it a few times, showed the guys where I wanted to stop and start it up again, turned on the tape machine and recorded it in one fell swoop, making up the lyrics as I went along—take one! I hollered the lyrics off the top of my head, articulating to the best of my ability my take on the great Indian legend of the spiritual beast of yore. As a bowhunter and nature-craver, the emotion was palpable and powerful. Rob came up with that wonderful fluid bass melody at the end, Vic the thundering double bass drum assault and history was made. To this day it is one of my and the audiences' and band's all-time favourites. We knew it was a killer but could not have known it would become a top requested classic American rock song for more than 40 years and adopted by so many American Indian tribes as their spiritual theme song, based on their historical religious legend of the mystical Great White Buffalo of their prayers. Mighty powerful stuff. I still get goose bumps every night we perform this intense rocker."

Equally valid candidates to live on in the live set might have been *Lady Luck*, *Living In The Woods* or *No Holds Barred*, although truth be told, the totality of these records, with these performances, arrangements and productions, sound at best, of their time, not in the least bit leading edge, as would some of the more fiery tracks on the *Ted Nugent* album. Nonetheless throughout, there's a big pile of Ted riffs and leads, his signature sound starting to form, the howl and twinning ideas up top, the snarling, predatory power chording down below. One final note on this transitory period, even though the fare is earthy, rootsy hard rock, there is indeed that funky, James Brown vibe of which Ted often speaks, but, let's face it, never really pursued much on the early Amboy Dukes records or indeed the rigid proto-metal angles of the Tom Werman era, plus beyond.

"The albums were, uh, poorly produced," says Ted trying to put a brave face on it a couple years later. "They're great, but total, total concept-wise, they were not. Have you ever seen me live? People who see it get next to it, right? Given the chance, it's gonna work, all right, so this is what I tried to get across on record, and it was not really gotten across on those albums. And for all the people who can see me, they can listen to the albums and go, 'Yeah! I can listen to the albums, I can see what's going on, it works, yeah, yeah,

yeah!' But it's like getting your rocks off over the phone; I mean, it's just not like being there, you know? I'm proud of the albums. I think *Call Of The Wild*, I think some of the songs are... I think the covers are great. *Pony Express* is a motherfucker. *Ain't It The Truth* is a motherfucker, *Below The Belt* and *Cannon Balls*, great, great! And *Tooth, Fang & Claw*... Fuckin' *Sasha*, phenomenal song about my little girl! *Lady Luck*, just, just great! *Living In The Words*, motherfucker! *Great White Buffalo*—love it! *Maybelline*—Chuck Berry should beat his meat daily for that one! *Free Flight*—beautiful! Great songs! But overall, as far as fire goes, as far as what's available on vinyl nowadays, it wasn't epitomized here."

Sasha in particular is a song that would take on resonance in later years, due to Ted's acrimonious divorce in late 1979 and the toll that always takes on the kids. The song represents a glimpse at Ted's sentimental side, his steadfast belief in family, and musically, a rare instance where he allowed himself the freedom to stray outside the package of persona and power chords he self-imposed upon his records. Asked about *Sasha* in 1980, Ted huffed, "Don't think for a fuckin' minute that I am out to live up to my image. I am never, for any reason, gonna limit my thought patterns. If I think jazzy, I'm gonna do something jazzy. If I think mellow for a minute, I'm gonna play the mellow. If it holds up as a musical composition, it will surface on an album. On the *State Of Shock* album, there's a beautiful melodious song called *Alone*, which isn't your typical *Motor City Madhouse*. Everybody said, that's not Ted Nugent. I said bullshit. I wrote it. I thought of it. The name's Nuge, you know?"

In any event, whatever one's take on the woodsy gumbo offered from *Call Of The Wild* through *Tooth, Fang & Claw*, there is no escaping the fact that it was underwhelming enough to warrant its lackluster response in the marketplace. Ted has said that through the entirety of the Amboy Dukes run, despite the band notching 200 shows a year, the two DiscReet albums had maybe moved about 100,000 copies each, and many of those sales occurred after the first solo album would shine the light in 1975.

In the band's waning years, beginning of '73 through the summer of '74, Ted Nugent And The Amboy Dukes would share stages with the likes of Captain Beyond, Dr. Hook, Joe Walsh, Bachman-Turner Overdrive,

Brownsville Station, Bob Seger, REO Speedwagon and ZZ Top, while also playing the massive Ozark Music Festival, July 19 to 21 of that year. By November and December '74, Ted's crew was no longer the Amboy Dukes, but rather the "Ted Nugent Band," with one of the last documented stands being a one week booking way up in Vancouver, BC, Canada, at the venerable Commodore Ballroom.

Not exactly all of a sudden, Ted Nugent was a long eight serious years into the business, as desperate for a hit as anybody with half his stamina would be. As hard work would have it, opportunity would soon knock, and Ted would be armed and ready to break down the door.

Ted Nugent
"Listen, Ted Nugent is available"

The gates to rock's biggest stages would open wide for Ted Nugent come 1975, and much of the credit goes to a fortuitous forces-joining between Ted's manager of a couple years, Lew Futterman, hotshot New York manager David Krebs, and a wannabe producer from Epic named Tom Werman. It's only rock 'n' roll, but it's a business.

"We had the option of staying with DiscReet, but I decided it's not going in the right direction and we gotta do something different," explains Futterman, picking up the tale of the Tedinator. "And I made the step towards breaking away and going somewhere else and seeing if we could really move him forward with his recording career. He continued to work quite well in person. He was earning a decent living in person with his performances, and of course having a couple of albums out did help, albeit not big sellers. He had his Midwestern and southern following. And I went around and we got turned down by 14 different record labels. I went back again to a couple of the labels and went to see different A&R people than the first time around, and one of the labels I went back to was Epic."

"Tom Werman was an A&R guy there, and he had not yet brought anything to the label that really had made noise. Tom and I hit it off well. I was I guess about ten years older than Tom—but we were both relatively young Ivy League graduates. We had quite a bit in common and so on. Tom said, 'Look, if you can give me a deal that's not going to be an expensive deal, and I can get involved with you in the production, I'll push to try and get a deal.' I said you know what? Let's do it. Let's do it and we did. We got the deal - it was a very low-ball deal. Then I went back to Ted and said, 'Look, I think that the problem we've had up until now is shaping the material. The problem is that your in-person performance is, to the greatest degree, all about energy. You can't really put energy in a bottle for recording. You've got to have shape. I said I've got an idea, and I'd like for you to give it a try'."

"And by the way, Ted's going to probably deny three quarters of this," continues Lew. "I like Ted and we see each other every now and then, but Ted, as you know, has a gigantic ego, and everything that happened good with his career was because of Ted. Anything else that wasn't because of him should be kicked to the background. But the actual story, the real story, is I brought Cliff Davies in from England. Cliff was not only a very good drummer who had been with quite a few good bands in England, including my band If, but Cliff was also a graduate of a music college and Cliff could write an arrangement for a 50-piece orchestra. He was really a trained musician, sight-reader, played three or four instruments in addition to the drums, and had a very strong sense of melody. I put Cliff and Ted together for like two months and Ted liked Cliff. Cliff was a very nice guy."

"So Cliff and Ted put their heads together and they really sort of started to knock things into shape. In terms of… like, trying to pull out of these riffs that Ted wrote something that resembled a melody. So Ted started getting more of a sense of that. Also to bring some clarity to the music, not just energy. Ted was very creative. Really, very creative, there's no question. Not only music but lyrics. A very creative guy. A highly intelligent guy. But not the kind of a person… very difficult to get him to do anything he didn't want to do. But he respected Cliff's musicality and he listened. We finally went into the studio, and when I listened to what they had, I thought it was really starting to sound exciting."

"At the time I was in very, very tight shape financially," continues Futterman. "I had actually gone back to school at Cornell and I was taking a masters degree in public administration, while I was recording, still, when Ted was under contract to me. I made a decision. I took my share of the advance and I plunked it into additional recording costs. I just bit the bullet and I decided, you know what? I want to make sure we put enough time and effort into this. In those days people used to go through recording of a hard rock album in three days and a cloud of dust. I treated this like a real… like one would treat a progressive rock album. Multiple layers of music and so on, really with respect for the music. With respect for Ted's music. A respect for his music that he, just from the habits of heavy metal, had never really given his own music that level of respect. It just wasn't part of the culture of heavy metal."

"And that's why... of course the classic that came out of those sessions was *Stranglehold*, which is really, virtually, an orchestral piece of heavy metal. I mean when you listen to *Stranglehold* there is marvelous dimensionality to that recording. I mean not just because I was involved with it, but just as a piece of great rock 'n' roll music. I think *Stranglehold*, more than Ted's biggest hits, was one of the all-time musical rock 'n' roll classics. We put a lot of time into the album, but it was not easy. I mean Derek St. Holmes, who is the lead singer, was a wild man. Nice guy, but a wild man. He was very immature. I mean he was the bane of Ted's existence for years; in fact we even threw him off the second album. Meat Loaf did the vocals on the second album."

"Anyway, we persevered; we put in the extra money from my share of the advance. Tom Werman went crazy. I mean Tom made his share of some musical contributions to it. Not what gets claimed in the press, but he made a couple of contributions to it. But Tom, at one point, actually went back to New York. He so despaired of us ever completing the album with all the fights with Derek and so on that he actually went back to New York. He wanted to disassociate himself. Then he thought... he listened to what we had all done together once we got back and said, 'Hmm, wait a second. This is pretty good stuff. Okay, let me go back. I'm not used to this fighting in the studio or people threatening to beat each other up, but you know what? Somehow the process is working'."

"So Tom, to his credit, decided to come back into the picture. Had he just stayed out of it I don't know what would have happened. The normal thing would have been defend yourself and make sure not to get fired and that would have turned the whole picture of what we were doing negative and who knows if they would have ever even put the album in. But he came back in, and to his credit—because Tom had very good taste in rock 'n' roll, and I gotta hand that to him—to his credit, he let his ears rather than his emotion take over. Hmm, wait a second. They may scream, they may yell, we may end up with a couple of people in jail before we finish the album, but you know what? It's a pretty good album. So from panicking he turned around and became a big supporter."

"We completed the album without a bad track. I mean despite all the fights, despite all the craziness, despite… and by the way, the craziness was not really from Ted. Ted, despite his wild man reputation, when it comes to business he's about as wild as your typical owner of ten pharmacies in the Midwest, seriously. From a business standpoint Ted is a very methodical guy. You show up on time, you do what you're supposed to do. In terms of his wild man reputation, it's got nothing to do with how he treats business. Ted is probably—in fairness to Ted—the most businesslike musician I've ever met in my life."

"Albeit when it comes to the music itself and what gets done was often over the years his worst enemy. You had to just fight with him tooth and nail to get product out that actually stood a chance at selling, but that being said, he was there on a business level and was there on time, put as many hours in as he had to, etc. unlike a lot of other musicians I've known over the years that it was just a miracle that you ever got an album finished because just getting them out of bed to show up was not easy. That's not Ted."

"Anyway, we got the album done, and then I had a big decision. Because we sort of had a handshake, that once we finished the album I was going to take over the management. I thought about it and I said you know what? I've been a successful manager, I've been a promoter, I've been a lot of things, but what I don't have is power. I don't have any power. We got a really good album, they were enthusiastic about it at CBS, at Epic, and what am I going to do to maximize the probability of success? I knew Steve Leber and Dave Krebs very well from the time they were office boys over at William Morris. A couple years older than them, not much, just a few. But you know, when one guy's 21 and another guy's 25, that's a lot of years at that age because you've had three years out in the world or four that the other guy hasn't yet."

"So I knew them from the early days and we were quite friendly, and I went to them and made a bargain. I said if I get Ted to sign with you for management, will you guarantee me over the next two years 100 shows with Aerosmith? They listened to the album. Steve had no ears whatsoever. Dave had fairly good ears; Steven, no ears. But when Dave said hey, this is good, this is really good, Steve, who is more the promoter type, said hey, I'm on board, too. They squeezed me on a piece of the publishing and this and that, whatever, that I went along with."

Or as Krebs himself remembers it, "A couple years after signing Aerosmith, I was at a CBS Records convention and they showed this video of Ted Nugent with a new album coming up and it was just amazing. I said I want to manage him. That's how we ended up on Epic. Aerosmith broke by themselves, but Ted Nugent broke off of Aerosmith by touring with them. So if Ted Nugent did a 50-day tour with Aerosmith and played before 600,000 people, you were really in the Coliseum in Rome every night, and the hands went up or down. For example there was a package out… a good friend of mine named Bud Carr managed Kansas, and he really begged a favour—to put Kansas as a special guest with Nugent opening and Aerosmith following. I said, 'Bud, I think you're making a grievous error, because this is not the kind of band that's going to be able to overcome Ted Nugent.' Well they didn't. But other bands… I think the Scorpions broke off of Aerosmith and Nugent, I think AC/DC broke off of Aerosmith and Nugent. You knew, because we had bands like Artful Dodger that we put out on these big packages, and we warned them that we thought they should play clubs and they convinced us we were wrong, and we turned out to be right. They couldn't deliver, not in that milieu, so to speak."

"But I made the decision," continues Futterman. "As I mentioned, I was back in school part time then, I was 37 years old, I had four children, this was going to be my last stab at the music business. If it didn't happen I was going to finish up my masters degree in public administration and I was going to take a job. At the time I was pretty left wing with my politics, which is a joke when you think about Ted who's somewhere to the right of Attila the Hun (laughs). Mindlessly so, but if you take my gun you'll have to pry my dead fingers off the trigger, that kind of thing. But listen… as Jean-Jacques Rousseau said, never confuse the artist and the man."

"Anyway, so we made the deal, and Ted agreed to go with them for management. The deal was they could not pull Ted from his Detroit management because I had a loyalty to them. I owed them. They had introduced me to Ted and I couldn't—now that it looks like success might be there—do anything that might compromise their position, and Leber Krebs agreed that Ted could stay with his agency, his Detroit agency. Sure enough he went out on the road with Aerosmith. Whether it was partially from that or just by the quality of the album, the first album, titled *Ted Nugent*, took off. It ended up selling almost three million copies or more, maybe. I lost track a long time ago, and that was the story with that. Then there's a lot more that goes on thereafter."

But outside of appreciating *Stranglehold*, Futterman demurs on the subject of whether anything else on the first Ted Nugent album contributed greatly to its hit status. "You know what? It's been so many years since I listened to the album. Listen, I'm not a heavy metal guy. Prior to getting involved with Ted, I had never for the purposes of enjoyment listened to a heavy metal album in my life. I mean did I hear them as part of my listening to what was then the popular genre of rock radio; the WNEW FMs of the world and so on. Yes, I was familiar with all the hard rock and metal groups, just on a very peripheral level. So I'm not a fan. I mean I came out of jazz and blues, and then of course progressive rock I loved. I even loved theater. In fact I had the first theater rock group that ever existed, a group called the Hello People."

At risk of a dodgy segue, "Hello, people" is what the - album was all about. *Stranglehold* was a bluesy heavy metal *Kashmir* for the ages, not so much blues but mid-Sabbath slow-burn with lots of jamming of various tension levels. The rest of the album was sparkled with short shocks of modern rock metal, from the barroom rock 'n' roll of *Snakeskin Cowboys*, *Queen Of The Forest*, *Just What The Doctor Ordered* and *Where Have You Been All My Life*—some proto-hair metal, others boogie-based by modern of riff— straight through the bull's-eye at the pure and Purple metal of *Stormtroopin'* and *Motor City Madhouse*. *Motor City Madhouse* was an early example of what would be known as speed metal (post-Purple's own *Fireball*) a contemporary of Aerosmith's brisk *Toys In The Attic*, which Ted raved about regularly. Chided once that *Snakeskin Cowboys* is a great Keith Richard imitation, Ted scoffed, saying "Hey, he wishes he played that stuff. Imitation? It fucking surpasses that. It's like without question influenced by him. Hey,

I used to know the first five Stones albums by heart."

But looking at *Motor City Madhouse* for a mad moment, here begins a tendency on many of Ted's heaviest songs, where the rhythm section is some combination of behaved toward downright timid.

Defends Ted, "Well it's always been me first, but with a nod to my team. I wouldn't work with anyone who I didn't respect deeply, their musical touch, opinions and history. It's great you mentioned *Motor City Madhouse*, because that was Cliff Davies who didn't have an extensive rock 'n' roll music history. He played mostly jazz from the band If. Tom Werman was only a huge fan of rock 'n' roll. He never played rock 'n' roll; he never engineered rock 'n' roll. But he sure knew it because he loved all the same stuff that I loved, and Cliff and Rob and Derek loved, and Tony Reale loved. Then you get us into 2014 with Andy and Tim and Michael Lutz. They are of the same mindset, and adulation of the original tone. It doesn't mean you have to stick with the original tone. You can improve and update and tweak it, but you start there. So it's raw and it sounds like a damn guitar, not some processed thing."

"But *Motor City Madhouse* is a perfect example," continues Ted, who proves he gets the point. "Because Cliff had never played (sings a double bass beat), the freight train thing (laughs). We recorded it, but he couldn't do it at first. Werman had a little strategy session with me, and I said, 'Well, play it with us now, and you go back in and overdub the double bass drum' and he did it the first try. I remember he had his sticks in his hand, but he held them... he held his forearms over his ears. As soon as he came in like we did when we recorded it live, live in the studio, then he went into the double bass drum (sings double bass drum). So I can understand to some degree what you're saying, because it's really meticulous, very controlled. Now, it's no surprise that all the greatest drummers in the world that I've worked with, whether it's Chad Smith or Tommy Aldridge or Tommy Clufetos or Denny Carmassi or Anton Fig or Steve Jordan or Carmine Appice or Cliff Davies or Mick Brown or certainly my new drummer John Kutz, because he happened to be a neighbour, and I was just shocked that he could play like this... but they all reference *Motor City Madhouse* as a dynamic moment in their drumming vision."

Hey Baby was like a Broadway show tune, similar in goofball old-timey rock bounce as *Magic Party*, a rare and finished unreleased track from these sessions, sung real laid-back by St. Holmes. In fact, Derek's soulful vocals are undoubtedly a huge part of the *Ted Nugent* album's appeal. St. Holmes had joined the band at the age of 22, Ted cognizant of his skills due to Derek's work on the Detroit scene, his band having backed up the Amboy Dukes the previous year.

"I was in a three-piece band called Scott," explains Derek. "Don't ask me where we came up with that name. We would open up shows for Ted. I would go out there and just slam it and try to steal all of the glory. The guys were going, 'We have got to get that kid in our band.' Ted would never bite on it. I don't think his ego would let him. In a weak moment, they talked him into it. I was packed up and headed to California. I was literally leaving—I had a U-Haul truck packed up with a car dolly behind it. I walked into the apartment to unplug the phone and it rang. Ted Nugent's agent was on the other line. This is after I had gone up to Ted and had dinner and hung around four or five times. Ted was never chummy enough to invite me in. The sixth time, however, they invited me up for an audition. I told them, 'Sorry fellas, I have been up there and he is not interested.' They said, 'No, I think this time he is interested.' I told them I was leaving for California as I had a job and everything waiting for me. They asked me to come over for a couple of hours. I put him on hold and I went out to ask my wife. She asked me where they were and I told them Jackson. She said, 'Go over there and do it. I will go over to my mother's house and wait for you.' I went up there and we played for 20 minutes and Ted goes, 'How many Marshalls do you want?' He didn't say I was in the band or anything like that. I told him, 'I will take two.' Those two Marshalls are still in his garage."

"I wrote that song back when I was in high school," says Derek with regard to *Hey Baby*, the second least Tedly song on the *Ted Nugent* record, next to marimba-jazzer *You Make Me Feel Right At Home*, that track's inclusion feeling like a nod to the instincts of Bachman-Turner Overdrive in this department. "I had to put his name on it and I had to give him half of the publishing or he wouldn't put it on the album. It was the only shot I had so I took it. There are a lot of cats still sitting in their bedrooms just because they didn't want to compromise. I compromised on a couple of different levels just so I could get to the point where I could live my dream. My dream was to be in a rock 'n' roll band, tour the country and play in front of tens of thousands of people. When the chance came for me to get songs I wrote on an album, I didn't mind sharing as long as I could get it on there."

David Krebs has always held a fondness for Derek. "Ted Nugent's a great showman, but Ted Nugent had a secret weapon that enabled him to break through and achieve a critical mass in my opinion, and that was Derek St. Holmes. Because Derek St. Homes is the voice of *Stranglehold*. Ted, whatever his reasons, has preferred to be his own lead singer for a long time. He's not a great lead singer."

"*Hey Baby* got some airplay," continues Krebs, on the band's outside-the-box pop proposal for a debut hit. "But I think Ted Nugent happened because he did a complete American/Canadian tour with Aerosmith. The trick was that Nugent wasn't—because he's a guitar player—really competition for Steven Tyler, who was a front man. If you're managing both, you don't want to be in that position (laughs) because only one of them is going to be the winner, and you'll be the loser every night."

"I think Nugent is a one-of-a-kind artist. Remember, as we move from the '70s to today, the amount of permitted sexism, or sexist nature of rock, became politically incorrect. So Nugent, if you look at what Ted Nugent represents, 'I got you in a stranglehold, baby' (laughs); that's pretty much the kind of... at that particular moment in time, and he was a great showman. Also, you've got to remember, again, part of the foundation of Nugent's stardom comes from the fact that there was a rhythm guitar/lead singer called Derek St. Holmes, who was the voice on *Stranglehold*, who was the voice on the song *Hey Baby*, which was a song the came off the original *Ted Nugent* album on Epic, that got us radio play. I would think that most rock fans think that on *Stranglehold* it's Ted Nugent singing."

But what a song... "Excitement, raw sexuality. If you get a chance (laughs), read the lyrics to *Stranglehold* and tell me what they mean, right? It's just the magic of the riff, and the chorus line. They're just brilliant."

So twin talents to be sure, but again, Krebs comes back to that package tour with Aerosmith... "When Aerosmith took Ted Nugent out, I think that really helped to expose him. We had a really ridiculously simple theory. It was if the kid was coming to see Aerosmith and buying Aerosmith records, we could sell them other records that were like that. So Ted Nugent, as an opener for Aerosmith was perfect because I've always thought it was a mistake to put a five-piece band with a front man in front of a five-piece band with a front man. So again, Nugent as a guitar player, was not in contention with Steven Tyler as a lead singer. It was a different kind of thing, and both of them benefited, because the show was amazing. I mean, they're both amazing live bands."

"Some of my early stuff was just mind-boggling," mused Ted back in late '77, forming a comparison between the weirdness of Amboy Dukes and Ted in the here and now. "It was so noisy and dissonant. But I think that's conductive to an individual style and to a marked type of music that I play." The first solo album? "I thought it just snagged the essence of my type of music. There's more presence involved, more crunch where it crunched and more kick where it kicked. My favourite music's always been James Brown. I mean, you could fill a river with the sweat that boy put down when he performed. Mick Jagger, same thing; Wayne Cochran, same thing. It's always been my ambition to be on the edge. One of the great experiences in life is to almost die, I would think. Every night I go out on stage and I don't think about it, but it inevitably goes down, that I put myself to the complete edge."

As regards the record's centrepiece, "*Stranglehold* just started as an encore somewhere with a riff that I attribute to Rob Grange on the bass guitar, and I expounded on that and expanded on that, and that jam session got such a grind going in the audience, I went, 'This ain't a jam; this is a damn song.' I started singing, 'Here I come again now, baby, like a dog in heat. You tell it's me by the clamour now, baby, I like to tear up the street. Now I've been smoking for so long, you know I'm here to stay. I got you in a stranglehold, motherfucker, get the fuck out of my way.' I mean that... I didn't come up with that. That was the attitude and the spirit of every concert and every music-lover that loved the fact that my band was so dedicated to delivering this energy and this tightness and this ferocious attitude and spirit every night."

Up into 2001, Ted explained *Stranglehold* to me this way: "A perfect example, may I dare, of what a musician who is driven by the music and who virtually in absolute terms craves to play and create and wallow and celebrate the musical ideas that he collaborates on, especially in an optimum setting that the virtuosos bring to my musical campfire. Again, if you examine the musicians who performed with me on those early songs, I give them great credit. On *Stranglehold*, we had a rhythm section of unbelievable blackness. We don't have any white influences. And Rob de la Grange on the bass guitar and Cliff Davies on the drums on both those sessions brought a thumping, pummeling, grinding, grunting, snorting rhythm and blues spirit to those tracks that is exactly what I envisioned when I came up with it. These are just classic jam licks turned into wonderful musical rock 'n' roll statements and again I attribute a lot of that to the rhythm section that Cliff and Rob brought to executing my musical vision. In the case of *Stranglehold*, the incredible, soulful, Aretha Franklin-like vocals that Derek St. Holmes brought and to the lyrics was every songwriter's dream. So I take plenty of credit for those mystical moments, but I give a gargantuan salute to my collaborators. There's a grinding, an absolute musical homage that we paid to our rhythm and blues motivators. Really, if you really pay attention, and get past the intensity of the playing itself, there is a James Brown, Wilson Pickett, Sam & Dave, Chuck Berry grunt factor that really spurred us forward. Those moments, they just reek of that dynamic, even when we play them today."

Reflecting back on the song with mutual journalist buddy Jeb Wright, Ted said that, "This earth-shattering lick came about from a constantly developing jam session and as usual, the lyrics were inspired by the pulse, in this case, sexually explicit pulse of defiance that permeated so much of me and my music more and more all the time. The song expresses my refusal to abandon my instinctive high energy, R&B-driven musical dreams in the face of constant pressure from management, producers, record companies, booking agents et al, to back down on the feedback guitar-driven music that I so love. Hence, 'I crushed your face' and to this day, this song is without question *the* sexiest, grinding pure animal love song of all time. Not only that, but the ultimate human beings, warriors of the US military, use this soulful soundtrack for inspiration to kill bad guys. And Kirk Gibson played it just prior to hitting that famous bottom of the ninth homerun, and the Chicago Blackhawks play it every night before attacking the ice to kick maximum ass on their hockey opponents. Then, of course, its use in the movies *Rock Star* and *Invincible* pretty much says it all. We can't wait to perform it every night and all real music lovers celebrate it with everything we got constantly—killer tune."

Enough said. As discussed, the serendipity of the totality of the *Ted Nugent* record had to do with picking proper people, from management, to producer, to one half of a new band, namely a hot-blooded smash-hit vocalist in Derek St. Holmes to Ted's very own John Paul Jones-styled theorist in drummer Cliff Davies.

"Tom Werman was my main producer and Tony Reale was my engineer and they both loved the attitude and sound of my music," explains Ted. "So they came in with a mother hen mentality to just make sure that what was caught on tape was actually what I did 300 nights a year live. So we didn't talk in terms of breakthrough or special this and special that. We just went in with the same attitude that I've always gone in with since '67 forward which is, dammit, this is important music, it's sacred, it is my statement, it is my heart, it is my vision, this is what I crave, let's do it the best we can. I just happened to have Tom Werman and Tony Reale and certainly a great rhythm section with Cliff Davies and Rob De La Grange (ed. just called Rob Grange on the albums—Rob thought his full French name to be too unwieldy), and Derek's vocals. They certainly brought a new quality edge to my musical expression and the performance that they invested in that recording. But it was ultimately Tom Werman and Tony Reale that captured it on tape so that we actually were represented accurately. So we all realized during the process that Tom Werman's pure rock 'n' roll understanding and fan approach to the music was optimized in Tony's capability of catching the edgy and specialized guitar tone that I have, and certainly Cliff's drums and Rob's bass and Derek's vocals. So it was really a work in progress that we had no idea was going to be any different than any other record until it was being recorded. And it was not identified as such just because of material and just because of our performances, but the fact that they were being captured accurately. We knew we had something really special but I think it caught everybody off guard when it went multiple platinum."

So it really did do well right out of the gates? "Yes, it really did. It started selling immediately upon release. I think they made 50,000 copies and those were gone. Everybody got a couple of copies in every record store in the world and they were snatched. They immediately went and did more and they were also snatched. I remember getting a call up in my hunting lodge, 'Ted, come home quick; we're selling 100,000 copies a week.' I'm like, 'okay, as soon as hunting season is done, I will.' I didn't care what kind of money was going through the pipeline; my hunting time is sacred."

Ted gives props to Tom Werman, but the first album gives production credit to Tom and Lew Futterman, the next record, *Free For All*, to Tom, Lew and his new drummer Cliff Davies. However, both Derek and Rob (and Cliff himself) would say Mr. Davies is really the true producer of both those records, and if anybody deserves co-production credit behind Cliff, it is engineer Tony Reale.

"We tried to get him just to sit in a chair at the back," says Derek St. Holmes of Futterman, "but on the first album, he was… you know, he was a producer coming out of the '60s. He produced a couple of hit singles for a couple of R&B artists, so he thought he was a rock 'n' roll producer. The only way that we got the deal with Epic was because Tom Werman said, 'The only way you're going to get this deal with us is if you let me produce it, or if you let me co-produce it.' So that's how we got our deal with Epic because Tom Werman's dad was in the hierarchy of Epic Records. He told Tom that if he wanted to make his mark and make his move, go find yourself some bands. So Tom went out, got out from behind the desk, called himself a producer, was musically talented a little bit, so he went out to try and find acts. One of the first ones he found was us, then after us he found Cheap Trick, then after that he found a band out of Atlanta—through my direction; I took him out to see them—called Mother's Finest, and he signed them as well. Then he signed Molly Hatchet. He had a pretty good run. He's a pretty smart guy."

"But Lew is the kind of guy… he would get on the talk-back," continues St. Holmes. "We would be recording and be in the heat of it. It was pretty intense, I would be right in the middle of singing a song and he would stop the tape and go, 'Um, Derek… uh, not sure if I like the way you pronounced "the".' Okay, so, picture that one. So after a while we just went okay, this is getting ridiculous; he doesn't get this. We've got to go for five or seven different performances and just hit it hard and not worry about it. But yes,

Tom was well embedded in Epic. I mean, he basically brought us the deal, and just said, 'Look, we want to sign you guys to a four-year deal, but I've got to be the producer or the co-producer.' It was no more or no less than that. But he had great ideas, and him and I worked really well together. I worked with him on different projects outside of the Ted Nugent deal. There is a band called LA Guns and I sung backup and fixed almost all the lead singer's vocals on that first album. Nobody knows that."

"It was a very strange situation," explained Cliff Davies, basically corroborating Derek's take on the situation. "You see, Lew Futterman, I've known him since about 1971, when I started playing drums in a European rock jazz fusion band called If. I was the drummer in If, when I produced a couple of albums with Lew, for If, did a bunch of writing and stuff. Then If broke up because Dick Morris became really sick, and in fact, he died a few years ago—he was a piano player and I wanted my own band. So Lew started funding this band called Strange Cure, and it was with a friend of mine named Paul Butler, who actually lives in Ottawa, Ontario, where I went to stay for a year and worked."

"So anyway, when we were doing this little project of mine, Lew called me one day and said, 'Hey, I want you to co-produce a Ted Nugent album with me. Ted is basically making a last-ditch effort to make some kind of musical career, and if he doesn't do it this time around, he'll probably become a professional hunter.' So I said sure, I'll come and co-produce. I showed up there, and Vic Mastrianni, who had been Ted's drummer for quite a while, a tremendous drummer, told Ted that he wouldn't play on the album if he didn't get some points or some sort of royalty. So Ted fired him and hired some sort of young guy who was very under-experienced and not particularly good. I think Lew had in the back of his mind, well, Cliff is a drummer too, so if push comes to shove, Cliff can do the drums on the album."

Which gives rise to a situation similar to that of *Survival Of The Fittest*, where the drummer pictured is not the drummer on the record… "That's right, his name is Brian Staffeld," says Cliff, "and that is not my photograph on the back of the album. Anyway, I basically showed up and it was a mess. They weren't very organized. The songs were kind of long and episodic, and Ted tended to lean in that direction if you let him. Basically we weren't getting any grooves. The young drummer was thrown out very early in the procedure, and it was decided that I was going to play drums as well as produce. We tried like hell—now this is the first album—couldn't get grooves, couldn't get anything, so we said, well, let's do it Beatles-style; let's overdub everything. So what happened was, the only track that was live on that first album was *Stranglehold*. Everything else started out with a click track and Ted's rhythm guitar, and once we got the click track and the rhythm guitar down, we would think about the melodies and the arrangement, making the changes, coming up with the studio version so we had the arrangement, in the form of a song. Then we would just overdub the drums, overdub the bass, and redo the guitar, which was the original guide guitar, and just go from there. We did the same thing on *Free For All*—it was all layered."

"I wrote a bunch of stuff on the first album," laughs Cliff, seemingly able to be amused at losing both production and writing credits on a hit album. "Actually, I rewrote most of the melodies. Ted couldn't really sing the melody, so I would rewrite the melodies, and sometimes I would change the chords if they were a little too boring. The only thing I ever got writing credit for were the two songs on *Free For All*."

"Tom was a guy who was like a wannabe," adds Davies, clarifying the political ins and outs of the Werman situation. "He played guitar and stuff in college and since he was a kid he always wanted to be a record producer and be involved in music. I think his dad was a big wig at CBS. He got himself a job at CBS as an A&R guy with some signing power - through his dad, presumably. I don't know whether he had some interest in Ted or whether it was a coincidence or whether Futterman actually went looking for Werman. But at that point, Futterman had a production company and before Werman and me joined the team, Lew Futterman produced a couple of albums for Ted, on the DiscReet label, Frank Zappa's label, *Call Of The Wild*, and *Tooth, Fang & Claw*. So like I said, at that point Ted went to Lew and said, 'Look, if I don't get a hit record soon, I'm going to hang it up and do something else with my life. I haven't had a hit record since 196...'" whatever it was, the Amboy Dukes thing. So Lew was financing the album, that we were doing in '75, and at the same time he was hustling for a deal. It was during his hustling that he came along Tom Werman, and got Tom to come out and see a few gigs."

"Tom said he liked the band, wanted to get involved, that he might be able to get him a deal and such. I think it really came down to the point where it became political. 'Well, I'll get you a deal for Ted Nugent if you give me a production credit, because I want to be a record producer.' Then he got himself started and had some credit on the very first album—but Tom did nothing at all. Didn't know anything about anything. He'd never been in a recording studio in his life. Most of the work... actually, the band at that point were on the road, so a lot of the time Tom Werman would go back to LA, and me and the engineer, Tony Reale, would sit there day after day after day doing drum overdubs, just layering drums over Ted Nugent's rhythm guitar, and when they had a few days off the road, they would come in, Rob would do some bass, and Ted would do some guitar and they would go back on the road and leave us to do drum tracks. So for a lot of the stuff, there was nobody there except me and Reale."

Asked how his sound had shifted from the Amboy Dukes days to the music that connected with millions, Ted figures, "It was no different at all in the guts and soul of it, but as we mature—which I'm going to start any day now, by the '70s, I'd already been doing it for 20 years, all right? So the little punk, snotty-nose Detroit motor city mad guy in the garage, over there in Redford township looking at the Detroit city limits, the uninhibitedness, the ferociousness of my Chuck Berry, Bo Diddley dreams, was as raw and unrefined as possible. Now, '70s, it was certainly as raw and unrefined as possible, but we could really play. The defiance factor, the outrageous Chuck Berry inspiration, throttle of the music was more important than ever, but we also made a conscientious effort to really musically communicate with each other. If you listen to the first Amboy Dukes manoeuvres, it was really chaotic, but because I was surrounded by heart and soul, dedicated, gifted virtuosos, and we're talking about 15-year old Dave Palmer on drums and then Cliff Davies in the '70s, they were the same type of musicians that wanted to play the spirit of the song. They loved the songs. All my musicians love the songs, but the craziness of real early youth had a little... as I'm saying this I have to stop myself, because I was going to say the clang disarray of the earliest music. I was going to say it was less clangy and disarrayed by the '70s. But

I have a funny feeling it was not. But there's a mystical element to practicing and focusing so much on the musical integrity, that our insanity level was at an all-time high, but we delivered it more effectively because we were a unified punch."

"You know it's one thing to just flail away with your fists, but if everybody directs the same fist to the same jaw, which is what we did in the '70s; we still loved the outrage and defiance of the rock 'n' roll origins, but we wanted to deliver it with a spirit of authenticity that we didn't know there was a spirit of authenticity in the very beginning. Blue Cheer did a damn good job, but if they would have kept going and focused, like the Amboy Dukes did and like my solo band did, they... I was going to say could have created a *Stranglehold*, but no one else could have created that. But that the integrity of that groove, what Cliff Davies and Rob de la Grange did in the rhythm track of the *Stranglehold* song and all those songs, was the song creator's dream execution of a musically dedicated refinement that lost none of the raw uppity outrage of the Chuck Berry, Bo Diddley influences. Did you get that, by the way? It was outrage in the beginning, but we became tighter because we were maturing as musical communicators."

Back to the necessary business end of things, and with respect to the happy meeting of minds Ted has talked about, Tom Werman recalls that, "I remember Lou coming to me and saying, 'Listen, Ted Nugent is available.' At that point I had heard of the guy but I didn't know anything about him. I said, 'Yes, and your point being?' You know, I hadn't heard about the Amboy Dukes. I hadn't heard very much of their music except *Journey To The Center Of The Mind*, and I didn't love that. So I went to see Ted because Labelle was playing in Chicago, and a bunch of us went out to see them because *Lady Marmalade* was breaking and it was a great free trip. A lot of fun. So while I'm there, Futterman convinced me to go over and see Ted at the Illinois Institute Of Technology, in their little auditorium. I couldn't believe it, again. As an A&R man you look around the room, you know? Because you're insecure. You say why am I the only one here? Why doesn't anybody else want this guy? It's so obvious to me that he can make great records. The same was true with all the bands. I was never part of any bidding war. Nobody wanted my bands (laughs). Yet it was easy for me to distil the pop out of hard rock. You know. I mean Ted was commercial even though he was hard. Same thing with Mötley Crüe. I'm a pop guy, not a metalist, and so I always saw my mission as getting radio play with these bands so that they could develop a huge audience, and then they could do what they wanted."

So why did Ted Nugent become so successful? "Well, he was one of a kind," laughs Tom. "Truly one of a kind. I mean he was overwhelming. He steamrollered the audience. I'd never seen anyone with the kind of energy that he exhibited onstage. I mean he came onstage and sucked up all the energy in the room. There was no room for anybody else to do anything. He was funny, he was fast, he had a fast mouth, he looked outrageous, he was tall with very long hair, and he was a pretty decent guitar player. He had these great songs that were all based around a rhythm guitar lick. Like the *Cat Scratch Fever* lick or listen to the way *Stranglehold* starts. He had been working on those songs for a long time, and that's the way it is for a lot of artists who are around for a while before they get signed, or who, in his case, split off from their band and then did his solo stuff. Derek was a great singer and Ted's just so confident and so arrogant, really; and ambitious. You know, he never doubted himself ever."

Into the guts of making the *Ted Nugent* album, and the personalities involved, Werman recalls that, "Rob was good; he was just a quiet guy who would do exactly what he was told. Ted had all the parts in his head before we came in. I mean I was there really more as quality control than as a music guy. I had ideas, I played percussion, I did certain things, but Ted wanted me there because he didn't trust Lew's rock 'n' roll energy. When I remixed the album… Lew handed in the album—I was away and can't remember where I was—and I was really disappointed with the mix. I said I need to remix this album. I went back to the label and got more money. I went back down to Atlanta and remixed it with the engineer. It came out much better. Cliff wasn't a rock 'n' roll drummer, but he was good, devoted to Ted. He was kind of brought in by Lew; he and Lew had done other things. He was a musician, yeah. He was a very bright guy. You know he committed suicide. I don't quite understand why."

"Anyway, he had a sound that I never cared for, but I couldn't really do anything about it. He was a pretty touchy guy, and I don't think he trusted us. I remember I walked into the studio the first time ever, down in Atlanta, and I remember he said, 'Aha, the man from the record label.' That didn't make me feel very good. His sound was too thin and wimpy. There was no beef in his snare. I thought he had pretty good chops, pretty good fills, but his snare and kick drum were just not aggressive. It's like chart drumming. I think that he rehearsed so much with Ted and Ted probably stopped him and said, 'No do that; I like that.' Ted ran the musical show. He really did, and you have to hand it to him. He really thought it all out."

Out of all the productions Tom would be involved in with Ted, he enjoys the first album the most, specifically its grinding epic hit single, a bold eight and a half minute slow burn to open the record… "*Stranglehold* is a monster," muses Tom. "I just loved it. I had a lot of fun doing it. We used tape slap on Ted's guitar. So all those answers and all those duets, those are not duets. That's me doing the fader on a tape slap machine, two 15-inch-per-second tape machines. We only had about three choices for effects in those days. You know, this is 1975. We had just gotten a 16 track (laughs). I remember when we sent the mix to Ted and he heard what I had done, he said, 'I really think it's great; I love *Stranglehold*, but don't ever do that again without asking me first.' I said, 'Yes sir!' (laughs)."

NME's Max Bell summed up the situation nicely, joining the ranks of those who had been rooting for Ted despite a tepid record, and thought that now, finally, Ted's time had come. "Once upon a time the idea of liking Ted Nugent And The Amboy Dukes was considered remarkably unhip. Poor old Ted and his boys were the butt of many a knowing jest, usually based around their supposedly ineptitude and crass handlings of some of rock 'n' roll's, uh, more simple trademarks. Nugent no longer needs to indulge in money-spinning Jack Elam leatherette guitar battles to earn his keep. Nugent's guitar style is all about eliciting a certain response, probably violent blood-letting hysteria, and he succeeds in unblocking most frustrating taps with his standard block bar rhythm chords. The rock 'n' roll plumber strikes again. Prediction: by the end of this year, Nugent and Bob Seger will have joined the ranks that separate small fish from huge monsters. This time he's sharpening his teeth on broken glass. I think you'd better get Ted Nugent before he gets you."

Free For All

"A liver-malt concoction of fun songs"

After an incredulous career sounding and looking like a mountain man acid casualty, Ted had learned to focus his primal urges on two last kicks at the Amboy Duke before going solo. The *Ted Nugent* album was the start of a long-brewing and then meteoric rise that found its steepest angle—creatively speaking if not commercially—with solo album number two, *Free For All*.

Free For All buffed up and shined a big Hollywood light on Ted's particular charms. Each track on the album was a mini statement on its own, each offering a new arrangement, riff, rhythm, velocity, indeed a new proposed vocalist, the album being split between three singers: Ted, Derek St. Holmes and a struggling conundrum called Meat Loaf (more on that later).

Ted positioned and articulated the record interestingly, back when the ink was still drying on the gatefold. Beginning first with the *Ted Nugent* album, he figured that it was "a step in the right direction. The DiscReet albums got a little more fire on them. Sound-wise. These have got a little bit more fire playin'-wise. I'm hip to this shit, but this new album, *Free For All*, is strictly a liver-malt concoction of fun songs. I'm strictly motivated by desire, so I'm not really interested in putting out a hit album."

Cliff Davies, professor of the band, as it were, sets the scene, as the band gets down to work on the apocryphal all-important sophomore.... "Why we were recording *Free For All* in Atlanta was because with the If band, with Futterman there, before I joined Ted Nugent, we did some recordings in Atlanta, at The Sound Pit, which was the same studio we recorded the first Ted Nugent album at. So Futterman was familiar with that studio, plus it was a really good studio. It had a Flickinger board, which was one of the first consoles with LED readouts and stuff, very cool. The engineer there, Tony Reale, was a stupendous engineer—died of a cocaine overdose many years ago; he was another one who really helped; he had some really good ideas. I mean, he was just magic on that stuff. He only did the first two albums, and we moved on. We moved to New York, because Lew's business was taking off so much, he needed to stay in New York. Then we started recording at CBS."

"So anyway, Lew gave Tom my production credit, I'm pretty sure because of political reasons, because there is no doubt of the fact that I did a lot of the work. Then when the second album came around, of course, at this point, Tom had some experience living through the first album, and he had more to do. He came up with an idea here and there that were pretty decent, but I mean, if you sit in the control room, pretty much sooner or later you're going to come up with a good idea (laughs). It wasn't like he didn't add anything to the album. It wouldn't have been any different without Tom Werman. But the bottom line is, Tom Werman became a producer because of those credits on the *Ted Nugent* albums. It gave him enough of a track record that he could go on and do more albums."

"*Free For All* was pretty straight ahead," answers Davies, asked about unique productions things done to the record. "We didn't do a lot of fancy stuff. I mean, like I said, the whole album was layered. There weren't any live tracks on it at all. It was kind of a weird album, because they already had a hit with the first album in '75, which I thought was a tremendous album actually. In retrospect, I look back and I think it's really cool. The second album, was a bit like laissez-faire. It was like we assumed we were going to have another hit. Ted was doing really well on the road, with attendance and playing with Aerosmith and everyone was kind of taking it easy, actually. We didn't really knock ourselves out very much. I think we did more overdubs and stuff like that. A little keyboards here and there, and maybe took more time getting the guitar tones and things. We had a little bit more budget this time around. But actually, for me, *Free For All* is the least of all my favourite albums. It really was, and I think, if Tom Werman had any influence on the *Free For All* album, it was to make it more poppy sounding. You know, more sizzle cymbals and stuff like that."

Continues bassist Rob Grange, "*Free For All* was a crazy album because the *Ted Nugent* album was a big hit, and they picked *Hey Baby* off the album to be the single. Again, great song, and Derek was new to the band, so that caused friction. So by the time the second album came along, there was a lot of turmoil going on because we would go to play live, and people would automatically think, with Derek singing, that he was Ted Nugent. I mean, they kind of made that connection. They heard Ted Nugent on the radio, and it was Derek singing, but they had never heard of Ted Nugent before in a lot of parts of the country. Because we mainly toured the Midwest. So we would go to concerts and they would hear Derek sing, and everybody would lock on Derek's side of the stage, because they thought, 'Oh, that's Ted Nugent.' Which caused a lot of problems. Then we got Ted Nugent on his own, and Ted Nugent on a riser behind the stage, and Ted Nugent was constantly running up and down the stage so everybody knew that he was Ted Nugent. So by the time we came to *Free For All*, there was a lot of inner turmoil in the production team too, because Derek and Lew didn't get along and Derek was going, 'Hey, I want to go in this direction with the band.' Ted was going, 'Hey, I want to go this direction with the band, and don't call it a band (laughs)'."

As regards the *Free For All* era, I told Ted that his show in Spokane, Washington on this tour marked my first attendance of a major rock concert. My dad took me, my brother, and a couple buddies down (three 13-year-olds), two hours south from my hometown of Trail, B.C., and Ted played that city's hockey barn, Be Bop Deluxe and Rex in tow. Ted, upon hearing this, answers, "Oh, that was that night that asshole pulled out the Ruger 44, back in 1976, was it? He brought a Ruger 44 Magnum out in the concert and they arrested him. They gave him the gun back and that weekend he went and killed five of his family. Good call, law enforcement! Good call, American justice system! That's what you do when a guy pulls a gun out in a concert and waves it around! That's nothing more than like, stealing hubcaps, isn't it? Give him back his fucking gun and I'm shocked he killed his family, aren't you!? Back in the real world, anybody pulls a gun out and starts waving it around you shoot the motherfucker. But I don't want to hurt anybody; I'm just a guitar player, what do I know? Jesus."

"Yes, that was that night," confirms Derek. "And really, Ted wasn't threatened. He didn't even know about all this. I saw what happened; there was a scuffle in the front row, but back then it was all festival seating so everybody was crunched up together standing up. This guy got in an argument with a man standing next to him, pulls out a 44 Magnum Smith and Wesson, I saw that go up in the air, and the security grabbed him, got him down on the ground, took the gun away. We get back to the dressing room and I tell Ted. I said, 'Ted, did you see what happened?' He says, 'No, you know I'm caught up in what I'm doing.' I said, 'This guy was wielding a pistol!' Well, then our publicist got a hold of it, and he turned it into: 'Man points gun at Ted; Ted stares him down,' blah blah blah, yeah. That's just like that biting heads off of bats deal. Same deal."

"Yeah, let me clear that up; that's really ridiculous," said Ted at the time. "See, the press loves to play games with me, because I don't talk about getting high and all that other drag, boring, decadent bullshit that everybody else talks about. So some of the things I say and some of the things that happen to me are really exciting to guys that write articles. You wanna know what happened in Spokane? I don't know. I didn't know anything. I never saw nobody with no gun. I never left the stage, I never stared at anybody. I never saw a gun. But what I heard happened was some guy pulled a gun out and as soon as it was seen, somebody smacked the guy in the eye and he was thrown in jail. There wasn't a note missed, there wasn't a song missed; I didn't even know it happened. I might have jumped out and sucked his eyes out of his forehead, but I wouldn't have stared him down. I would've just gone to my high note and melted that goddamn bullet before it got to me."

In actuality, the Spokane incident happened on the tour for the *Ted Nugent* album, not *Free For All*, as discussed in an April '76 Rolling Stone article, five months before *Free For All* was issued, with, incidentally, the *Ted Nugent* album sitting at about 200,000 copies sold at that point. "There is no righteous outlet for aggression nowadays," said Ted. "So everyone's got this pent-up little ball of fire in them.

The line is negative versus positive. Every bit of violence, energy and aggression that is perpetuated from that stage is totally positive. What does some doorknob with a gun have to do that? The guy should have his hands cut off."

Nugent then took the opportunity to get his views across on gun ownership, not the first time he'd spend column inches talking about arming America to the teeth, and certainly not the last. "Everybody should carry a gun and every time two assholes argue, one or both will shoot each other. For the first 20 years everyone is armed there would be absurd amounts of unnecessary deaths. The way the situation is now, you and I can't carry them, so who's got 'em? Assholes, criminals that do it against the law. If we all carried guns and were hip and on the ball like I fuckin' am…"

"We were recording *Free For All* while the retro rockets were still screaming fire on the *Ted Nugent* album," continues The Nuge, back to the present-day, looking back with fondness. "Obviously the whole attraction to my music is the live performance of it. Everybody at Epic Records was so tuned into that, that they wanted that imagery on the cover, me doing the things that I do live, representing that outrage. So we did those photos and I remember that they weren't prepared for the numbers that was selling either so there were two or three printings and they had some different fonts used," this last comment referring to the curious variations in the typestyles used in different printings and in different territories.

Indeed, what a cool cover… Ted's here, no he's there, Ted in action, Ted's a pop-up doll, Ted smiling and rocking, looking like a cross between Frank Marino, Les Dudek and a beaming David Lee Roth. Did he rock those… slacks? Yes he did. It didn't hurt that he proffered a friendly greeting on the back of the thing, sayin' "To all you muthas I'll call friends. I'm glad to have you with me cuz here we go again, Ted Nugent." No, the pleasure is all ours, as it was when Kiss wrote us those little notes in the *Alive!* album one year earlier.

Adds Earl Steinbicker, partner of photographer Jim Houghton, on the record's photo shoot, "Those would have been studio shots. We also did *Cat Scratch Fever* and the famous shot of Ted bound and gagged in a straight jacket, which I think were just used for promo. *Free For All* would have been done in the studio as we absolutely refused to do live work."

Once inside the music, one is shocked to hear Ted pulling a pretty innovative move, taking a tight-knit band with two perfectly serviceable vocalists and adding a then little-known outsider called Meat Loaf, for lead honours on six of nine tracks, his printed credit smooshed right in there after/with the band's, no indication of how large a role he played on the album.

"Well, I had gone back to the '60s with Meat Loaf," explains Ted. "Meat Loaf had a duet in Michigan back in '67 called Stoney and Meat Loaf (a '71 album ensued, reissued when Meat Loaf got big with '77's *Bat Out Of Hell*). Stoney was this beautiful red-haired gal, which I guess Marv (Meat Loaf's real first name) had always surrounded himself with a babe to do duet lead vocals. Even before he was ever heard from, he was doing that. They sang these unbelievable versions of rhythm and blues classics that immediately got my attention because I knew them all by heart. He put a lot of soul into it; they were authentic. They were definitely projecting that Motown rhythm and blues pop, and a direct descendent of James Brown's showmanship. I don't know if Marvin would tell you that or not. There's no question about it. From vaudeville to James Brown's excitability. Meat Loaf is the real McCoy, which is why I had him on some of the songs on *Free For All*. I knew that I had a couple of tracks on there that would be perfect for his pipes so I called him and he did it. I like guys who have heart, and he's got a lot of that. But again, there's another example. All the English bands that influenced me—Stones, Beatles, Yardbirds, Deep Purple—I mean, all of them were direct descendents, Cream, Hendrix, direct link, not distant link, a direct fucking link to Howlin' Wolf, Bo Diddley, Chuck Berry and James Brown! So that's why that music still holds. That's why there's such a thing as classic rock. There's not going to be classic hip-hop."

Word has it that Meat Loaf can be a pretty a cranky guy… "Oh, I've never seen that. All I've ever seen is a very jovial, courteous, conscientious, loving man. That's all I've ever seen. Then I think if you met his daughter, you would see that it's a genetic imprint. They are Midwestern. They have a great hospitality spirit. They're kind people, goodwill, and they have a real decency about them. I've never seen him get angry. You know, we should all have the emotion and weaponry of anger at our disposal. I think angry is really good. When you see a judge let a child molester out, I think you should be very angry at that judge so it motivates you to get rid of that judge. I think anger is a beautiful emotion."

"Well, that was easy," says Tom Werman, on the decision to bring in Marvin. "They were having a lot of behavioural problems at the time. And I wasn't in charge, of personnel. The guy who owned Ted's production contract was Lew Futterman, who gets co-production credit on all the albums (laughs). He fired Derek, and he said, 'He doesn't have his shit together,' and Lew was the vocal specialist, so he thought. I said, 'Listen, I happen to know this great singer. He auditioned for me, but I don't know what to do with him. He's a killer singer. He's available right now.' He said, 'Get him on the phone!' So we flew him down, overnight. He walked right into the studio and finished the... you know, I think Lew was trying to teach Derek a lesson by saying you know, you're not indispensable to this band. So we're going to finish this. He liked the vocals so much that we kept them. Very interesting, but not obviously a logical match. Ted was loathed to use ringers. Meat Loaf and one piano player once and that was it."

Lew Futterman offers his take on the odd order for some Meat Loaf. "What happened was when we got started Ted was having a lot of trouble with Derek out on the road. Derek thought he was supposed to be a rock 'n' roll star so the way you do that was you throw chairs out the window and so on, that kind of crap. Ted of course did not approve of that at all. Kill a moose or something, that's one thing, but you don't throw chairs out the window (laughs). That kind of acting out was not his story and we were having increasing trouble with Derek. Derek caught the ear of David Krebs who got in his mind somehow that Derek had a lot more to do with the success of the first album than he really did. When David started to hold Derek up as a potential future star and so on, that just exacerbated Derek's immaturity, to the point where about the third day of recording, Derek became impossible. We had the one hit album out, Ted was now starting to headline himself, albeit still doing the big stadium tours with Aerosmith, and Derek was totally carried away."

"I'm not the kind of guy... my strengths, yeah, I'm creative in the sense that I know how to bring people together, like Cliff with Ted. I knew what was missing and I knew the shape. Was I able to come up with the idea for Hello People? Did I create If with an idea? Yeah. But in terms of musical ideas, that's not my background. I mean I can't even play the radio in tune. I get creative ideas and I'm a very good policeman, but I never was a musical producer. In other words I didn't say, 'Hey, well if you change this note or change that note it will make the melody better.' It just wasn't what I did. I mean I wrote some lyrics to some songs and so on but they were uniformly B-sides. Realistically it's a gift, and I didn't have it."

"The label didn't get really involved there," continues Lew. "Coming off that first big hit album, I had a lot of power. I had a lot of power, because remember, I was the one who brought him to Epic, I was the one who made the concessions necessary to make the deal, I was the one who brought Cliff into the picture which radically changed the shape of the music, and I was the one who found the studio down in Atlanta that we could get at a price that enabled us to do a $100,000 album for $20,000. So I had put all the pieces together. So despite Dave Krebs—who is a very smart guy and I'm not in any way denigrating Dave—is... not only in terms of what he was able to do in the music business business-wise and so on, but just as a guy in general, he's a highly intellectual guy, a very bright guy. Just like with many manager-type guys, guys coming out of an agent background, he was a little star-struck and he thought Derek was a star."

"So when we were arguing about Derek one time, he said to me, 'Lew, you're the luckiest guy in the world. You just stumbled into it. You don't know what you're losing. You're trying to kick Derek to the side; you don't know what you're losing.' I said okay, but in the meantime it's still my bat and ball so I'll be captain, and I had a tight contract, so nothing much could be done. I said, 'Derek, you're fired for this recording.' I had met Meat Loaf previously, and Meat Loaf was looking for a deal and so on. He hadn't made his own deal yet and he really needed money, and I made a deal with Meat Loaf and I gave him some money to do the lead singing on the album. Ted sang a couple songs, too, but Meat Loaf sang most of them."

"In any event, by having Meat Loaf available it took away Derek's power. Of course Derek came back afterwards with his tail between his legs and behaved for a couple of albums. He did go back out on the road and do the shows and so on and sang the songs that Meat Loaf had recorded. We did the album. It wasn't as good an album as the *Ted Nugent* album, but it came out good, it sold well, and Ted's career moved forward. Derek sort of got his act back together, enough so that he was tolerable to be out on the road. He and Ted had numerous battles afterwards, but you know, it held together enough so that we got quite a few years out of the band."

Offering an additional psychological profile of Lew's management partners, Tom Werman recalls that, "Leber was really of Broadway; he took care of the Broadway scene. Krebs was the rocker. He was a very, very insightful, very inquisitive listener. Good listener. He'd say, 'Werman, come in and sit down here,' and he'd ask me question after question after question. He didn't tell me things, he asked me things. They were probing questions. I didn't always know the answer, I didn't always have a good answer for him, but he was a very bright, very nice, very accessible manager. Not easy, you know. He was tough. But you respected him because he knew his stuff. He didn't just yell at you and tell you what he wanted for his clients. He was always analysing. He was very good, very interesting office. A lot of great people in that office. He'd ask me about songs. I don't think he asked me specific questions about the artists as much as he did about trends and what would you say if you were a kid doing this and what do you think about that and do you like this band? Stuff like that. I mean, he didn't ask me any questions that really had to do with the day-to-day management of Ted; he just did a really good job."

For that album, subsequently, vocal-wise, we saw a three-way split between Ted, Derek and Meat Loaf... "I don't remember the split," continues Tom. "Ted always sang a few. He wasn't a singer, but he was a vocals stylist, kind of like Jagger in the early days. I don't remember any specifics to the songs. I just knew the time and the behaviour and how we were doing. The albums that followed up big hit albums were always far less enjoyable. Because they had weaker material usually and weaker production values and less time. Because the band had to be out on the road. For example *Dream Police* was done in 30 days, start to finish. In those days, for mixing included, that was ridiculous. That's because they had to go on tour. Meanwhile, we had to shelve that for eight months after we finished it because *Budokan* sold so big. Anyway, that happens, and *Free For All* was one of those—a follow-up."

"As a band, the four of us wanted more of Derek's singing," adds

Grange, "because he has a good upper range, and a good melodic voice. So when it came to turmoil on the second album, Derek split. He said enough of this. So then they got Meat Loaf, pretty much undiscovered, and a really cool guy, and he could sing so loud in the studio, blow out the diaphragm on the microphone. The guy was just amazing, a strong singer. But it didn't really fit where we were at, at that time. It kind of stuck a finger in the band. Eventually Derek came back and they sorted it out, and we were back on the road for the *Cat Scratch Fever* album. But a lot of the stuff, like *Stranglehold* on the first album, I wrote the bass line, and that's a pretty well-known song, but I didn't get credit for that, really. It was my idea to put a phased bass on, and I wrote all my bass lines. Like on *Free For All*. Yeah, played through a phaser – that was my idea. In fact, I basically came up with that bass line, and Ted said over the microphone in the studio, 'Rob, why don't you save the phased bass for your solo album, man.' The engineer, Tony Reale liked the song, and said hey, this is really neat, a cool sound, let's keep it. So we kept it, and of course, the rest is history."

Come '77 and continued troubles with Derek, Did it look like there was any shot at all of Meat Loaf actually joining the band?

"Well, he had a good thing going with his existing band," notes Rob. "He was right in the middle of his *Bat Out Of Hell* stuff and all of that. Really, to us, we were street rock 'n' rollers from Detroit, and he was more Broadway, kind of. He wanted to stick with that because it was going in the right direction, and he just came in to do the sessions and then he was on his way to do his other deal. I don't know where it would've gone if Derek didn't come back."

And Cliff's take on the tale?

"Well, I don't know how much you want to print, but basically, Derek was like a street punk. He was very uncouth, and when we were cutting the first album, he thought he was going to go in and do his thing. He soon found out was that you don't do that. The producer tells you what to do and how to do it, and you're supposed to follow direction. I don't know how many times Lew Futterman barely stopped from punching him in the face. Incredibly rude, incredibly difficult. I'm just giving you background."

"So basically, nobody got along," continues Davies. "Derek hated the producers, they hated him. They went out on tour. Now, I didn't tour the first album. This young kid who they replaced Vic Mastrianni with, who wasn't good enough to play in the studio, they decided he was good enough to play live. So after the album was finished, which we recorded in '75, I went back to London, and carried on with my little supergroup. They got Brian Staffeld and went on the road, and they had an incredible year, obviously, they had a new management team in David Krebs and Steve Leber, which was the biggest management company in the country. They were touring with Aerosmith, big auditoriums all over the place. I completely forgot about Ted Nugent. I went back to London and got on with my stuff."

"About nine months later, Lew called me up and I talked to him for awhile, and he said, 'Well, remember that album you came and helped me co-produce?' 'Yeah, you mean the one that I didn't get co-production credit for?' (laughs). 'Well, it sold a million units.' I dropped the phone. Because it was just like a Band-Aid and super-glued kind of album, I was amazed that it sold a million units. Anyway, he said, 'Well I'd like you to come and co-produce the second album too.' It was the same thing, had Brian Staffeld in the studio, couldn't get a groove, didn't work out, so I parachuted back in from London to do the second album, *Free For All*. Lew decided well, you're going to have to play drums and co-produce it because Staffeld just isn't making it. So we went about it the very same way we did before. Everything was layered on *Free For All*; there were no live tracks."

"While we were there," says Cliff (getting around to finishing his Meat Loaf!), "Derek was a really crazy guy. So I'm in the studio doing a rough mix or something, Derek and Ted and Rob had decided they were going to go home early. There was a lot of tension between Werman, Futterman and Derek, just the usual same old shit, and it was actually worse now, because Derek was a star-had a hit album now, and is a bigger asshole than ever. So one night they go off, and Rob says to Ted, who's driving the Lincoln Continental, 'I want to get some gum.' So they stop in the parking lot of a Piggly Wiggly or something, down south. Derek decides he wants to get something too. So Ted stays in the car listening to the radio. Rob and Derek walk into the store. Rob gets his gum, Derek decides to be a smart-ass and shoplifts a can of tuna, puts it in his shirt, and as he's going out, the security guard notices that Derek has something in his shirt. So he says, 'Excuse me young man, I think you've got something in your shirt,' and Derek takes a swing at him. The guy ducks, maces Derek's face, completely fucks up and messes up his face. They call the cops, they take him downtown; they find three joints in his sock. So now he gets prosecuted for shoplifting, for violence or some kind of assault and also he had three joints in his sock."

"He came to the studio the next day, after they let him out of jail, his face looked like a fucking basketball. It was all swollen up, he can hardly talk, and Lew Futterman said, 'I've fucking had it. I've had enough of this. We've got a million selling album. All we gotta do is produce something halfway as decent, we've got another million selling album and we've got this fucking jerk doing circus tricks.' He says, 'Derek, you're off the album—get out.' So we kept the tracks that Derek had already done, and Werman got in touch with Meat Loaf. Meat Loaf I guess was trying to get some sort of a deal with Epic Records. Werman's dad was part of CBS. It was very political between Werman and the record company, so they basically just parachuted in Meat Loaf, and he just took over where Derek left off. We did what we had to do to finish the album and by the time the album was finished and we were out on tour, they went on tour, Derek was better and everything."

Then, says Cliff, money started becoming a looming, deal-breaking issue… "Ted was paying everybody $200 a week, and I said well, it's $750 a week, or I wouldn't go. So he paid me $750 a week, to play for the band through that fall. We did a big long European tour, Ted's first European tour, extremely successful, and when we got back to America he said, 'You know, I can't afford you, Cliff.' You know, $750 a week (laughs). Ted already was a millionaire from the first album. I said, 'Well, that's fine with me. You just tell me when you want me to leave and I'll go home.' He said, 'Well, what we're going to do is, we're going to get this guy in here that management has come up with. He's going to watch the show and we're going to rehearse at sound check, and when he's ready to take over, you can just go home.' I said, 'Well, that's all very well, but I need something more definite.' So we got a definite date, and I made him buy me the ticket right then, so I had the ticket in my hand to go, and we went out on tour. This guy not only ended up being a very bad drummer, he was a complete fucking asshole. So everyone hated his guts. Everybody refused to work with the guy. So one day Ted came to my room and said, 'Well, this guy isn't really working out, Cliff; you're going to have to stay longer.' I said, 'No thank you very much, I'm going home. I don't see anything here for me. You're trying to get me out of it and now. I mean, if you don't do it this time, you're going to do it next time.' We're in the middle of the tour. I was going home in two days."

So did this other drummer ever play any live shows?

"No, never played with them. So I was going home in two days, so everybody panics, and the management flew in and they were saying, 'My God, oh my God, you can't do this, Cliff.' 'Yes I can. You told me I can go home on a certain date. I've got my ticket. You're not interested in me being in the band. Ted isn't interested in anybody making any money, so what's the point of staying anyway? I'm going home.' So there was a big conference, and they sit down and they get everyone out, management comes in the room and said, 'Well, what would it take to have you stay?' 'In order to stay in the band, I want 10% of the tour net, and I want 1% of all record sales.' The management said, 'That doesn't seem like too big of a deal.' 'I want the same thing for Derek and Rob. I'm not going to play in a band where we're all making a hundred grand a year, and they're making $200 a week. It's fucking ridiculous.' Anyway, because of me being an upstart and not really giving a fuck whether I was in the band or not, that was my bottom line, really. I had other things going on in London and they bit. They fucking bit on the whole thing, and signed us all up and gave us contracts. It was only because of that whole political situation that went down that we actually made any money."

So everybody got that?

"Everybody got that. In fact, they gave Derek an extra 5% because he was the lead singer. I mean, my best year with Ted Nugent, I made $250,000."

In terms of the production duties for *Free For All*, Grange confirms Derek's and Cliff's assertions, saying that, "Lew Futterman or Tom Werman really didn't have much to do with anything. Cliff Davies produced those albums. I think Cliff got co-producer or whatever. But those albums are produced by Cliff Davies, not Lew Futterman. I think we were Tom Werman's first project. He would show up and bop around the studio and everything but he wouldn't really offer anything, as far as ideas or anything.

He was a nice guy, cool guy, a record guy, but Cliff was the one who produced those albums, got them to sound good. Tony Reale the engineer was good. Lew was mainly on the phone all the time cutting real estate deals, back in New York. In fact he would say, 'All right, wait a minute, I can't hear the telephone.' We were right in the middle of doing the album. 'I'm talking to my guy. Could you guys keep it down? I'm on the phone.' We'd go, 'We're doing an album here, man!' So Lew is a nice guy, but he didn't have a clue as to what was going on. Didn't have a clue. He hasn't produced any other rock bands since then. I think before us he was doing a jazz band. The fact that he signed us was totally bizarre."

"Like I say, Derek and Ted and I were three Detroit rock 'n' roll road dogs," continues Grange, now in real estate himself. "All we did basically, we rocked; we just rocked, all the time. Cliff came in and he was a polished studio musician. He knew how to work the board. He knew how to get the sounds in the studio and get them to work in the studio, on the board. So he really kind of took us in, cleaned us up, introduced us to French wine (laughs), and it worked. It just clicked. It was just amazing. When he got in the band, he straightened out the meter. Because a lot of times in the live show, Ted would start singing and he would push. Push means he would race. He would start speeding up. Cliff would reel him in like a metronome, and so suddenly the music started sounding good, instead of just being racy all the time and meters all over the place."

Although Werman figures *Free For All* went on to do as good as the first one, he says that, "*Cat Scratch Fever* is probably still the biggest seller because it had the big single. Again, I remember, being in Atlanta at the Omni, when Ted did that song for the first time. I called my boss that night and said, 'Ted wrote a single! Ted wrote a single!' You know, and I was sure of it. So we went in and recorded it pretty quickly after that. The first time I heard it was at a show, live. I thought, boy, this is a single. That's what I was attuned to, singles. So of course, I'm going to be more pop than say Butch Vig, Nirvana. He's a grittier producer, no question about it. He embraces chaos and I reject it. I was good for a time, a place in time, a time in musical American culture. But the producer always has a certain approach to music. Even if he says, 'No, I'm the chameleon; I do whatever the band wants me to do.' That's not true. I mean, we're all trying to make our band's sound like our favourite bands. So I always tried to make my bands sound like The Who, the Beatles and ZZ Top, whichever they were nearest.'

Ted was nearest ZZ Top, I imagine?

"Well, I don't know what he was near. You know, I didn't do a lot for Ted in terms of arrangement. I did a lot for Ted in terms of sound and presentation and song structure. But Ted knew exactly what he wanted in terms of parts. He sang all the parts to all of his musicians, and he told everyone what to play. When we walked in the studio, it was really easy for me. I was more quality control than anything else."

So was there a Tom Werman sound, a production quality, a stamp, even if we might concede this would come with Werman projects from beyond the Ted years?

"If there was, I would like to think that it was a fluid, locomotive rhythm. A prominence of rhythm guitar, doubled rhythm guitar licks, around which songs are based. That's the way I listen to music. The strongest thing to me about rock 'n' roll is the good, elementary, catchy, basic guitar lick, as in *Girls Girls Girls*, as in *Cat Scratch Fever* and a number of songs that were big. Everyone knows what a hook is, but I prefer to build a song around a real driving guitar hook. Probably the best example of that is ZZ Top; I love their drive. I always try to get a good solid drive in a song."

There are certain tricks used to get a huge guitar part, or to make the riff prominent... "Yes, certainly by doubling, but by helping it to roll along through percussion, through reinforcement, through other instruments playing accents for beats—you know, there are numbers of ways that you can do it. Tailoring the drums to serve the guitar, rather than vice versa."

Back to the record at hand, *Free For All* opens with the title track, a bright sunny funky number that, along with Aerosmith's *Walk This Way*, should receive more credit as a pivotal rap metal original. Ted sings this one, instantly establishing himself as American stadium rock's first David Lee Roth. Somehow, as a turbulent teen fan listening, looking at the cover, and being immersed in all things Cheech & Chong circa '76, the guy comes off as some sort of Mexican bandito.

"When we got into *Free For All*, the actual song," recalls Rob, "Ted had this funky riff and I'm going, man, what am I going to play to that?! So I just came up with this bass line which was really simple, and it really fit in with *Free For All*, and actually really made the song. So as a band, we really… I still call it a band, because we really kind of wrote everything together. I mean, even if you look at Ted today, he's never had any hits as big as those hits. If you can imagine, even when Derek and Cliff and I got together in Fresno, a few years ago, we invited Ted, but he didn't come. Just the three of us together… there's just something about us playing together, that really works."

"I would probably say the *Ted Nugent* album was probably, to me, one of the favourites, but I also liked *Free For All*," adds Rob. "We really had a momentum going into *Free For All*, and the whole thing going on with Meat Loaf and Derek and all that, it kind of chopped that album in half—it's like listening to two albums. But I still see on the statements that I get, that the hottest selling albums of all his albums—and he's been on a lot of albums—are *Ted Nugent*, *Free For All*, *Cat Scratch Fever* and *Live Gonzo*. Those have been his hottest selling albums in 30 years. So when you go to see Ted live, he plays mostly songs from those albums. Like I say, we all wrote those songs. Think about it—has he written anything like any of those albums since then? So who really wrote the albums? He is a mega-millionaire, and I wouldn't be selling real estate and Derek wouldn't be playing in a bar band if he had treated us fairly."

"Well, just listen to the guitar riffs, the basic foundation of those songs, what I call the guitar theme lines of those songs," Ted remarks on the opening two tracks of the album, the aforementioned *Free For All* and the blistering modern metal cruise control of *Dog Eat Dog*. "I mean, you can tell where they came from. They came from the same place that all my licks come from, and that is relentless touring, relentless feedback opportunities with a live audience. When it's all said and done, Martin, I may be a musician and I may be good at this and that, but ultimately I'm just a rock 'n' roll fan. I crave the sound and the electricity and the primal urgency of the rhythms, so I execute on the instrument. Because I've played all my life and practiced intensively all my life, I'm able to execute the things I hear in my head on the strings. *Dog Eat Dog* is the perfect example of a lick (sings it)… I mean, it's just such a grinder. I was surrounded with such virtuosos that they were able to execute it in its optimum form. It's a perfect live song and we still do it to this day."

Asked by Jeb Wright about the *Free For All* riff, Ted recalls, "I was backstage in Pittsburgh, Pennsylvania around late 1975. I've told you in the past about how *Great White Buffalo* and *Cat Scratch Fever* and all of these great songs come from me tuning my guitar. It happens that they sound great on the tuning meter, but they also sound great through a loud amplifier in the dressing room. There is a difference because the volume creates multiple tones and frequencies and sonics and you tune a little bit differently. So, I will start a lick and all of the sudden I go, 'Damn, that's a cool-ass lick. What is that?' The coolest string on the guitar is one that rings open. I was wondering how many open strings I could get out of an E chord one day. So, I went up there to that fret, and I made sure I had all of the open strings I could, and I started flailing on it. I was literally creating it in the dressing room and I started singing, 'Never before I have a turned on you, you looked too good to me.' I was talking about my audience. 'Your beady eyes, they can cut me in two and I just can't let you be. It's a free for all and I heard it said that you can bet your life. Stakes are high and so am I, it's in the air tonight.' It really is a stream of consciousness. I never sit down and think, 'Hmm, what would be a cool lick?' I just pick up the guitar, turn it up and start slamming on it. It is all derivative of that Bo Diddley and Chuck Berry grind. It is just the next extension of that. Billy Gibbons called me up last night from Detroit, where he performed with Kid Rock. We were talking about how we first got started and how we could play all Chuck and Bo and Lonnie Mack songs. Whether it's *Tush* or *Sharp Dressed Man* or *Free For All* or *Cat Scratch Fever*, I guarantee you that there is honky tonk and boogie woogie and Chuck Berry inside there."

St. Holmes, who makes *Dog Eat Dog* the best vocal performance on the album, comments that, "Day in and day out of travelling on the road, and meeting people and running into situations, I think we just felt it was a dog eat dog world out there. I think we would always try to put a womanizing female slant on it. Well, I wouldn't, but Ted would. Back in those days we tried to write everything from the crotch. But I think that's pretty much *Dog Eat Dog*. You know, we would read the newspaper then, 'kamikaze from the hundredth floor...' We were driving the limo going to the airport or something after a gig, and we would read about some guy who just couldn't handle life, and he just jumped out of a window in New York. We were just, wow, how do you do that? We would just take it all, juggle it and throw it out there, and that's where a lot of those lyrics came from."

Writing On The Wall is the album's longest track at 7:10 and it is sort of Son Of *Stranglehold*, slow, churning, and again, here come a few Mexican melodies, underscored by Meat Loaf's piquant vocal skills. "*Writing On The Wall* I love," notes Ted. "I consider that one of those grinding rhythm and blues mid-tempos that is just so damn sexy. I enjoy those kind of licks." But is it heavy metal? "You know, I've never liked the term heavy metal. To me, heavy metal represents some stupid white guy who hasn't learned personal hygiene yet and wears a leather jacket or a Levi jacket because it's the trendy thing to do, which I spit in the face of. I think that's all just cheap and transparent and meaningless. I was influenced by all things black and rhythm and blues. I've never been influenced by heavy bands. Obviously the Yardbirds and the Stones and to some degree the licks on the Led Zeppelin records. But heavy metal has never done anything for me. I don't consider my favourite bands heavy metal, my favourite bands being Aerosmith and Cheap Trick and Van Halen and ZZ Top. I think those are all rhythm and blues bands. In the case of Van Halen, it's just rhythm and blues-tinged pop with a real rock 'n' roll energy level, mostly delivered by the front men, David Lee Roth and the incredible style of Sammy Hagar. As a functioning band, Eddie and Michael and Alex are the consummate high energy rhythm and blues rhythm section. They are so rhythmical, they can't just be lumped in with that. I certainly wouldn't insult them by calling them heavy metal. I consider heavy metal things like Judas Priest, which I enjoy, and Black Sabbath and Dio and I just think it's too Caucasian for me."

Closing side one is *Turn It Up*, a compact corker of a track, a happy-go-lucky number that I always gang-grouped with *Draw The Line's Bright Light Fright* and *Let's Make It* from Derringer's *Sweet Evil*, which in totality, sounds very much like a classic Ted Nugent record. On *Turn It Up*, the sweet, high innocent pipes of Derek St. Holmes match perfectly the fun pop-rock energy the band musters, all culminating in a big carnival-coloured wall of sound as the track blusters to conclusion.

Incidentally, while working on the record, Ted had told the Thom Gardner from Back Door Man that he was pretty sure the album was going to be called *Turn It Up*, also noting that the record would include a track called *Bloodbath*. Gardner also wondered out loud with the Nuge if he would have joined Purple when Blackmore left, if asked. "I love 'em, but I love me better," quipped Ted. "I've got more to offer on my own. Let's put it this way. If I didn't already see the flames comin' out of my own little world, I would've jumped on it, 'cause I do, I've always loved Deep Purple. You know, 1968, *Hush* and *Journey To The Center Of The Mind*, dig it, both of us were in that early splurge-type of thing, so I can definitely get next to Deep Purple. Plus they've got some outrageous jams. *Highway Star*, that's motherfucker music."

Gardner also asked Ted to clear up this business about "guitar battles." Obliging, Ted says, "There's never been a guitar battle; they were billed as guitar battles. You see I've had a long, dubious career. There's been some dry spells where I needed all the help I could get in order to keep the cash coming in. Different people in the organization would think of different gimmicks, other than the normal gimmicks I use, and one of the gimmicks was the old contest attitude, the old competition gig. So I battled these guys. Frank Marino... give me a break, and Mike Pinera, who's a motherfucker, really good; it was always a jam, a duet. I always try to outdo these guys in a little off-the-record manner, though."

"The truth will be known, I never said I was the best. That's like saying, 'Who's the best fuck?' I mean, who's to tell? It's up to the women and with the best guitarist it's up to the ears of the people. I can go, 'Hotdog is the best food,' but... I think that within the non-structure of my type of music, even though because we are all earthlings, there is a type of structure involved, though it's very unlimited. You should touch upon all the extremes. I don't think you have to always stay in key. You know, people say, 'Oh, it's painful.' That's good, painful's great—I need more pain. I need more amps so when I want to get loud it can get just disgusting, just wrong, so loud it's wrong— that's good loud. Then it should get so quiet... Remember we used to play, fuckin' all of a sudden the thing would go shoop, and I play without the fuckin' amps and then everybody'd go (looks around, bewildered). Then when they were like that, we turn it up again and they'd go, 'Aaaaahhh.' It's the extremes, the real slow, real fast, real soft, real loud."

"A lot of people say I don't play nasty and stuff; that's a lot of shit. *Hibernation* and *Migration*, that's the ultimate in taste. I mean there's a little bit of everything. *Baby Please Don't Go*, that's the ultimate in raucous noise. More noise, less notes, more distortion, more noise, more trash, more assaults on the ears, then mellow, then loud. There's nothing you shouldn't be able to do. That's why Hendrix was what he was, extremes. That fucking guy would take a note and send it to Zeus and catch it on the rebound, you know? There's nothing like that these days, except for an occasional, you know (points to himself)."

"Probably 50 or 60," figures Ted, when asked about how many players had cycled through his band already by this point. "The reason I've been through so many musicians is because I've got things I like to do and don't expect anybody to have to change what they want to do, to do what I want to do and I will certainly not fucking change what I want to do for what anybody else wants to do. If you can dig the Ted Nugent trip, come and we'll have a great old time. But then everybody starts going their own way and they want to chase their own animal and that's cool. But I don't want anybody chasing their animal on my time. But a lot of times, I can dig their animals. Like Derek, the guy that sings with me now and plays guitar. He and I are from the same school of rock, and a lot of the stuff he does, I can dig, and I can get my rocks off on his ship, so I say, 'Hey, bring that ship around so I can take a ride on it.' So he writes songs that I can get next to and we do them."

Back to *Free For All* and on side two, we're immediately hit with the album's second of three malevolent rockers, *Street Rats* again featuring Meat Loaf gliding over the top numerous percussion textures driven by a classic open air stadium riff. Ted beams with pride: "*Street Rats*, *Turn It Up*… those are my babies! *Street Rats* is just one of the greatest guitar riffs in the history of electronic middle fingers. I still perform that lick on stage all the time. I enjoy both of those songs." Incidentally, *Street Rats* is a track on which Ted played his solid body replica Gibson Byrdland, a rare occasion given that he says the thing weighs a good 40 pounds.

Next up is *Together*, on which Ted uses an MXR Phaser. It is the record's lone ballad, sounding like a mildly funky, reflective Pat Travers moment. Nonetheless, it is a track that sticks in Ted's craw. "*Together*, I don't care for. That was one of those back door sneak attacks. I think Cliff Davies wrote that and I just never enjoyed it. The guys thought we needed a ballad and I just somehow acquiesced. I must have been out quail hunting or something. I just don't care for the song."

"That's kind of where *Together* came from," adds Grange, referring to a pool of songs he would write, some of which would show up on his *St. Paradise* project of 1978. "Cliff and I wrote that, and that's kind of where *Light My Way* came from and where *Hey Baby* came from. It all came from that same pool of songs. But Ted wrote good songs, and he had great ideas. This limitation was his vocal range. You know, he's good at singing stuff like *Cat Scratch Fever* and *Free For All*, but you can't really put him on *Just What The Doctor Ordered* or *Hey Baby*. It's just not going to work. The same thing with Derek: He would've been uncomfortable singing a song like *Cat Scratch Fever*, maybe because of the lyrics. It's just not Derek's style. He's more of a blues-based singer. I always thought the two together really kind of complemented each other."

"But I love *Hammerdown*," Ted enthuses, with respect to what is the album's crowning vicious metal moment, even Meat Loaf raising a considerable snarl for this classic riff rocker. "I'm editing my Ted Nugent *Spirit Of The Wild* TV show right now that won awards for the last three years on the Outdoor Channel and a bunch of network affiliates, and I used the *Hammerdown* intro lick for mood-setting and tension-setting."

Perhaps loosening the bolts on side two along with the down-wound bass meander of *Together* are the tracks *Light My Way* (heavy but poppy and camp) and *I Love You So I Told You A Lie*, which sounds like sour Kiss mash.

"Derek and I wrote *Light My Way*, which is a cool rocker," notes Grange. "I've got to look at my gold album on the wall here, to see what's on here. I really like *Dog Eat Dog*; that was a cool tune, and Derek did a great job singing on that one. Again, we all just kind of put those tunes together, but he got all the writer's royalties on it. But no, I really enjoyed playing in the band, and lucky to stay with it and keep going. I think I was one of the longest guys in the band, from the Amboy Dukes. It was a great time, and it's too bad we couldn't get together and do stuff together, just play together. Actually I think that would be good for Ted, because Ted really does need some material. He writes good stuff, and the stuff the he did with Damn Yankees was really good, but the tough part is, he can't stay in a band environment very long. Like he would come to town, and he would have different guys with him now. Even with Damn Yankees, that was a great band, talented people, and they did two albums and they dispersed. So Ted is a good guy, but he is a tough personality to be in a band with."

Ted remarks that, "*I Love You So I Told You A Lie* should have never been on there. I can't believe how tolerant I am of bullshit. I hate the song (laughs). I just never figured it out. I was convinced somehow by production team members, primarily Lew Futterman, that the song needed to be on there just so those guys had a song that they had written on the record, like somehow we were some kind of commune. I don't like the song. I liked *Light My Way*; that was a Derek and Rob composition. That's a great song to this day. Derek's got an uncanny rock 'n' roll rhythm and blues touch."

Cliff's lone writing credits on the album are for *Together* and *I Love You So I Told You A Lie*, the two Ted has denigrated. "Well, really, me having a couple of songs on the *Free For All* album was a bit of payback, because I didn't get proper credits on the first album," explains Davies. "It was like pulling teeth. Ted did not want to do anybody else's tunes (laughs). But I basically wrote the tune for the band, right there in the studio, and Rob helped, came up with a cool bass line for *Together*, which is kind of like part of the gist of the song, so I gave him credit. I think he gets about 25% credit. There was another guy. But Rob Grange, I mean, some of those bass licks on those first three albums are astonishing. Back in those days, '76 especially, Rob was quite often in bass player polls as a favourite bass player. He was a favourite bass player among bass players. He's still very good. I mean, I played with him a couple years ago and he was still playing great."

"That is part of his name," answers Cliff, asked about the two ways Grange presented his name. "That's his name. His actual family name is De La Grange. It's a French name, and for some reason for a long time, he decide it was too fancy for rock 'n' roll, so he called himself Rob Grange. But now he calls himself Rob De La Grange again. The other one, *I Love You So I Told You A Lie*, that was basically my attempt at writing a pop hit. In fact, everybody agreed that it was a pop hit, but Ted refused to release it as a single, because it was one that he hadn't written. You may have been talking to a millionaire, had we released that as a single. Actually, you're not."

"I wrote that song and brought it to Ted," says Derek, with respect to *Light My Way*. "In those days, you kind of wrote the whole song, but you had to give Ted a piece, to put his slant on it. So I wrote a song called *Light My Way*, and I think the bassist is credited as well. I was kind of into the MC5, and I was into Iggy And The Stooges, and I stole a little bit from each one of those bands, and put that song together. Ted liked how fast it was, so he got a kick out of that, and he came up with some of the lyrics. I came up with most of the music. It's kind of *Kick Out The Jams*-ish. That's where I kind of got the idea for the lyric. A couple of those guys come from the down-river Detroit area where I come from, and I was always a big fan of theirs, and I've since been able to speak with Wayne Kramer a couple of times now, because we're both from sort of the same neighbourhood. There was some talk about getting together with them and going out as a second guitar player in MC5 a couple years ago. But that's kind of fallen to the wayside now. But any chance I have to work with those guys, I would be there in a heartbeat. Because I come from the same tradition, the same vibe."

Did Ted let you play a fair bit a guitar on those early Nugent albums?

"No, I always played one rhythm on all of them, and then they would bury me in the mix. I would play one rhythm on every one of the songs. Sometimes not every song, because there were songs where Ted would say 'I've got it, I'll do it,' but of course on everything that I co-wrote. On the first album I co-wrote *Snakeskin Cowboys*, *Just What The Doctor Ordered*. Back then we didn't even know what a credit was, but he wasn't saying. He didn't share that. So we didn't have any idea back then that co-writing, you know, you get part of the money. We didn't know the mechanics of, how do you make money from an album? We do need to know those things, and nobody was quick to tell us. So when we finally found out, ooh-wee! I co-wrote the melody for *Stranglehold*. You know, that's one of the biggest songs. Never got a dime for it. The only thing I get off that is, you know, record sales, or

CD sales. Quite a few years ago I was pretty—what's the word; I forgot about all that—bitter I think is a good word, and then 15 years ago I said you know what? Can't do anything about it, got to give it up. I've got to let it go. I can't give it any more power, because it just takes up space in my brain."

"Well, basically it was the Ted Nugent show," explains Cliff, asked to address the extent to which Derek's guitar work can be heard on the album. "And Derek was extremely young, very inexperienced, never been in a pro band. It was like his ego was hurting all the time, because it wasn't really a band. I mean, Ted was presenting it as a band for publicity reasons, kind of thing. We were a band, but in actuality, we were Ted Nugent's backing group. I mean, we were very, very involved in the arrangements and the writing. Derek was very inexperienced, and he couldn't write melodies, so I would write the melodies and teach them to him, and he would sing them. As far as Derek is concerned, there is actually quite bit of very good Derek guitar here and there. He is a tremendous rhythm guitar player. We actually ended up with more rhythm guitar from Derek on the album than Ted would've liked, I think. But if you listen back in there, there is some really cool second guitar work going on. You know, Derek wasn't upfront where Ted was, which is where he wanted to be, which is probably why he is whining. But he certainly has presence in the rhythm section. He certainly made an incredible difference to the feel. You know, me, Rob and Derek were really the heart of the band. We were really a band on our own, and Ted really like floated over the top, sort of thing."

I mention to Derek Ted's disdain for *I Love You So I Told You A Lie*, which St. Holmes says comes as no surprise. "He didn't write it. He doesn't like anything he didn't do."

Ted says the same thing about *Together*. "Yes, exactly," notes Derek. "And that song too, I was supposed to sing that one. I sat at the piano... I liked that one!"

Which brings up a pressing question: just how democratic was the Ted Nugent band? Or more pointedly which albums from the catalogue might be deemed at least somewhat democratic? "There weren't any," quips the Nuge. "The *Ted Nugent* album was a dictatorship. *Free For All* was basically a dictatorship until I considered the recommendations of *Together* and *I Love*

You So I Told You A Lie. My spine got a little jelli-fied on those. *Cat Scratch Fever* was a dictatorship and I've given and taken a lot after that, but not anymore (laughs)."

Derek figures it came down to egos. Case in point: "We played Madison Square Garden after the first album came out. They go, 'Please welcome Ted Nugent' and the lights go up and we start playing *Just What The Doctor Ordered*. The whole audience is looking at Ted. I stepped up to the mic and started singing, 'Got my guitar when I was ten years old' and you could see every head and eye in the crowd look over to me. I got the biggest shit-eating grin on my face. I found out that no one was told I was the singer. That is probably when a whole bunch of tension started."

"It was hard. I knew I was the Steven Tyler of the band but I wasn't getting any recognition in the press at all," explains St. Holmes. "When the people from the magazines would get there to interview us, they were told to only talk to Ted. Occasionally a couple of them would come up to us afterward and say, 'I was told not to talk to you guys but that is ridiculous. You're the fricking band.' I said, 'I know it, man.' Actually, that is when all the trouble started. It was all Ted trying to keep all the glory on Ted. He is still that way. I love him and we are like brothers but working together just does not work. I can work with him but he can't work with me. He is so jealous. He can't stand that I can step up there and just fricking open up my mouth and nail it—he has told that to me. He said, 'Derek, if I had your voice then I could conquer the world.' I said, 'Well guess what? You don't.' I was always every bit as good as him as a guitar player and he didn't like that. They would turn me down in the mix. I have people come up to me when I play my club dates and they tell me that they had no idea that I could play guitar like that."

Derek in fact wound up leaving the band temporarily during the recording of *Free For All* – it's a subtle distinction, versus our previous discussion of his being aggressively pushed out.

"I left because I didn't like the way the producer was making us sound. Lew Futterman and Cliff Davies produced the album. Tom Werman was there as well but I didn't have any beef with him. He was glad the first album went platinum so he was not going to make any waves. We were rivaling Led Zeppelin at the time. I wanted that thing to sound like a Zeppelin album. They wanted to turn it into a high energy pop record. I got into an argument with Lew and he said, 'If you don't like the way things are going then we can just replace you.' I told him, 'Well, then I guess you are going to have to.' We were recording in Atlanta and I flew home to Michigan. They got Meat Loaf to come in. He recorded *I Love You So I Told You A Lie* and *Street Rats*. I had already sang them and they were in the can. I gave them my best rendition of Paul Rodgers and they would have been awesome. But Ted is spiteful and vindictive so he canned all that and they used Meat Loaf. They took all the tracks back to the label and they played it for them. Everybody freaked. They went, 'Who is that singing?' They said, 'That is Meat Loaf.' They said, 'Who was that other guy? We need to get the other guy back or we are going to get in trouble.' So they called me up and offered me the job back. I got a little bit more money too. Now I was making ten dollars instead of nine—I'm teasing. I went back. We recorded the *Cat Scratch Fever* album in London and the producer and I butted heads again. We just never really got along. I always thought he was in the way. He was an armchair, drinking wine and reading the newspaper type producer. Every now and then he would put his paper down and say, 'I'm not sure if I like that.' Here we were busting our ass and he was sitting there reading and drinking wine."

The below expanded version of the story from Derek repeats some of the salient points, but, again, it's interesting to note the subtle differences in the telling...

"I had sung all the songs. And we got in a fight halfway through the album, and I was just full of myself, and I guess so was he. Neither one of us were going to back down. It was silly. Silly crap! But if we had a mediator... and we should've had management there. We were so volatile, we should have had management there all the time. We needed a judge, all the time. So Ted said, 'I'm in charge of this deal, and you're not, and we're not doing it your way.' I said, 'Why don't you sing the album?' 'I'll just get a new singer. We don't need you. We do not need you.' I went, 'okay, this will be interesting.'"

"So they went out and got Meat Loaf. I remember even catching one of the phone calls, when Meat Loaf called in. I was sitting in the studio and I just always ran over and picked up the phone. He said, 'Hey, this is Meat

Loaf.' I said. 'Wow. Let me just talk to you for second. Let me just tell you what's going on.' It turned into a power play. 'I think if I could get my way, I can make this album sound like something.' He said, 'Well, Derek, I need the money, and they've offered it to me. I've got to take it.' I said, 'Well, okay man, you know what? I dig it. I understand, you've got to have the money, but I really wish you could stay out of this deal'."

"So, sure enough, they let him come down and sing the rest of the songs. They took the material back to the label, back to New York, they sat around a board meeting, played them the new material, and they all freaked out and said, 'We don't know who this guy is, but get rid of him! Get the guy who sang *Stranglehold* back.' That's exactly what they did. I got a phone call out of the blue, and I was already at home, starting to get another band together. This is like two weeks. I'd had enough; I was ready to get busy. I get a phone call and they say, 'Hey, we made a mistake; we'd like to bring you back in.' I said, 'Well, number one, more money. Number two, I'm singing the songs.' You know, I got a chance to straighten out maybe three out of 15 things. Albeit not enough, but I came back and stayed for *Free For All*, *Cat Scratch Fever* and *Double Live Gonzo!*. The live album was my last go and that was it. California Jam 2 was the last show that I ever sung for him for ten years."

"But yes, I was on those songs because I had already sung them," continues Derek, clarifying the timeframes. "In the beginning of the album, I had already put down at least one or two vocals on every song. So I had completed what I was supposed to do. We were still working on a couple of things. I think we were getting ready to sing *I Love You So I Told You A Lie*, and that was written by Cliff Davies and really myself. Again, really not knowing what co-writing was, I didn't get anything for that. That ended up that was the only song I really wanted to sing and I didn't get to sing it. Cliff was really upset, because we kind of wrote it together with kind of a Bad Company/Paul Rodgers-type vocal, and then what we got was a theatrical, dramatic, *Hammerdown*, goofy Meat Loaf thing."

Continues Derek, "This was Lew's doing, not Tom's. Werman and I are best buddies and we always got along well. He just happened to not be there that day, and Lew Futterman was turning it into a fricking high end-y frequency circus that day. I was just trying to spread my wings a little bit because I thought I was the lead singer. It turned out I didn't have as much power as I thought I did, so, you know, 'If you don't like it you can quit; I'll get somebody to replace you.' 'Well okay, see you.' Ted wasn't even there. He didn't even know about that. Then when Ted found out that the producer had canned me, he didn't have the balls to call me up and fix it. He just thought, well, maybe this is easier. I'll just let it... I don't know, Ted has always been jealous of my guitar playing and singing. Forever. Except for now. I mean, we are older, we're smarter, he's more mature, and he says, 'Derek, you've got an incredible voice. Let's utilize it.' You know, we should've done that back then. But who knew? We were just a bunch of punk kids."

In terms of press, Rolling Stone continued with their favourable treatment of Ted. "Having a million-dollar seller as last year's *Ted Nugent* album was, has not noticeably soothed the savage breast," wrote Billy Altman. "On *Free For All* one need only listen to the breakneck mania of *Turn It Up* or the extended whine of *Writing On The Wall* to realize that he isn't resting on his musical achievements. Trophies and awards must go up on the wall at Nugent's house in the same spirit as moose heads: gratifying to look at when you're back from safari, but of no use on your next trip to the jungle. Each song on *Free For All* leaves you gasping for breathing room; no space is too small for Nugent to cram in a grand, searing riff, and his long solo on *Together* is so sinewy and melodic that I found myself staring at the turntable in disbelief. But I do believe. And when Nugent fades out of the album's final track, *I Love You So I Told You A Lie* with a quotation from the Stones' *The Last Time*, I share with him the knowing smile of those who believe in the sound, and often the fury, of rock 'n' roll."

Cat Scratch Fever
"He's a hollerer, not a singer"

W as *Free For All* too smart, slick and challenging for the blue collar hard rockers that made up Ted's army? Possibly so, and yes, weirdly, *Free For All*, way back at the second album of many, is the most polished, most richly arranged, most dimensional and even serious record of the entire Deadly Tedly catalogue. And alas, it failed to build, appreciably, anyway, on the motor city mania of the debut. Ted was doing well, no question, garnering those column inches, playing the hockey barns and even headlining them, but what he needed now was a hit—not a hit album; that comes second—but a hit single. *Free For All* was the type of album that built quiet respect, but its reception lacked the contact high of the electric inaugural Ted spread.

"A really good manager wouldn't have had me go in and record *Free For All* while the *Ted Nugent* album was still going up the charts," reflects Ted. "Relax. Only half of *Free For All* was as good as it should have been. *Free For All* shouldn't have come out until *Cat Scratch Fever* and maybe there would have been no *Free For All* and half those songs would have gone away and just the best songs—*Free For All*, *Turn It Up*, *Dog Eat Dog* dwarfed the less than best songs on *Free For All*. You know what I mean? And that's what a real manager should have done. Because I am so gung-ho—have you noticed this? – I am so possessed by making the next song and jamming the next recording, that somebody's gotta slap me right between the eyes and go, 'Hey, shut up, sit down, and let's finish this first!' Because I can't wait to do the next lick."

Still, *Free For All's* representation of the sophomore slump concept is a storyline that has entrenched over the years, similar to that of Van Halen with *II*. Both were nothing like their shadowing debuts, but really, at the time, more serious critics were actually applauding the growth. But it all means jack squat to the wider world without three infuriatingly repetitive minutes of mind-numbing ear candy—the hit single.

To encapsulate or paraphrase the following fevered oration from Nugent, with the song *Cat Scratch Fever*, Ted didn't go to radio, radio came to Ted. "It's not to be understood. I was oblivious to radio demands. I was oblivious to radio requirements. I was oblivious to commercial considerations. I remain to this day pure and absolutely unadulterated and untainted in my singular craving and demand to just create the music from my guts, from my heart and soul. I love radio, but they can kiss my fucking ass. I play music for me and those people in the audience that are communicating on that primal level. Now, coincidentally, the radio that resisted *Stranglehold* and *Motor City Madhouse* finally had so many requests for those songs that they became a huge team player for Ted Nugent. I can't thank them enough. To this very day that same connection that music made in the '70s, I can turn on a radio station right now, somewhere in America, and you will hear *Cat Scratch Fever* and *Dog Eat Dog* and *Motor City Madhouse* and *Stranglehold*, because it was pure and relative to the primal scream that we all celebrate immemorial. It's a timeless consideration. But I did, fortunately, have sound technicians; Tony Reale, certainly Cliff Davies and my band mates, had great ears and were really critical. Certainly Tom Werman and all my team, Lew Futterman, they listened critically to make sure the chaos factor was delivered in an impacting, in-tune, tight, effective manner. So radio immediately jumped on that, because how could you not?"

"You know what? I'm a lucky guy," contributes Ted, who finds himself in a giving mood. "Once again, my gravity-defying career is the manifestation of great music and especially great rock 'n' roll. With all humility, I attribute it to the Tom Wermans, to the musicians, to the Cliff Davies and Rob de la Grange and the Derek St. Holmes and today to Mick Brown and Greg Smith and my team. My team loved the music. They're my team because they were attracted to my musical creation and wanted to celebrate it and enhance it and by their dedication of their incredible talents, those songs will stand the test of time eternally. Now I have some great ideas because I'm so inebriated by those original Chuck Berry, Bo Diddley defiant licks, that it takes a team of gifted individuals who have better ears than I do, that can make sure that the clang factor is not lost, but it is also deliverable without breaking things. Even though we want to break things, you can't listen to music if it keeps blowing up stuff. So I want to deliver it like we're blowing up stuff, but I have teams of professionals who keep it from blowing up stuff so people can actually buy it and listen to it. How's that for an answer?"

"My answer will not only be in response to the *Cat Scratch Fever* right place right time, but I believe it is approaching universality with musicians everywhere, that we are reflecting our life's experiences," continues Ted, not buying that there was anything particularly timely about that song bisecting the state of rock radio in America at that time. "We are a mirror to the world around us. I've been really privileged and humbled by jamming with the Bo Diddleys and Chuck Berrys and Bon Scotts and Keith Moons and Jimi Hendrixes and getting on a stage with Heart and Cheap Trick and Aerosmith and ZZ Top. You gotta be kidding me. What a communication opportunity that is and my reading of all those great musical moments and great musical creativity is not that we came up with it, but we fed off those audiences. Remember, every band I know played hundreds and hundreds of concerts every year. You cannot—even the condition some of them were in—you cannot escape or deny the pulse and the vitality of that audience who was there to celebrate the music you're celebrating. So as you play a concert, hundreds of concerts later, *Cat Scratch Fever* was a direct result of the feedback from the people who were cheering me on and giving me this dangerous level of confidence that made me just pursue my musical dreams with zero inhibitions. And I believe that every great song came from that relationship with the audience that taught us what connects with them best."

Sure, *Cat Scratch Fever* was a hit, but the timid totality of the playing, arrangements and above all, the anemic production... Lew Futterman is hesitant to give Tom Werman a whole lot of the blame – or credit. "Was he more involved? You know, I really can't say that. To this day, I really do not know. Other than being there in the studio and making his astute comments about the quality of takes and so on, I mean I don't know what Tom brought to it creatively. I have no recollection of Tom ever being involved actually in the arranging of any of the numbers, and certainly not in the songwriting, which was always... the songs came in before we ever went into the studio. What later is in the press is another story. As far as the big hit single, *Cat Scratch Fever*, Tom has zero to do with it. *Cat Scratch Fever* was me... and a giant fight with Ted."

"Ted came in with this great riff for *Cat Scratch Fever*," continues Lew, discussing a track that, frankly, was not head and shoulders above any of the other songs on its namesake platter. In other words, maybe it was just Ted's time. "Ted was very creative in that respect, and he came up with a great lyric. Ted is a very, very talented lyricist but what Ted didn't have was a melodic sense. He could write riffs, not melodies. Part of the reason he had no melodic sense is Ted could hardly sing a note. I mean he really... he's a hollerer, he's not a singer. He has a very unmusical voice by nature and getting Ted to actually sing recognizable notes, as opposed to being in the cracks—and this is coming from a guy who can't sing a note. Don't get me wrong, I can't sing, but if somebody is a little bit off I hear it in a second, but I can't sing a note."

"But Ted was a guitar player who made an attempt to sing and really, a very talented writer of riffs and lyricist. He was not melodic. He came in with *Cat Scratch Fever*, which was... it was sort of thinking about being a melody. Cliff, who was very musical and had a very good sense of melody, sat down with Ted at the piano and these quasi notes that Ted was singing, they actually found the place on the piano that it could be a note and that worked. They sat down and they sort of turned it, note by note, into a rather melodic heavy metal song."

"Ted was insistent on singing it and the truth was the nature of the song, Ted's phrasing really worked very well with it. Certainly would work better than Derek's phrasing would. Ted had the right phrasing for it because he was a genius with riffs, and he sang riffs—he didn't really sing melodies. So how do you take *Cat Scratch Fever*, which is sort of a riff looking for a melody and once you get the melody, get a guy who really sings riffs, not notes? So what we did on *Cat Scratch Fever* was a heavily produced single. The way we did it was we first put down the basic track. Then we put Ted singing live so you'd have the right feel. Of course it was very unmelodic. Then we took the basic track with Ted's phrasing, which was right on, and we brought in a group of English rock 'n' roll background singers, who sang the notes as written by Cliff, which were based on Ted's basic thrust towards a melody and his riffs, and you know, sang with Ted's phrasing. Phrasing was terrific. He had the sense of how he wanted the song to sound, he just couldn't make them… he couldn't hear the melody in his head until it was there for him to hear."

"But he had the sense of the song. It was his song, his creativity. It was a matter again; we're coming back to the issue of shaping. Ted… it's not like in any way I was Svengali or something, not in any way at all. Ted always had the great creative ideas. They just didn't have shape. That's why I said I was a very good traffic cop. That's what I was good at. I was good at getting people around Ted who would help him take his very creative, very good ideas and put shape to them."

Of note, the background singers Lew used were a ragtag bunch, namely utilitarian journeyman Alan Spenner, Rory Dodd, known for doing backups with Meat Loaf and Boz Burrell of Bad Company fame. But how does this vocal story end?

"So let me tell you, because *Cat Scratch Fever* is actually quite melodic. So now we put on the backing track. We've got the singers and they're singing the harmony and so on and then one of them even does a bad but in-tune melodic… does Ted's lead. Now we got the whole thing, but with Ted's phrasing. We've got it on the tape. Ted records on top of it and now Ted is hearing essentially his own melody. The melody that he sort of wanted to come out, but that his own melodic limitations kept him… he's hearing his own melody in the shape that it should be. He had no trouble singing on top of it quite melodically. I mean he hit every note. So now we've got the basic backing track, we've got the instrumental backing track, we've got the vocal backing track and we've now got Ted singing his own phrasing, exactly as he conceived of it, but hitting all the notes. It's really a song now, hitting all the notes. Then Ted took it and he embellished it with the things he liked and then we gave it to him and said, 'Okay, you've got a structure. Now do you want to add some more rhythm guitars? Do you want to add whatever you want to add now? Maybe re-do your lead? Whatever you want.' Because we had 16 tracks to work with. Of course now it's a very different thing. The techniques… but then, 16 tracks were plenty."

And by this point had you removed the other vocals?

"Oh, no, not the backing track because remember, on *Cat Scratch Fever* you do hear backing vocals. You hear them. I mean we never removed them completely. They're not prominent any more, but it's sort of like singing along to your favourite tune. Everybody's a pop star singing along with their favourite record. Because you're hitting the notes that you're hearing. Ted took it and cleaned it up. Of course I had his voice fairly prominent in the track, which is not the way we normally recorded his voice. At first he was very concerned about it, because in his own way he was humble about his own singing abilities. When I first presented it to him, almost like a pop song, where you could clearly hear the lyrics, he was, 'No, wait a second, that's not rock 'n' roll.' 'Ted, you've got a hit single here.' I said, 'and this hit single is going to do a lot for your career'."

"Finally he said okay and he got into it. He picked up on it and he got enthusiastic about it and embellished it with a lot of things at the end. He really got into… once he decided, yeah, you know what? It did work. Then he got behind it. It wasn't like, oh no, this is what they're going to put out under my name? He had good sense. It was a fight, but he picked up on it and said hey, I think we've got a hit. Needless to say we did. *Cat Scratch Fever* was the No.1 heavy metal single. It wasn't the No.1 pop single, but it was the No.1 heavy metal single. It was a career-changer because it broadened his appeal beyond just the heavy metal audience to the general hard rock audience and I think, enabled him… that song more than any other enabled him to become a stadium performer."

"*Cat Scratch Fever* is getting a much stronger response than the earlier stuff and we think it's a better album," noted Cliff Davies back in '77, surprisingly doing more than a few of the interviews. "We've been performing the title song, *Wang Dang Sweet Poontang* and *Death By Misadventure*. But we are fast becoming a hard-working studio band too. Ted and I are a very good combination. I'm very much into production as an art form and spend hours at the desk fiddling with the knobs. Ted is into generating the energy and rawness and the results are good: *Cat Scratch Fever* doesn't sound polished and chrome-plated. We don't use a lot of tricks. We play very high energy, frenzy-level rock 'n' roll, and it works."

What is of interest here is that Cliff is claiming deep involvement in the guts of record-making with Ted and so is Lew, at least with this one song (the vast majority of his comments concerning the wider catalogue modestly have him admitting to doing very little!) Talk to Tom Werman and he feels he was a big part of the sound as well. Yet Ted is the boss, but giving much credit to his unheralded backups. Yet in what are almost like unguarded moments, he betrays his quite extensive studio skills and input. Indeed, for a guy with as much take-charge ego as Ted, the totality of his oration really plays down his contribution to the production process.

"Until Cliff finally left the band, Cliff was always very, very involved with the arrangements," concludes a clarifying Lew, asked if Davies was still the secret weapon at this point. "But Cliff was a very self-effacing guy. He never demanded a lot. I don't know the ins and outs of the eventual squabble they had over money and so on because I was no longer in the relationship. I tried to stay out of it because I was still friendly with Ted and I was still friendly with Cliff. So I don't know the details. I was focusing on my own life. It's not that I don't want to discuss it; I don't even know most of the details because by that time I was a real estate developer. When they had their first battles, I was not even in the music business anymore."

As *Cat Scratch Fever* hit the stores in May of '77, *Free For All* was about to go platinum. It really did seem that hit single or not, the next album would be platinum in no time as well. As for cover art, Ted's amusingly Cheech & Chong-ish Tex-Mex look and vibe as gotten across one record back would fly the freak flag once again. Ted radiates manic and as we flip the cover over, we find out why: he's being handled roughly and by a sweet Sally that likely isn't his wife back home on the farm.

For the new record, the band forsake use of the Sound Pit in Atlanta and headed for the Big Apple. "We all wanted a change," said Ted, playing it up on the press trail. "I wanted the album to be noisier. I think the engineer who worked on the last two Epic albums was great but I don't believe the Sound Pit was conducive for a real ringing album. This time we wanted more wood, more glass, more concrete. I want the sound ricocheting off the fucking walls! On the last album there was an attempt at a slight decrease in attack. On this album that is not allowed!"

Ted plays up a gritty, funk-infected track on the album called *Death By Misadventure*, one of the album's under-rated songs, a scattershot rocker buttressed by a cool instrumental break. "That's a great song, great arrangement. It's about Brian Jones really. I've always been anti-drug, though. It started the first time I cut myself with a razor blade. I knew right then the drawing blood from your own body is not cool. Actually, it's just a matter being opened up to the situation and seeing people drop like dogs with knives in their gut and needles in their arms. My whole stand on the subject is a man is a lesser man as soon as he endeavors in drugs or booze. I'm the most on-the-ball person I've ever met. If there's a catastrophe on hand, I'll be the first to overpower it. If someone pulls a knife on me, I'll be the first motherfucker to punch him in the eye. If someone looks at my family wrong, I'll be the first to de-leg him. It relates to music too. If my drummer starts a beat, I'll be the first to jump on it. If I hear a riff in my head, I'll go immediately to my guitar and work it out. I never miss an inspiration."

Ted came equipped for this 1977 interview—as he would, amusingly, time and time again over the years—with a warning, "These new songs are devastating and I want you to be prepared. You should be naked when you listen to them but be sure to have some lumberjack, log-rolling boots on for traction."

"You should hear the copy I have of that one where I am playing harmonica on the beginning of it," adds Derek St. Holmes, concerning *Death By Misadventure*. "Ted thought, 'He is putting too much of himself into my music and I can't have it.' We rocked. It wasn't just Ted. Everybody was as good as the next guy. Nowadays, Ted likes to surround himself with hired guns. The only time he has done well is when he surrounded himself with people as good as himself and that was when he did Damn Yankees. He didn't last but two albums because he couldn't be the boss. I have had many a night with Tommy Shaw where he would say to me, 'Derek, how did you ever endure him?' I told him that we would just threaten to kick each other's ass. Finally, I did that and that is why I wasn't in the band anymore."

Perhaps foretelling the break-up of the band that would come, Ted made clear that, "Derek wrote a song with me called *Live It Up*, but I did most of the writing myself. There are ten or 11 songs on the album – and they're all giants. The songs are shorter, but there's *more* guitar work, not as many stretched-out solos, but my songs don't have too much vocal to 'em anyhow." As for the lyrics? "Boy meets girl, boy eats girl, girl eats boy, girl pukes, boy kicks girl's ass, just your average love stories." Bringing up *Live It Up…* in fact, that was the only song not wholly written by Ted, who is also much more of an engaging singer on the record than Lew gives him credit for, his ragged voice the perfect foil to Derek's, a bit of spice to the gumbo in the manner Peter Criss or Ace Frehley add to Kiss, or Keef adds to the Stones, only here that voice had most of the lines.

"I think that rock 'n' roll should be played by impulse and unvarnished," said Ted to Rolling Stone, pretty much nailing the *Cat Scratch* credo. "When you write a song, you should develop the essential thrust of the given lick and not change it. I don't want any tricky musicianship! Fuck that! I hate it! I want drive! Hammerin' away in unison, strictly reinforcing the thrust of the rhythm. No alter-rhythms, no counter-rhythms, changes and groovy syncopation and all that fuck-all. That's what gave me trouble with musicians, because they all wanted to be tricky and clever and impress their musician friends. I could give a flyin' fuck."

Along a similar tack, Nugent articulated that, "The hardest part is finding people to play my music who have the talent to play it well without losing the feel of its basic appeal. The basic pounding of rock 'n' roll is boring to a real advanced musician and I consider myself a very advanced musician. But it still happens to be what I feel. My band are all superlative on their instruments and with me, they know it's time to drive. They know it's got to be Hammer City, and there's no place for tricky quadruple piddle-diddle jazz licks at the end of the phrase. It's time for a boom-crack, boom-crack. It's time for the Neanderthal rhythms which are to be played with precision— which is as difficult as playing the tricky lines."

Hence the amount of turnover his band had seen with the charade that was the Amoby Dukes and was about to see again – just as they were hitting stride. "In the pursuit of satisfying their egos – not to get the spotlight, not to get the credit, the interviews, the fulfillment of speaking their peace the way I do at the drop of a hat – has got to be discouraging. But there are people who are going to be comfortable with this position and they're going to be good. I have to find the ones who are going to fit both requirements – and it's not easy." As well, these supplicants must keep up with Ted substance-free… "It isn't demanding on a healthy, intelligent individual, though. The minute you act stupid and your stupid actions take away from your physical and mental well-being, then you fall by the wayside. In more specific terms, as soon as you start getting drunk and stoned, you fall. It's as simple as that."

Interestingly, concurrent with the making of the album, Ted also brings up a track called *Walking Tall* that wouldn't even make the cut, showing up years later however on the *Out Of Control* box set. "That song is actually about walking tall and carrying a big bone. It's just a song about the attitude of being your own bad self and don't take no shit from no shinola."

But back to the album as it would be issued, Ted speaks accurately in that the songs, on the main, are shorter, but more so that they seem more immediate, more gathered around riff and little else, certainly over and above the thoughtful bunch that filled up *Free For All*. There's a rootsy *Hibernation*-like instrumental called *Home Bound*, on which Ted plays up one of his half dozen or so signature sounds, his sinewy, coyote-howl twin leads, as inspired by George Harrison, twin leads that criss-cross in and out of feedback, another one of his overt characteristics, both in the studied studio and on the showbiz-buzzing stage. "That's a song I wrote about the feeling I get when I'm about to go home after touring," says Ted, in the same chat, describing the new album in total as "smooth yet urgent." "It's not mellow, it's a great song. Sure I'm mellow sometimes. I get mellow a couple of hours after a show; I go to sleep. Now that's mellow. But that's as mellow as I ever get."

At the heavy end, there's the frantic *Wang Dang Sweet Poontang*, the similarly brisk and snarling *Sweet Sally*, slight boogie structure notwithstanding, the latter, like the album's hit, another example of Ted singing along with his riff. *Fist Fightin' Son Of A Gun* is near as heavy, and even more boogie-woogie (if that's possible), Ted being a class example of how proto-metal from this era seemed to near subconsciously lapse into boogie licks between the forging of forward-thinking metal structures. Heaviest of the lot is album closer *Out Of Control*, a fiery lick-licked rocker energetically sung by Derek. A notch down is *A Thousand Knives*, mid-paced but still squarely part of the metal world as it existed in the late '70s. Then below that, there's the relaxed *Bolero* recline of *Live It Up* and the rhythmically daunting yet poppy *Workin' Hard, Playin' Hard*, replete with more twin leads, its odd riff recalling the James Brown ants-in-your-pants dance of *Great White Buffalo*.

Sweet Sally and *Wang Dang Sweet Poontang*… according to Ted, he's on his way to some sort of a concept album there. "Some of my best songwriting shit comes from when I'm surrounded in the fervor of rock. Every time I plug in, I create. I write about things I get into, like *Wang Dang Sweet Poontang*, that's about pussy. *Sweet Sally*, that's about American pussy. Most of my songs are about pussy. I really get off on seeing all the young chicks in the audience. You know what my life is like? It is very well-defined. I get up five minutes before we have to leave for the airport, I get on the plane, I get off, I go to the sound check, I rehearse, I snag some backdoor youth and I have sex, I toss her out, I do interviews, I play in the tuning room, I take a huge shit, I get head, I rupture the masses with my guitar playing, then I snag some more pussy and go to bed. If I'm not doing the above, I'm talking to my road crew, my truck drivers, my T-shirt sellers. I'm totally the product of my own desires. I am the nucleus. I have life licked."

Assessed *Melody Maker* when confronted with the latest Ted spread, "With a couple of exceptions – *Stranglehold* and *Dog Eat Dog* are the two that immediately come to mind – the songs haven't been catchy enough to stay in the mind. All that changes on *Cat Scratch Fever*, where Nugent has come up with some real scorchers. Best of all is the title track, which sounds like a cert for the US Top Ten. But it's not all smut (harmless though it is). There's a really excellent instrumental, *Home Bound*, which has all the power and musicianship of the classic *Migration* from *Tooth, Fang And Claw*, where you can really hear the rock-solid support that Nugent gets from his talented band (doomed, I'm afraid, to be forever in the shadow of their gregarious leader—but not to be forgotten). Their playing is great throughout and Ted's on top form; coupled with a selection of fine songs, it should all add up to the smasheroo hit Nugent has deserved for years."

All told, *Cat Scratch Fever* turned out to be a fairly rockin' album, if jarringly midrange sonically and somewhat stiff, especially in the light of

Ted's railings over how funky he and his funk brothers are and were, no matter what the era. It is of no matter and almost fortunate, fortunate that Ted was smart enough here up into the late '70s to not let too many of his roots show. After all, even in '77, he was a veteran for which the front edge of hard rock should have been somewhat unknowable, although, granted, *Cat Scratch Fever* is no *Sin After Sin* or even *Long Live Rock 'n' Roll*. In other words, old-timey musics like blues, boogie, southern rock and soul singing are built into the fabric of much of these songs, even if Ted blasts them with so much guitar, music history barely makes a peep.

Cat Scratch Fever, the album, would vault to No.17 on the US Billboard charts, rising to No.28 in the UK and No.25 in Canada as well, with the single hitting No.30 on Billboard. More importantly than fleeting chart numbers is the fact that the record has amassed triple platinum status, receiving that certification in March of 2001, remaining to this day, far and above the best-seller of Ted's elsewhere solidly performing catalogue.

Double Live Gonzo!
"We got him some bigger sticks"

In the time-honoured tradition of Kiss, Blue Oyster Cult, Humble Pie, the Allman Brothers and most amazingly, little Pete Frampton, it was time for Ted to send Mr. Excitement flying off the stage and onto black plastic and to roll the dice in search of that weird phenomenon, the smash hit live album.

"We may have thought after three studio albums, why not do a live album?" recalls manager of the moment David Krebs. "It gave time off to also write. Plus Ted Nugent as a live act is magical. There's a certain kind of excitement that you could capture live that you probably couldn't capture in the studio and Ted Nugent never suffered from having to deal with hit singles, so…"

Double Live Gonzo! wouldn't necessary send Ted into the stratosphere lop-sided with the live versus studio, the way Kiss or more so Frampton had gone, but it did sell a bunch of pancakes, keep Ted in the news, and most importantly, demonstrate what a monster Ted was live.

This is key. If Kiss or BOC think they had a problem with their mousy studio albums set against the explosive roar of the live show, well, Ted fitted right in there as well. Let's face it; the productions had not been the best. In fact, *Cat Scratch Fever* tracked the lightest of the three so far, *Free For All* the most skillfully rendered, *Ted Nugent* quite accomplished for 1975 and for a debut record. Fault also must be placed with the drumming, Cliff clearly not a rock 'n' roll wild man, his beats minimalist and polite.

"I guess I was a fancy drummer to some degree," muses Cliff, a characteristic clearly not in evidence on the Ted Nugent albums. "Ted and I butted heads a lot, because some of my heroes growing up were Buddy Rich and Tony Williams, jazz; John Bonham was a tremendous drummer, Keith Moon was a good friend of mine, I thought he was a cool drummer. Basically, I think Ted would have rather had someone who played the beat a lot more and played less fills. But because I was a busier, flashier drummer, I think it made us sound more exciting. Ted had a tendency to want to dampen other people in the band, so he shone. You know, he wasn't worried about being upstaged by backing groups. Especially when Derek was in the band. I mean, Derek was very, very hot on stage. He looked cool as hell, he looked great, played good guitar, and Ted was a little frightened of being upstaged. With me too. I had been with If, I had been with Roy Young Band, people who knew what I was. So he stopped the drum solo in the show, because it took too much applause (laughs)."

As mentioned, it was more so Cliff's musical skills away from the drum kit that helped craft these songs that were now so successful live. "Well, I play piano. Right now, I teach jazz, classical piano, for a living and percussion. I'm involved with this nonprofit organization. I came from a musical family. I have a really heavy musical background and by the time it got to Ted... do you know the Roy Young Band? A late '60s band in England. I think Roy Young moved to Canada. But I was basically the chief writer and brass arranger and orchestrator in that band and that was late '69. I did that for a couple of years and then when I joined If, I became the main writer and orchestrator and arranger, so I had a lot of background in that kind of stuff. So I was able to whip out things, play piano; you know, I play guitar. I actually played guitar when I was young. But I don't actually play guitar. I'm an orchestrator, composer, arranger. I play most things, even though I can't play them all the time. But most of the stuff I did on piano, the arrangements, composition."

So here the Ted Nugent gang are on stages all over America leveling town after town (the album is recorded mostly in B-cities, time-honoured supporters of hard rock in the '70s) and Cliff responds, blowing it up, exploding all over the record. Perhaps the most forceful indication that Cliff was almost a different drummer left to his live devices is demonstrated within *Gonzo!'s* opening salvo, a caterwauling wall of sound that quakes way for opening riff-rocker *Just What The Doctor Ordered*. As has been theorized, one can understand this idea that Cliff was browbeaten by Ted to keep it simple on the studio albums—after all things could be changed, erased—but let off his leash live, where Ted maybe felt less threatened by someone who had to stay behind him and also sit down to do his job.

Cliff certainly doesn't slight Ted as a worthy guitarist, even if he could be inconsistent... "I think Ted went through a period when we were on the road, in '77, and '78, where he was just an unstoppable guitar player. I mean, he was playing and playing gig after gig after gig and we would often do these things where at the beginning of a song... of course, when you do a lot of tours, the songs get longer and longer and more episodic with more tricks and things, so in '77 to '78, and even into '79, well, more '77 and '78, he would like drop to his knees under a single white spotlight and there'd be like a 15 minute guitar intro—and it would be fantastic. He would be so agile and so on top of it and you would go wow, this guy can really fucking play. Then you would have a week off and he would go home for a week and work on his four-wheel drive vehicle and he would come back playing with his knuckles (laughs). So he wasn't very consistent. He could do it, but he just had so much going on in his life and he had so many things he was doing all the time, I honestly don't think, up into '79, that he really had time to sit down and actually practice playing guitar. He would do it in the dressing room or something like that before a gig, but he definitely waxed and waned when it came to guitar. I think it was maybe the 1980 tour, when he was really starting to slack off a little bit."

That image of Ted on his knees, attacked with his own weapon, is captured viscerally on the front cover of *Double Live Gonzo!*. Implicit in the shot is Ted losing control, losing his hearing, losing his mind, as the feedback exponentially multiplies out from his hollow-body Byrdland. One can almost picture Ted throwing it down in panic and leading a frantic exodus from the B-city hockey barn like a scene from a B-grade horror flick swarmed by killer bees.

"Everyone listens to the guitar," continues Cliff. "It's the Ted Nugent band and it was a guitar hero band. He wasn't, but Ted wanted to be like a Jeff Beck or an Eric Clapton, but he just didn't have the dedication. He wasn't a real musical guy. He had a tin ear. He didn't know when his guitar was out of tune. Sometimes I had to tell him, 'Well, you're playing a minor here, Ted; it's supposed to be a major.' He didn't know anything about music; he just picked up the guitar and played the damn thing. It's his own licks, his own runs, so oftentimes it's very different from anyone else. He often made them up himself. Rather than having learned a diminished scale, he would make up a Nugent scale (laughs)."

In any event, besides raucous, lively, rock 'n' roll-gone-mad performances all over the place, *Gonzo!* issued in January of '78, offers intrigue with respect to song selection. Three Amboy Dukes tracks are on offer (well, *Baby Please Don't Go* is a cover), *Hibernation* mellowing us out, *Great White Buffalo* charming its way into our hearts, welcoming us to the world of countrified Ted. Bravely, Nugent fills a whole side with these two songs, turning slightly more than a quarter of the album ambered and Amboy, an odd circumstance considering that there are absolutely zero songs from *Free For All*.

Boldest move of the batch, however, is the paired set of non-album tracks, *Yank Me Crank Me* and *Gonzo* both being robust heavy rockers which, seemingly to underscore the friction with Derek, are sung by Ted, not to mention completely penned by Ted. Unfortunately, however, both songs seem a little undercooked, like *Cat Scratch Fever* filler, simple of riff, with vocal melodies that follow these simple riffs.

What's left is a lone offering from *Cat Scratch Fever*, unsurprisingly the smash hit title track and then all the redneck classics from the debut album, again, a curious mix of songs, especially given that the performances used were mostly from the summer of '77, well after *Free For All* was road-worn.

"*Double Life Gonzo!* was certainly not an embarrassment," mused Ted four years after the fact, expressing some reservations about the album, again, the bane being "the producers"—always the producers. "But I'll tell you straight, there are moments on that album I cannot listen to. I cannot listen to *Stranglehold*. It's a piece of shit. A piece of shit! Fucking producers demanded we use that version. The son of a bitch is too slow, it's out of fucking tune, it's a shitty performance. I got a cassette of the song done in Dubuque, Iowa on a foggy afternoon sound check and that version stomps the dogshit outta the one used on *Double Live Gonzo!*. *Great White Buffalo* is one of my all-time favourite songs. I can't even listen to the cocksucker on that record. It's an embarrassment. How could they have fucking chosen that version? Aaaaargh!"

Double Live Gonzo! would surpass its predecessor on the charts by hitting No.13 on Billboard, on its way to triple platinum status (although remember that each record of a two record set is counted, giving *Gonzo!* a double count). The album went platinum about as quickly as *Cat Scratch Fever*, inside of a few months, although the road to triple platinum was a long one, the album receiving that certification in April of 1999. *Yank Me Crank Me* would get trotted out as a single, rising only to No.58. It emphatically did not become a regular rock radio staple. In fact, even in 1978 it was played less than tracks like *Just What The Doctor Ordered*, *Snakeskin Cowboys*, *Stranglehold* and *Free For All*, earlier catalogue songs that weren't even issued as singles.

"Everything got raced live," laughs Rob Grange, asked to sum up this landmark live record. "You get out, you've got a few thousand people there and they're excited... everything—believe me, everything—goes fast. But like I say, Cliff helped us a lot in the live shows. He got the stage monitors all dialled in right and he really worked it. When we first got him, he played kind of light and jazzy and of course Derek and I were into early Jeff Beck and heavy drums, Small Faces and stuff. We got him some bigger sticks and got him to play heavier. So once he kind of moulded into that it worked really well."

Clearly though, by bearing witness to the strength of the metal mania within this record's grooves, Ted was giving it his all. "It occurs three or four times a year where I pass out at the end of the set," said Ted in the fall of '77. "The other night I passed out after the second song. First of all, that makes me a bit cautious because I don't want to hurt myself, but it also made me proud to realize that I'm on the edge. I'm literally at the point of demanding far too much of my body. If you blink at my show, you'll miss more than most people put on in their whole show because it's the ultimate high intensity, high energy rock 'n' roll music to ever be exposed on the face of the earth."

During the same chat, with *Music Express*, he also lamented that all the pyre at a Ted show, unfortunately, was not controlled by his road crew. "I don't know what the system of education is," ruminated Nugent, at the trend of the day, tossing powerful fireworks up on the stage. "They're there to have the riot of their lives, there's no reason to throw missiles at people. Do I have SALT talks prior to every gig? Anybody who can't have the finest, most intense high energy, free-for-all, uninhibited time of their life without putting another person in jeopardy, that person is wounded. I realize I inspire it every night. I scream at those kids and shout and I want them to go nuts; I want to eliminate anything negative in their brains. I accomplish this every night. I want them to sweat, get raucous, get outrageous, but don't jeopardize anybody, man."

"That's still when Ted was under contract to me," begins Lew Featherman, offering his recollections of the *Gorno!* period. "I mean I stayed involved with Ted and with *Double Live Gorno!* and so on, where I brought in Rick Browne (credited as Assistant to the Producers), a kid from Cornell, who I met when I was up taking my masters degree. Rick was about 20 years old when I met him, enamoured with the music business, a very bright Cornell student. I was back up at Cornell, 37 years old and working on that masters degree. But that album was pieced together from innumerable concerts, with augmentation afterwards and everything. I mean *Double Live Gorno!* was quasi-live. In other words we augmented all kinds of stuff. We'd have a really exciting overall performance but we would have… the rhythm guitars were just not kicking ass the way they should be. We pulled them out as much as we could within the framework of the technology of that day and we could put on brand new electric guitars, rhythm guitars. So that was a quasi-live album. You could still get away with that kind of augmentation without disclosing it back in those days, because there were no laws, no rego or anything that said everything had to be disclosed. Now you really have to. Truth in advertising and so on. But it wasn't the law and we did whatever augmentation we did to keep the feel of the live performance but make the music as good as it possibly could be within the frame of the technology."

"It was a great album, but it was worked over quite a bit," affirms Weiman. "All live albums were. But Ted was a great live act. I think it was probably more appealing to the buyer, or the fan, to have a live Ted Nugent record than a canned Ted Nugent record. Because you could actually pick up on and hear the energy; you could hear what was going on. It just translated better. He recorded more faithfully. It translated more faithfully from the stage to the record, I think."

As to why there were no *Free For All* songs on the record, Tom first of all says he'd never noticed, also venturing that, "the probable answer is that it was a function of Ted's live set. We took most of that album from a San Antonio performance and apparently he didn't enjoy playing *Free For All* songs live. They didn't come out so well or needed too much work. Because you could replace or repair a few things, but you didn't want to completely make a synthetic live album."

"I was never really a good analyst of musical trends," continues Tom, but then nailing the appeal of a record like *Double Live Gorno!*. "But I know why the music I made appealed to adolescent males. They're pissed off. They're angry, they're frustrated and they've got a lot of aggression, a lot of testosterone. One thing I used to take pleasure in was knowing that all across the country on Friday night, there were teenagers playing my music while they got dressed, while they drove to where they were going, and when they got there they were listening to it as well and it served a real purpose, I think. Which was to help them. I remember having that realization when I took my boss to see Ted Nugent at the Lansing, Michigan ice arena; must have been '75. I saw the kids come in almost to the person wearing the same things. They wore motorcycle boots, jeans, leather jackets and T-shirts. They were incredibly active and loud and it seemed they were trying to get something out of their systems, you know? I know that some of them were drunk. I mean, there wasn't a lot of control at that time with the crowd and I remember thinking after the concert, I can help these people. I can give them something that they need. That's what I did, basically. Not out of... it wasn't an altruistic thing (laughs). I enjoyed it too."

"The concert business was still young and just operated very loosely," continues Weiman. "I said gee, these kids, this is something I haven't seen before. Because I was from the east and the Midwest was almost a redneck thing, but not in a derogatory way. A lot of these people probably came in pickup trucks; a lot of the pickup trucks probably had gun racks. I thought to myself, we can help these people. We can help these people satisfy their craving for the kind of party music that Ted really delivers. That was the deal, really. I think that Ted was probably the ultimate, the goal of every hard-partying music listener at that time. Because he was extreme. Very few people got as out there as Ted, especially on stage."

Specifically on Ted's presentation, Weiman says that, "At that time he had, for the time being, given up the loincloth and the bow and arrow, which, I guess he'd done with the Amboy Dukes, or possibly by himself before we signed him. But when we signed him he had a new band and there was more rock 'n' roll. He still played the frontiersman, the snakeskin cowboy, but, you know, it was after, I think his first three or four albums that he went back to the severe, almost insane. He would shoot flaming arrows on the stage, into dummy deers on the other side. He used to do that in the studio too. He actually brought his dummy deer with him (laughs). But you know, like Alice Cooper, there was theatre, drama, a little bit. He didn't wear any makeup, but he wanted everyone to see who he was, and that's why he would run around, climb the walls, climb vines, climb ropes, shoot arrows. He was kind of like Elvis and his karate moves."

"Everyone does one at a certain point," says Tom, back to the inevitable documentation that the above concert experience required, in the form of a live album. "The labels love them because the budgets are very small. You go out and record four or five dates with a remote truck and you know, I don't know exactly how much of this went on with other artists, but I'm pretty sure a lot of it did. You would bring the tapes back into the studio, you would keep the drum track and you'd do a lot of fixing. Especially the vocals! It wasn't just the performance; it was that all the other instruments were leaking into the vocal misc, because you would have these amps blasting ten feet away. So every live album was a pretty polished live album, and when you heard *Double Live Gorno!* and you went to the show afterwards, or vice versa, you went to the show and then you bought the record, it was always considerably better than the live show. Then again, here you took songs that were already done and in the can and you just gave them to people in a different format. It was live versus studio and I think people cared about what a band sounded like live, knowing that you could do all kinds of tricks in the studio."

Fans most definitely cherished them, judging from some of the huge hard rocking success stories of the '70s. "Because it was the real deal, they thought," figures Tom. "And many times it was. The Who, *Live At Leeds*, that was mostly the real deal, and I remember it just floored me. I never really got The Who until *Live At Leeds*. I mean, the energy, the ferocity, you couldn't get that in the studio, just couldn't. Because in a studio you would make a record like a layer cake. You'd just add a track, add a track, add a track, maybe combined with... and add more tracks. It took something out of it."

The mainstream press got it as well. "More than Springsteen, more than Jackson Browne, more than Johnny Rotten or Joey Ramone, Nugent is the true hero of '70s rock," wrote John Swenson, reviewing the album in *Circus*. "He's won all his battles in the trenches, not on the record company promotional drawing board and his relentlessness has finally paid off. He plays in an anachronistic rock style, a fastfingers metal boogie that most people thought died out with Canned Heat and Ten Years After. But his sense of what those rock 'n' roll (read carefully—not art) fans want to hear and his near chivalric dedication to pure rock values has identified him to rank and file rockers as one of their own. But Nugent's trump card is that he's so much better live than on record, so much the frenetic, jumping and jiving crazy that he embodies the rock 'n' roll values so many of the 'cool, detached, alienated' New York punkers claim to be searching for. It's all here. Nugent's live album gets him down cold and that means *Double Live Gonzo!* cuts Kiss *Alive!* to shreds, turns the Stones' recent live disc to a puddle of scrap vinyl and rivals any other documentary set since The Who's hoary *Live At Leeds* for sheer unaffected rock power. Nugent is also his own best spokesman, screaming in that strangled cat howl before, during and after songs, asking in his strangely polite way after the enjoyment of the audience, delivering one of his motormouth wraps that move about the same pace as his solos. So his evaluation of his own guitar in his introduction to *Stranglehold* pretty much says it all—'This guitar right here is guaranteed to blow the balls off a charging rhino at 60 paces' (wild screams of approval from the audience)... 'This guitar just refuses to play sweet shit...' Nugent just doesn't know what it means to pace himself."

Swenson's references to punk were wholly relevant to the times and to

The Nuge. Ted covered a lot of column inches stating his opinions on punk, basically cutting it down seven ways to Sunday, although on the positive, Ted acknowledged that it came from the same fire that spawned the Rolling Stones or The Amboy Dukes. Ted was a big target for punks and writers who liked the punks, 'cos of his big mouth, his huge commercial success, his talk of craft, his anti-drug raps, his long hair, his white slacks, his large redneck life, even his positivity… basically nothing about Ted was punk. If in the UK, the enemy was Yes, Tull and ELP, stateside, it was Ted, Aerosmith and Kiss, and don't get them started about Styx, Boston and Kansas.

On the press trail for the record, Ted was asked to contrast the construction of a live record versus a studio spread. "Well, when I walk in the studio, I'm doing me, they're doing Ted Nugent compositions. There is an inescapable relationship between the studio and the stage, however removed they are. There's no way anyone will ever capture live performance on record because you just don't have all the elements. You don't have the face-to-face, body-to-body, flesh-to-flesh, volume-to-skull; but seeing how my entire inspiration comes from stage and the intensity thereon, I secure that whole desire for that intensity in the studio and that's where these songs come from. Now, the studio offers an element of extended creativity that is not available to me on stage, unique to the studio where I can overdub and I can really get immense satisfaction out of that. I think the people who like the rock 'n' roll that I play do so because they've seen me live. I have a lot of fun and everybody wants to have fun and nowadays everybody craves the release of worldly burdens from their shoulders and Jack, when I get to the concert, I'm telling you there's no worldly burdens on nobody's shoulders. That's why you got all these elements of super chaos-extravaganza-extremo-beyondo-wombo-live-it-up-o. There's an element of uncontrollability."

Double Live Gonzo! would be the last record featuring the classic lineup, the lineup that made the first three albums so magical and authoritative. Soon Derek would be out. So would Rob Grange. Cliff wasn't too happy either.

"Honestly, I think it was we were together too closely too long, too much," sighs Derek, summing up the turmoil in the band at that time. "We just toured constantly and you know musically and ego-wise, everybody was developing their own styles and coming up with stuff. Everybody that was in a band with someone, as history shows now, everybody comes up with their style of music as well and it's the little piece that you get when co-writing with somebody. Then all of a sudden you go, 'Well, my co-writer won't let me get all my ideas out; he likes to do his own songs. I'd like to do my own album.' What we didn't do quick enough, is that we should've gone off. Our management company should have slowed the touring down and we should've been able to go and get our rocks off, basically. Go and record our own music."

"I mean all four of us, because everybody was musically talented. Rob Grange, Cliff Davies, down to Ted, down to myself and if we had all gone out and done that and then come back in a year, we would probably still be together. Cliff is an incredibly talented musician, great voice, great songwriter, great producer, great arranger and just a great player. I mean, he plays five different instruments—drums are just one of them. We still stay in touch. He lives in Atlanta so I see him. If he's not doing something on the weekend or something and I ask him to come out and play with my band, he does. Incredible. Let's see, Rob sells real estate in San Diego and he still plays bass. Two Christmases ago, we all flew to Fresno, California and played a club. We invited Ted, but he didn't want to come. So we played this club, we filmed it and we recorded it and the three of us got up and did all those songs and it sounded like the fricking record. We hadn't seen each other for 30 years. But yes, hanging around with Ted back then, with him in his state of mind in that timeframe, he was incredibly intense. Incredibly driven, as we all were driven. He was the spearhead and if we disagreed with a few things here or there, we had to roll with it."

"Management didn't slow down on touring us – their motto was: strike while the iron is hot. We should've taken a year off. Everybody could have regrouped, because it got to the point where I got tired about listening to what Ted had to say and he got tired of listening to what I had to say. When we were on stage, it was one of the only times we got along and enjoyed it. Then there were times when we would be driving in a car together talking about everything other than music, then when we get to the stage, we didn't enjoy it. We'd look at each other and I didn't like what he was doing and he didn't like what I was doing. But there were many nights, because of that friction and tension, we were freaking incredible. I've gone back now and looked at some of that old German footage and California footage and English footage, and we were... wow."

Rob Grange chimes in, offering his memories of playing live with the band. "Well, we toured a lot with Aerosmith and a lot with Golden Earring and Montrose. We toured a lot with the original Lynyrd Skynyrd band, who died while touring on the road. If my memory is intact, I think we may have been touring with them when their plane went down. It was a very somber time because we had just all seen each other and then they were gone. They were so full of life and a great band. Many times we'd arrive at the Holiday Inn and it would be surrounded by police cars and we'd think to ourselves, 'Yup, the Skynyrd band got here before us.' We'd arrive to a fight in the hotel lobby or in the hotel bar and mostly likely it was the Skynyrd boys. After their plane went down, it had a lasting effect on everyone out on the road and the risks we all took to travel in a band. The fact that their songs are still played and loved to this day is a tribute to the memory of them and their sacrifice. Golden Earring, those guys told Derek and I, don't leave the band because you are making a big mistake. Then we played a lot with Foreigner, and those were probably the primary bands we toured with. Head East, as well and in fact Van Halen opened up for us on Ted Nugent shows."

Of note, one Madison Square Garden show, at which Skynyrd were supposed to co-headline with Ted Nugent, occurred approximately three weeks after the plane had gone down. Ergo, there was no Lynyrd Skynyrd, but this show would feature the band Rex. It would be a significant show for that band, as this was the show that broke up Rex, with Smith being courted at that show for his play at teen beat movie stardom. The Golden Earring dates of which Rob speaks occurred during December of '77, approximately through the mid-west. Golden Earring had been out with both Rex and Legs Diamond during the previous month, before hopping onto the Ted dates.

I asked Rob what Ted's and management's attitude was toward backup bands. "To be perfectly honest with you, Derek and I always encouraged bands that would attract more girls. Because a lot of people who would come to see us were young adolescent teenage boys who wanted to be guitar heroes. Derek and I were always going, "Where are the girls?!' (laughs). So we would always try to get bands that attracted girls, like Aerosmith and Babys and Montrose, to the concerts. We toured with Montrose and also with Sammy Hagar when he went out on his own; Sammy had a pretty regular band that he brought in from Sausalito and they were really good. We would always see Sammy. We toured a lot with Journey and Neal (Schon) would always come back to talk; he was a great guy. Foreigner's singer Lou Gramm, he was a really, really nice guy. Lou I think was working at a record store or a clothing store or something? He got the gig to sing in that band. Yeah, he was always very gracious and humble and very thankful to be there. They were a great touring band."

Cliff doesn't remember the circumstances around the Skynyrd booking, but says, "Could be, but we played Madison Square Garden a dozen times. Really, people think of Madison Square Garden as a big place, but they ripped it down and now they've got a new Madison Square Garden. But the old Madison Square Garden only held 14,000 people. It wasn't very big. At that point in Ted's career, he could easily fill a 14,000 seat venue. That wasn't difficult at all. I'm sure it went off without a hitch and nobody skipped a beat."

Cliff also says that similarly, "Bon Scott died when AC/DC were touring with us. We were off the road at the time, but they were currently touring with us. Our favourite band to play with was AC/DC. They always opened the show for us. They were by far the greatest rock 'n' roll band at that time other than us. They were fantastic. They hit the stage running every night. They were hot every night; I mean, they warmed the audience for us every night. It was just a fantastic match-up, it really was. I was pretty friendly with Bon Scott and I used to party with him sometimes, not get too close to him, lest I should be dead (laughs) from various substances. The wildest tour we ever did was with Stevie Marriott and Humble Pie, Bon Scott and AC/DC, and Ted Nugent. There were some great stuff on that tour; boy, between Bon Scott and Stevie Marriott, it was totally crazy. We did a lot of gigs with Nazareth opening the show for us. They became really good friends of ours as well. We did a whole American tour with Golden Earring, who we became extremely friendly with."

Other stage-sharing memories include Starz and aforementioned Rex. "We hung out a lot with Starz because they did more gigs with us. When we did the Starz tours, they were always like a three-act show. It was always such a crazy, crazy thing. When it's a two act show, you didn't tend to hang with the other band, but with three, you spend a lot of time shooting the breeze. I do remember Rex being a cool guy, and sitting down and shooting the breeze with him on a number of occasions. But it was literally a blur. We would do 29 gigs in a row and take two days off, 25 gigs in a row, take two days off. It was relentless. Towards the end, we were on the road so much, that by the time we got to mid-'79, we were zombies. We really didn't have much of a break since 1976. We would fly into the gig, do a sound check, go to the gig, disappear, come back the next day. More like that: less and less hanging around."

For Europe in '76, in support of *Free For All* (the *Gonzo!* recordings draw from that tour as well as the more recent *Cat Scratch Fever* dates), "it was with Black Oak Arkansas; they were our backup acts for the first tour of Europe," recalls Cliff. "Lone Star were one of those first on a three-act show things. Especially if it was in Germany. You could do certain places on your own, and you could do double gigs, which we did with Black Oak Arkansas and then with a festival or at a bigger gig, you'd need a third act and that was Lone Star." But Ted never felt threatened by up-and coming-back-up bands. "No, not all. He had ultimate confidence that we could wipe the floor with anybody."

"Oh, brilliant, absolutely brilliant," remembers Lone Star's Kenny Driscoll, asked about Ted's treatment of the band. "To me especially. At that time, I lost the plot with my band; I was getting fed up with them because they were all into Scientology and I couldn't handle it. So I would be in Ted's dressing room a lot of the time and we were jamming. Derek St. Holmes wanted to get a band together with me – he was adamant about it. He was living in Flint, Michigan. So I sent him a letter, because I couldn't get him by phone. I heard back from him three months later and that was that. But Ted's band, they were very nice to me (laughs). It was our first proper tour and he gave us all the volume and everything. He had his Byrdland guitar, which is semi-acoustic, but it screams like a bitch, feedbacks like crazy. Then I saw them on the next tour, because we were friends. Whenever they came to this country, I would see them. I don't like his animal stuff. I'm a vegetarian (laughs). But I mean, I always liked Ted; we always got on really well."

Back to what would be the final recorded document from the original band, years later asked to respond to the pervasive tension in his band between its armies of lead singers, Ted says, "No, no, no, all of those guys can out-sing me, sing-wise. In fact, Derek jammed with us in Las Vegas recently and he still has great pipes. He's jamming with us at the LA House Of Blues and Anaheim House Of Blues. I'm just giddy about it."

So you've buried the hatchet with him, somewhat?

"I don't think there was ever a hatchet. With all due respect, I think Derek—he may admit this or he may not—was delusionary. I mean; the real premise of those guys splitting was that I was holding them back. But I would ask you, Martin, if I was holding them back, why didn't they move forward? Of course it's true. If I was holding Rob de la Grange back, where's his record? That was 30 motherfucking years ago. If I was holding you back, when are you going to do it?! Fuck you. There's an ego thing. A lot of people don't realize I have an ego because I have a gargantuan amount of confidence. But it's not confidence in me, rather confidence in my understanding where I come from. So I'm the only guy who celebrates Howlin' Wolf and Muddy Waters and Lightning Hopkins every single night by name. And Chuck Berry and Bo Diddley. I'm the only guy who pays homage to those by name, because that's where this comes from. I don't give a shit about stardom. It's not even in the top million. It's not even on the list! I mean, a good shit is on my list, okay? A good piss. A nice overcast day with a north breeze is on my list. Stardom isn't on the list. It couldn't be more inconsequential."

"But to too many people, it is," continues Ted, who even since this interview, has gotten up to guitarin' with Derek on a semi-regular basis. "Derek had some terrible, terrible, bad advice when we were really starting to sell records. From girlfriends and wives. 'He wouldn't pay me enough.' They were claiming he wasn't getting enough spotlight. I've got to tell you, talk to any of my lighting directors. In fact, I'm waiting for some interviewer to talk to one of my crew. When you talk to the light man, ask him what I talk about more. Ask them if I talk about my getting lit more, or my bass player, drummer and vocalist getting lit more. Ask them what I talk about. I always identify, 'You've got to get them there. We've got to get these guys.

If I ever turn around and don't see my guys lit up, you're fucking fired.' I tell the sound man, 'I want the drum's enormous. I want the bass and Derek's voice enormous!' So why I've been labelled a hard guy to work... in fact, Martin, do yourself a favour. Get his number from Linda and call Craig and Mike. Call Tommy Clufetos and Barry Sparks. Call Jack Blades. 'So, I understand Nugent's a prick.' Let them tell you what I'm like to work with. I'll tell you what I'm like to work with. I'm a fucking dream to work with. If you believe in the music. Because it's all about the authenticity and the spirit of tight-knit, streamlined, rhythm and blues, heart and soul rock 'n' roll. If that's what you're into, we're going to get along famously. You know if you're posing, you're going to get hurt."

"Well, the problem is, you see, Derek thinks he's a star," sighs Cliff, in conclusion over one component of what you've probably figured by now is a big grubby mess. "Derek doesn't realize that nobody knows who he is. I mean, he had a real tough break. As a kid getting into music and trying to make a career out of it, to be Ted Nugent's lead singer and guitar player was probably the worst thing he could have done (laughs). He was always just a sideman even though he was a lead singer. But actually, you talk to people today and they are convinced that Ted Nugent sang all the songs. You tell anybody about *Stranglehold*, they'll tell you Ted Nugent sang it. But it was Derek. Derek's voice, on the very first album... it went a long way to making that album a hit. He sung brilliantly on that first album. But that's what it's like for Ted right now. Ted tells people he sang on *Stranglehold*. I mean, he really wants people to think it was all him and it was nothing to do with anybody else. That is his goal in life. I mean, I've had arguments with people up and down, where they swear to me that Ted Nugent sang *Stranglehold*. There was no lead singer in the Ted Nugent band, that Ted Nugent sang all the songs. There are people who are like ready to pull a gun on you. 'Listen, I know my Ted Nugent, man!' Really serious. It's just egos gone crazy."

Finally, where did the great Leber Krebs organization sit within this tangle of motivations, the motivated, and the motivators?

"Leber and Krebs were a couple of incredibly filthy rich Jewish assholes," says Cliff. "They were sleazy. Steve Leber had been involved with New York show business and Broadway for many, many years before he was involved with Ted Nugent. Had the reputation of being like the fuckin' Mafia. He was the sleaziest guy in town. David Krebs… he was the kind of guy that when he was young, when he went to kindergarten, he went in a limousine. That's how rich his parents were. He got into rock 'n' roll, pretty much for a lark. Honestly he didn't need the money. Neither one of them needed the money. So it was just like a project for them. They had so many acts and they were so big. They had so much going on that they couldn't pay attention to individual acts. It wasn't really like having a manager at all. It was very strange. It wasn't hands-on, the way it maybe could've been."

Where did they end up? What are they doing now?

"I think David Krebs is running some sort of a national Republican magazine. He was a staunch Republican along with Ted. Leber, actually, he could be retired right now. I mean, they were both quite a bit older than us. I'm 59, so he could be in his mid to late 60s, said he might've hung up his hat. But they were both filthy rich. Yeah, it was all about money to them. I can never understand people like that. You know, why does it have to be about the money when you've already got more money than you can possibly spend? I mean, Aerosmith was David Krebs' favourite band. He, quote, 'discovered' them in Boston and they had this horrendous management deal. They paid David Krebs like 40% management. But for that, David Krebs spent all kinds of money, millions of dollars… I mean, they are a superstar band today. He made them into that band, because they were his little guinea pig. Now, when time came for Ted Nugent to sign a contract, a management contract with David Krebs, he enlisted the help of Lew Futterman, the producer, who had been involved in negotiating record contracts and management contracts before and was friendly with Ted. When he went to negotiate a management contract with David Krebs, Lew Futterman played hardball. Instead of paying 40% management to David Krebs, Ted only paid like 15%. So what did they do? They put all their energy into Aerosmith, because that's where they were making all the money and as a result, we were always on the back burner. Because they were only getting 15% from us. So it's like being too smart for your own good. You know, you think you're going to make more money because you're paying less management, but management isn't going to put as much into you because they are making three times as much from someone else. So there was a lot of that kind of stuff going down."

You get what you pay for... "Exactly! The other thing is, Ted always resented it," continues Cliff, confronted with the idea that Ted Nugent was successful because of the sum of the parts, half of which wouldn't be around for the next studio album. "Because, I mean, when we were back on the road in '76, Ted would get up at fucking dawn and hit as many radio stations as he could. Have a nap in the afternoon and then we would do a three-hour sound check. I mean, he was really good. When we were on the road, he was really fuckin' into it. The rest of us were partying. When Ted was at the radio station, on his fifth radio station, I was at the pool drinking Heineken (laughs). So he resented somewhat, the fact that we became famous because of him. In fact, he spent the last 20 years systematically removing our names from anything he could. I mean, the greatest hits album, which is released now, there is no mention of Rob or Cliff or Derek as musicians. The only reason I get mentioned is because I was the producer and the producer's contract says I have to get a credit. But he has systematically tried to remove our names from anything and everything."

Cited the quote from Ted with respect to his benevolence as an employer, Cliff remarks, "Well, that's complete fucking bullshit. I mean, like I said, he took the drum solo out because it was getting too much applause. I mean, he wasn't a stupid man. He knew he couldn't go onstage and put everybody else in the fucking dark—he wanted to look good. What made him look good was good for him. If lighting the rest of the band, for whatever the reason, was part of the show, then that was good. But I mean, he really was not a fair guy to work with. In fact, the guy is a mean-spirited prick. He really is. I hate to say that about anybody and I'm not out to put anybody down, but he's a nasty person. He's an asshole. That's just him. I mean, whether it was because his father was a Marine Corps drill sergeant and beat him up too much... You can imagine the kind of rumours that float around. I don't give any of them any kind of anything at all. But the guy's a prick. He's an egomaniac. He's egocentric, self-centred and he doesn't give... I mean, he gives to charities. He's not a mean guy in that way. You know what I mean?"

"Ted is one of these guys that wants to be the leader," continues Cliff.

"He's a megalomaniac. When we got in the argument with him when I was going to leave the band, I held out for some points and then wanted to include Rob and Derek, it wasn't so much that he had to give me that money. It was that he didn't get to make the decision about who got the money and how much it was. You understand what I'm saying? At any time you take the decision-making process away from him, then that's a bad thing. He wouldn't have necessarily minded. I don't think at that time… I don't think he was in any state to negotiate with anybody, because things were flying so fast, in every direction, but the best case scenario would've been to leave it up to Ted and say, 'You tell us what you would like to pay us. How much of a percentage for it to be worthwhile for us, without gnawing at you.' If we had gotten to that point, where he could make the decision, things would've been a lot better. The problem was, the manager, David Krebs made the decision. He took the decision-making process out of Ted's hands and that's when it went bad."

As our examination of the post-*Gonzo!* break-up of the classic Ted Nugent lineup winds down, it's obvious that I did take up Ted's advice and asked a few people what it's like to work for Uncle Ted. Yet even those on the outside… they seem to be cognizant of the situation. "Ted and I go back to when he opened for Jimi Hendrix back in '68," adds yet another opinion from the deep past, Orville Davis, bassist for Rex and Starz, both back-up acts for the Nuge. "Ted and I, we talked on a few occasions and on one occasion he approached me about playing bass when I was touring with Rex, out there. It just finally came down to where it was two rhinos butting heads. I've got respect for Ted's longevity, but sometimes I felt that he treated Robbie pretty crappy and Derek St. Holmes pretty crappy. No actually, I don't think he did, I know he did. It was what it was, you know?"

In closing, while Ted does a bit of a scan of his long, rollercoaster career to date, he offers this philosophical kernel… "I never, ever, ever gauge any of my personal appreciation based on commercial success. It's a nice manoeuvre and it's enjoyable. I certainly spend the money, but my personal moments have nothing to do with anything commercial. The drive of my life comes from moments with my son in a fishing boat or with my wife on a mountaintop hunting goats in Hawaii. These are the moments that drive the quality of my life. I certainly appreciate with all my heart and soul all those people that have supported my career and bought my music and celebrated the intensity and the touch that it represents. But some of my favourite moments recording-wise never made me a penny. There were moments that were less than perfect, but then, it's a roll of the dice, ain't it, boobie?"

Weekend Warriors

"Ted Nugent wasn't really a recording band"

As discussed, the most significant move in the Ted Nugent camp come *Weekend Warriors* is the ousting of the band's golden crooner Derek St. Holmes.

"Unfortunately what happened," explains Ciff Davies, "and this was 1977. We're out on tour with him through '77, and Derek is being a complete jerk, he's trying to upstage Ted, getting in his way when Ted's trying to run around. In Passaic, New Jersey, I think it was, it came to a head, when Ted was out on stage. Derek used to, like, drink Jack Daniels out of the bottle and he was always coked up, did a lot of cocaine. Derek and Ted came to blows in the dressing room and Ted said, 'Look, I can't take your fucking shit anymore; you're out of here.' So a big panic went down, the management flew in and they decided that Derek would finished this tour in '76. We would then do Cal Jam 2, in the spring of '78, which would be Derek and Rob's last gig and then they would form St. Paradise and I would stay with Ted. Which is exactly what happened. We went through the end of the year in '76, we met up and did Cal Jam 2, which was the last gig that we did together. We went straight into the rehearsal room with a new bass player. Well, we had been doing it before, with Cal Jam as well and we ended up rehearsing with Charlie Huhn and the new bass player and didn't even skip a beat."

"When Cal Jam happened on 18th March 1978, I was once again oblivious to any considerations other than my band's gonna kill tonight," recalls Ted Nugent on this milestone show for the band, quite possibly, given that's it's the last hurrah for the classic lineup and Ted at his apex of fame, the most magical moment of the band's storied story.

"I arrived on-site at Cal Jam 2, in Ontario, California, 15 minutes before

I was supposed to go onstage, with African blood, guts and mud still on my boots, as the last white guy to get out of the Sudan alive. I was in the Sudan 48 hours prior and I ran with the natives who saved my life from the rebel murdering forces that blew up the Khartoum airport. I literally came out of my safari camp with only the bag carrying my toothbrush and some lion claws and some Masai fighting jewellery, commandeered my way on a Red Cross plane out of Juba, Sudan. No one knew where I was because all communications had been cut off, there was a war going on and they were killing everyone. I commandeered a Red Cross plane, again thanks to the black Africans that I created a blood brotherhood with—they saved my life. I got on the Red Cross plane, flew to Cairo. I'm muddy, bloody, hadn't seen a bed or a shower in ten days. We were literally escaping the rebel forces. My guns, my bows, all my trophies and skins and all my animals, all my possessions were back on a mound of earth in the rain-drenched floods in central Sudan. I commandeered a seat on a flight from Cairo to London."

"When I landed in London, literally by all logistical considerations, I couldn't make it from London to Ontario in time to perform. But my crew was going, 'Don't worry, he'll be here.' My management's going, 'Oh my God, this is a million dollar date, Ted Nugent's headlining, Cal Jam, we have half a million people here, what are we going to do?' My guys are going… Craig Colborne went, 'He'll be here. Everybody relax; just set up the stuff.' My band was pacing, my band was already in a weird place because they were quitting right after the show—did you know that? They literally quit right after the Cal Jam 2. Hysterical. I go… I literally got… I ran through Heathrow airport, I mean, stinking like a camp dwelling. Hadn't slept in anything but on the ground in ten days. At Heathrow I got on one of those supersonic jets, the Concorde and had the pilot radio ahead that I'm coming to Kennedy airport in New York. When I landed they took me in a police car to a TWA jet that they had wait for me, landed at LAX where they put me in a helicopter and I got backstage 15 minutes before I was supposed to go onstage. I hadn't seen any of my band or family or friends in three weeks, I hadn't touched a guitar in three weeks, so that intensity level that you see when I hit that stage, I still had African blood and guts under my fingernails when I climbed that stage at Cal Jam 2. So I know it was an awesome event, it was a day of rock 'n' roll infamy, but for me it had much bigger, badder, outrageous considerations because of what I had just gone through to get there."

"The audience was awesome," concludes Ted. "It was perfect. It was just a sea of unified celebration for my music and my band, Derek St. Holmes, Rob de la Grange and Cliff Davies who performed as God meant dedicated musicians to perform. It was a great, great day."

"True story," recalls promoter of both Cal Jams Don Branker. "24 hours before the show, he's in deepest, darkest Africa some place and I don't remember the country he was in. He was hunting wild boar with a bow and arrow. We had to fly him from Africa into London, into Los Angeles and then helicopter him in and he made it, which again is one of my... Because Nugent was a headliner, you know. So it was always a fear for me. We were tracking planes. Did he make the plane? Yeah he made the plane from Africa, yeah he made the plane from London, yeah he's in Los Angeles, he's on the helicopter, helicopter is on its way and he went on. Nugent was an interesting guy to work with by the way. He does no drugs at all and doesn't drink and allows nobody associated with the show to be doing drugs at all. You would not think so looking at him. You know what I mean? He's straight as an arrow. Now of course he's a right-wing conservative and you know, his true colours are there. Leber and Krebs at that time were managing both Aerosmith and Nugent and they both were with the same agency, so it was pretty easy. So it was a packaged deal, putting them on the show. He did a great show. I mean he really did, if you like Ted Nugent. I'm always a great fan of his and I had worked with him a few different times by now, but he did a great show."

"But like I say, we had to fly him from Africa to Ontario Motor Speedway in 24 hours. That was a challenge but we were able to do it. Ted showed up, walked onstage, he'd only been there for maybe an hour, two hours in the country, walked onstage and played a set like never before. He's appeared many times on my shows and he knocked 'em dead. Did the Ted Nugent that you all want. He was as excited as the kids were; that was the other interesting thing. Ted's... I think one of his lines was if only he could have been in the audience and watched himself play, he would have enjoyed it. He would have been his biggest fan. He had perfected his show. Didn't miss a beat—very impressive, very impressive."

Ted's arrival was a disaster averted but in actuality, an even bigger potential disaster waited in the wings, concerning the headliner of the day, Aerosmith, who, as alluded to, was another Leber Krebs act.

"Let me start off from the beginning," relates Branker, setting up the tale. "Show starts up with Bob Welch... Bob Welch just had Fleetwood Mac. Stevie Nicks and Mick Fleetwood came and played with him, so that was a good start, you know, in the morning. You had Santana—Carlos who never could do a bad show. I've done probably, I don't know, 30 or 40 shows with Carlos from the very beginning when he first started. Never did a bad show; everybody loved Carlos Santana. Then it went into Dave Mason who had his following. Then you get into Heart, which was the most phenomenal show I've ever seen a girl rock band do. I mean they just blew me out. The vocals were just phenomenal, the sound that they had was just phenomenal. Foreigner, absolutely just destroyed the stage, this sense of great songs, because they were riding three No.1 songs off their first album, *Cold As Ice* etc. They just gave a great performance."

"Each one of these acts, remember, they're looking at a crowd that is a mile long. You can picture that. It's 350,000 people. You can't... from the stage because I do all the announcing, so I had to see it all the time. But it's like the earth curves before you see the end of the crowd, you know what I mean? Of course Ted was really hot and had been hot with *Cat Scratch Fever*. He had never really had a hit. He'd always been a good hard rock band, but he hadn't actually had a hit record at that time there. So he was very, very hot at the time."

"Now, Aerosmith was just coming back into their own again you know, a little bit, actually right before their demise, to be honest with you. I think *Draw The Line* album was the one that had just come out then and so they were hot with that. They did a great show."

"But I had a problem with Aerosmith. Honest to God, true story. I've got only one more act to play and that's Aerosmith. I get a call on the walkie-talkies saying, 'Donnie, can you get to Aerosmith's trailer? We've got a problem.' Those are not words you want to hear, you know. The problem was that my caterer, within the rider, which is one page of how much I'm going to pay them and the rest is 49 pages which is the lighting and the sound and all the technical requirements and of course the catering requirements. In there was two pounds of jellybeans and no black jellybeans. My caterer had missed it and left the black jellybeans in it, so they called me in to tell me that they weren't going to play. Which of course to me would have been a full-scale riot. I don't know how many people would be dead, how many of them would've been hurt, but I know it would have been horrible. Because in order to gain access onto the inside of a two-and-a-half mile oval Indianapolis-style track, there were only two tunnels in. You've got to go underneath the tracks. So nobody could leave it in a very fast way if, God forbid, there was a riot."

"But nevertheless I told them, 'Well you are going to have exactly the amount of time it takes for me to get from this dressing room to the stage. I will make the announcement that you don't want to play because somebody forgot to take out the black jellybeans. I'll pack my wife in my car and watch the riot at home on TV. That's how long you've got.' By the time I hit the stage, they were running behind me. I went up on stage and said, 'Ladies and gentlemen, let's give a warm Cal Jam welcome to Aerosmith!' Of course they did a great show. Now I did not know at that time they were on hard drugs. That was unbeknownst to me. Of course I wouldn't have known that, so now I understand a little bit. I don't forgive them, you know. I probably won't watch *American Idol* because of it. I'm still upset with Steven."

"It was all Steven. I had never met Steven before. Their managers were Leber and Krebs. They were the ones... each dressing room had a little room into it and then there were big trailers. So I had a little room like a little office into it and then the dressing room was the bigger part of it. I just went into the office part and Leber and Krebs told me and then this guy walks out. I had never seen him before and to be honest with you, I had been up for four days. Even a one-day festival is four days worth of work, you know. You are building a city and I'm responsible for everyone out there. So all I see is this guy walk out with a bunch of... you know a big mouth, the biggest mouth I ever saw in my life besides Mick's and a bunch of silk handkerchiefs. He's telling me he's not going to play because somebody forgot to take his black jellybeans out. I know that if that shit happens that my show is not complete and I would have to refund the show, because they were the headliners. Not forgetting the riots and all that other kinds of stuff. I mean it's a whole quagmire of nightmare for me. It was all Steven."

"Generally they were groundbreakers, back then," says Derek, intimating, as Krebs himself does, that he and Steve Leber had quite a bit to do with the execution of Cal Jam 2. "They were making things happen that are commonplace now, but were not normal back then. They were the founders of putting together quite a few of these huge festivals. To that date, there were just maybe, I don't know, three or four? I'm not talking about Monterey Pop Festival. I'm talking about Woodstock and huge events like that. They came up with a huge bunch of them. California Jam 2, California Jam 1, there was the Day On The Greens. David Krebs is who I worked for mostly, hand-in-hand. I talked to David all the time and he's always done well by me. I love him like an older brother, because he's always been good to me. I just saw him, because I was just in Manhattan before Christmas and we got a chance to sit down and have lunch and we chatted about things coming up."

"I was a very big proponent of stadium tours," confirms Krebs. "So I really spent a lot of time putting together Cal Jam 2, which was Aerosmith and Nugent co-headlining for 300,000. But the expense of converting an open field for a rock festival with a low ticket price at that time, the break-even split figure was, I think, 207,000 tickets. So I said after that, this is totally stupid. Why don't we try to get into some stadiums? So the next one we did was at the Cotton Bowl, which was an 80,000 seater. I always thought this: if you're my fan and I can get you to see me perform outdoors in a stadium at night and follow my show with fireworks, I have then put forth an indelible impression on your psyche, okay? So in '79 we did maybe five or six big festivals. Each one we gave... I think we did one in Toronto. Didn't we do the Canadian World Music Festival and we gave Canada either two n's or two d's? That was our trademark. Texas had two x's. We did it with Michael Cohl, I'm sure."

An interesting side note: as throwback to the days when headliners at club shows would go on at a reasonable hour, with the baby bands playing deep into the morning hours, the "headliners" of Cal Jam 2 were actually Frank Marino's Mahogany Rush and Rubicon, the funky pop act that would morph into Night Ranger. The idea here was that Branker could spread the movement of the crowd out of the place, projecting that some fraction would stay for the two baby bands, avoiding a stampede to the exits after the last kerrang of Aerosmith. In any event, disaster was avoided, with the show ending at midnight, albeit, two hours later than planned.

Wrote Sylvie Simmons of Ted's set, "There was a crush around the stage as around a thousand heavy metal clones squeezed up against the chain-link fence salivating and chanting for their hero. Looking half-crazed and half-starved, a product of all that aeroplane food, Nugent leapt on stage a parody of himself and lunged into *Cat Scratch Fever*. It was sweet inspiration to the crowd's psychopathic element, who pogoed (a necessity of having less than an inch between your feet and the next person) to the brain-mashing music, taking in every word of his repetitive machine-gun wraps. The girls love him to talk dirty. *Wang Dang Sweet Poontang* was dedicated to 'all that sweet California pussy,' the very same words use the last time he played LA. One could wish that he'd find another fetish just to make a change—saying the same thing 200 times a year does get a bit predictable. In fact, that's just how Nugent sounded. A half-crazed, arrogant product of raw meat and junk food, less acrobatic than usual, under the false impression that he was playing to thousands of deaf people. Nugent plays about the best powerhouse rock around, but that's not to say he isn't getting stale. Heavy metal music per se is getting stale. It would be better if he gave his band (competent musicians all) some of the stage exposure instead of singing, playing, soloing and soloing and soloing under the spotlight (of the 19 pictures on his *Double Live Gonzo* album, all 19 are of Teddy) all of the time. However, that's about as likely as asking God to play a saint. And Ted Nugent is worshipped."

Even though Cal Jam 2 would be Derek's last gig with the band (he would return, on and off, starting four years hence), the straw that broke the camel's back was a fateful dustup months earlier.

"We played some theater in Passaic, New Jersey," relates Derek, in conversation with Jeb Wright. "Ted wasn't even at any of the rehearsals before we started that leg of the tour. The rest of us were proud of our playing and we rehearsed for the gig. Ted shows up and we start playing and he is stumbling around like he is playing with his knuckles. We had to pick up the rest of the show for him. We get backstage and he turns it all around—with about 40 people around. I am not for that. If you have a difference with me, then let's go in the next room and let's you and I talk about it. Don't put on a show in front of 40 people because you never know what you are going to get when you push people into the corner like that and start embarrassing them. Ted was doing that—he thought he was a big shot. He started screaming at the drummer who was a little skinny English guy; he wasn't going to say anything. Then he started going after Rob and Rob just totally ignored him because he was the same size as Ted and he wanted to beat his ass but he didn't because he was raised better."

"I don't think I was raised better. By the time he got to me I had already had a six-pack of Heinekens and half a bottle of Jack Daniels. When he started to run me down in front of 40 people I just said, 'You know what—you just got done playing out there like you were playing with your knuckles. You always brag about how you think you're as good as Jimmy Page and how you think you are this rock god guitar player but we carried your ass out there tonight. I am sick of it.' He jumped up and he ran across the room in front of all these people. I guess he was going to fight. He was rushing across the room and there was water on the floor in front of the buffet table and he slipped and fell to his knees in front of me. I grabbed the back of his head—I was going to fricking drill him. I didn't care; at that point I was over the edge. Just as I reared back, his brother, who is standing behind me, reached his big arms over me and grabbed a hold of me. While his brother had me held, Ted punched me in the face and kicked me in the balls in front of all these people. The roadies jumped in and broke it up."

"The people from the label were just appalled. They were not with us on the road hearing him putting us down every chance he could. If Ted would have said, 'Derek, you played good tonight' three nights a week and then yelled at us the other two then that would have been all right. But to have him yell at you all the time for three weeks on end is too much. He never came up and said we sounded good. So we ended up having a fistfight. When they pulled us apart, I told him, in front of everybody, 'Ted, take this job and shove it up your ass.' He goes, 'Oh no, you're fired.' I go, 'Whatever. I am out of here. I've had enough.' I got my stuff and walked out of the room and into the next dressing room. People were freaking because the label saw this. We were touring on *Cat Scratch Fever* and we were just getting ready to put out *Double Live Gonzo!* and the band is fricking history."

"The manager, David Krebs, comes in along with his publicist Laura Kaufman and they start to calm me down. Krebs flat out told me, 'I need you to go back in there—I don't care if you have to lie. I need you to go back in there and tell him you're sorry and that you don't know what you were thinking. You have got to stay with this situation for another three months until we can get your record deal signed and then I can get replacements.' I told him that I was not going to do it. They had to talk me into it. He told me, 'Trust me. This is going to be good for your career if we do it this way.' I thought about it and thought about it and then I got up and went in the other room and said, 'Hey man, I'm sorry. We are like brothers and this is all my fault.' Ted says, 'Do you really think that?' I told him that I really did and he said, 'Let's try to make it work.' From that point on I was done. I stuck it out because we had to do California Jam."

"That was our very last show," continues Derek. "Ted never touched a guitar for 30 days because he was in Africa. He was washed-out in a monsoon and he lost his rifle and his packing gear. He missed a couple of flights and he was lucky he got there. Meanwhile, us three trusting souls, the band of merry men, had been rehearsing for two weeks just so we would sound good. Ted jumped out of that helicopter and put on his stage clothes that were sitting there in the dressing room. He strapped a guitar on and he walked out on stage and started playing. He had the two guys there that were going to replace us there as well. The next night they were going to shoot *Don Kirshner's Rock Concert* with the two new guys. He thought that he could go on *Don Kirshner* and everyone who had not seen the band live would think that they were the two guys on the record. It caused a ruckus in the community for the people who had seen him live. They were third stringers anyway as they had never played anywhere but clubs. I remember the singer, Charlie Huhn, coming up to me after the show—he doesn't know me. He comes up to me and he goes, 'So, whatcha gonna do now, man?' I didn't even answer him. I looked at my road manager and I pointed to this kid who was like a foot away—I pointed right in his face. I said, 'Who is this kid? You need to get him out of here.'

He goes, 'I don't know what you said but you got to go.' That was not a good day for us. The last thing I needed was some young little whippersnapper, who is going to replace me, to come in and get in my face and ask me what I was going to do now. I thought to myself, 'You rookie. You have no idea what you're in for.' I saw him seven years later and Charlie goes, 'Derek, I hope you are not mad at me.' I told him that I wasn't. He goes, 'I had no idea.' I said, 'I know you didn't. But you know now, don't you?'"

"I am telling you the truth. I am just telling you what I saw and what happened to me," continues Derek. "It is not a Nuge slam. He is cool. He is a good guy. He is a lot older now but he is still not ready to handle Rob, Derek and Cliff in his life again. I don't know why because we only made each other better. Even his daughter comes to me and says, 'I don't know why dad doesn't have you singing all the time.' Look what happened to Aerosmith. Those guys never have to work again. It is not that we are trying to cash in on all the money but how about getting paid for what we produced? What we produced in the '70s can be revisited in the 2000s. When we got together for the recording, it was awesome but the thing that was missing was Ted's part and him putting his flair to it. Rob Grange impressed me. He has not missed a beat. Cliff lives about 20 miles from me so we occasionally play together. To play with the three of them was a dream come true and I have the DVD to prove it."

Discussing in 2000 the long history of bad vibes in the band with Goldmine's Michael B. Smith, Derek explains that, "Once we started to get good—we had done that first Epic record with *Stranglehold* and *Hey Baby* and *Queen Of The Forest* and *Snakeskin Cowboys* on it—I can remember things were beginning to be stressful. I knew I was good at singing and playing and writing and I was starting to stretch my wings on some of that stuff. I think they started thinking I was getting too big for my britches and they started to hold me down a little bit. I couldn't figure out why, because nowadays you try to hire the best people you can to make the thing happen and you just manage it correctly. There started to be a little tension. It started to wear on all three of us, Cliff Davies, myself and Rob Grange. It started to put a wedge in between us and Ted, and before you knew it, he had three disgruntled employees on his hands. We had all quit at different times and if it wasn't for David Krebs, his management at the time, the whole thing would've fallen apart a lot sooner than it did in '78. Ted was being a hard-nose and saying, 'If they don't like it, they can leave.' We could have left and he would've been left high and dry. When we left, he went on to do *Weekend Warriors*, which kind of rolled off of the success we had built for a little while and then it was over."

"People were saying, 'Where did Ted go?'" continues Derek. "But it wasn't the same band anymore. It just isn't going to sound the same. I guess during the '70s, we just hung out together and saw too much, you know? We weren't getting a cut of things and it took David Krebs to say, 'Hey, you need to cut these guys in on something. We are making hundreds of thousands of dollars here and these guys are making a thousand bucks a week or so and they're making it happen with you.' So we got cut in. But it was too late. It was water under the bridge by then. We weren't really happy, because we knew that he was forced, kicking and screaming to do it. The only saving grace for the day was that hour and 15 minutes on stage. You deal all day long with the trials and tribulations of touring and being in a rock 'n' roll band for what—an hour and a half on stage every day? That was it. That was your safe zone. It was just not the dream we had all thought it might have been. We were all disheartened."

Cal Jam 2 was commemorated with the *California Jam 2* double album, which flopped badly. Only CBS acts, i.e. Epic and Columbia artists, were included on the album. Ted shows up at the end of side two, with *Free For All* and *Snakeskin Cowboys*, production credit going to Cliff, Tom and Lew.

More importantly, *Weekend Warriors* would be issued in September of 1978, wrapped in a gem of an album cover featuring a bold 'n' brash illustration by Jeff Cummins. "Originally, Oui magazine (based in LA), commissioned the Ted Nugent piece for an interview/article with Ted," explains Jeff. "To be honest, at that time, I'd never heard of him! The art editor sent me some pics of Ted playing live and wanted a kind of 'G.I. Joe' thing, with machine gun-guitar etc. The original artwork was kind of A4-shaped with the gun end bleeding across the opposite spread, above the text. When Ted saw the published article he wanted the artwork for his next album cover! Oui sent the artwork back to me and CBS then asked me to 'square up' the blue background—luckily there was just enough room on the art board to do this. This is all pre-Photoshop don't forget. Also, they wanted me to add the Fender logo to the amps and make Ted's legs more muscular! Best of all though, CBS then asked me to 'move some the hair from in front of Ted's eyes, so that we could see more of his face.' Yeah, like his face would be there waiting to be revealed once the hair was removed! I explained that, as I had based the likeness on a photo provided of Ted, with hair cascading forth, his face beneath the hair didn't actually exist. They sent me loads of Ted photos and I kind of made it up in the end. Later, the cover art received an award from the Society Of Illustrators in New York and was exhibited at their awards show in the Eagle Gallery, I think it was called, in Manhattan."

The painting celebrates one of Ted's signature looks, namely the white slacks and although we can't see it, the pinned on tail at the back, which is emphatically in view in the Cal Jam footage. Guns and guitars complete the picture, getting across the idea that Ted will be hunting for hard rock domination carrying this latest batch of songs over to the radio station, but more importantly, stages all over the Western world.

But it almost didn't happen. First idea was Ted in a tuxedo. "The tuxedoed look," shuddered Ted, telling *Creem* about it in 1979. "Well, I tried the tux and that doesn't work. In fact, I didn't try, I just knew it… Have you ever seen any of those pictures? Man, this would fry your little buns off. We did some photos down in Florida. First suit I ever owned. It was a Florida suit, beige. I don't know what kind of material it was. I just felt a bunch of material 'til I found something I liked… Fuckin' 1200 bucks on the suit—three-piece, extra pair of pants, just fuckin' incredible! Then to top things off, I wet down my hair and slicked it back… Looked just like a fuckin' queer in Gentleman's Quarterly. There are those pictures floating around under lock and key that maybe this year will surface. In fact, Gentleman's Quarterly wants to use them. It was dangerous. I could be sitting here right now with you and you would refuse to believe it was me. I just looked like such a gay ranchero."

Leading up to the album's birthing, Ted talked a good talk of having 40 songs to pick from for possible inclusion on what would become *Weekend Warriors*, including *Good Clean Fun, Meathook, Bloodbath, Sabertooth, You*

Can't Stop Me Now, an instrumental called *Hacksaw* and *Jailbait*, which would resurface three years hence on *Intensities In 10 Cities*. He also crowed repeatedly of *Venom Soup* and *Name Your Poison* and both as possible titles for the new album.

"I actually think that *Weekend Warriors* is one of Ted's better albums," says Cliff, "which is really gritty. It was the first live album; did a lot of it live, in an old studio in New York, CBS Studio C, which was actually an old cathedral, converted into a studio. The same cathedral that Take Five was recorded in, actually, which was pretty cool. But yeah, we had some pretty good success. It was moving right along..."

As contrast with the "poppier" vibe of Tom Werman, Davies says he, "always tended to take the more rawer approach, a bit more lo-fi, a little bit more like rock 'n' roll. The same way like a lot of The Who records were. I can't remember the guy's name now, but he had a way of making it lo-fi rock 'n' roll so it sounded cool. I wasn't really into like 20,000 cycles on the cymbals and 50,000 cycles on the bass drum. It's too much like Fleetwood Mac or something. Like I say, when we got to the third album, *Cat Scratch Fever*, we made that much rawer and then when we got to the *Weekend Warriors* album, I really went all-out and made it scrappy, almost like a punk album. But that was happening. Punk was coming out and people were tired of hi-fi. Everybody was coming out with really lo-fi records that were distorted and had all this fuckin' energy and power which hadn't been sucked out of the record with black boxes and gadgets. That's what I really wanted to do with *Weekend Warriors*; I wanted to get rid of all the overdubs and gadgets and the boxes and just get down to the rockin', punk, Ted Nugent energy. I thought it turned out quite successful, from that point of view."

"You see, Ted Nugent wasn't really a recording band," muses Cliff. "For example, you had bands like Pink Floyd, great band in the studio and when they go on tour, it's just really a bonus for that band. I mean, it's like, they don't make a living out of touring; they would rather be in the studio playing music. Ted was exactly the opposite. Ted hated the recording studio. He wanted to be on the road, he was a live performer, that's what he was, a tremendous live entertainer, the best I've ever seen and that's where his thing was. So funny enough, what happened with our records, because they weren't really that good compared to the other records that were out at that time. It wasn't great writing or anything. There's nothing really profound on there, but it was basically the tours that sold the albums. We would go on tour and all of a sudden the albums would sell like crazy. You've got to remember we were the last really big pre-MTV band and so we were out there slogging away. We worked like 29 gigs out of 30 days, for months and months and months, all over the country. Because that's what you did that back then. You toured to sell records and MTV didn't start till 1981. We were the last of the big pre-MTV bands."

"He got less involved actually," explains Davies, with respect to Tom Werman, who shares the production credit on the album with Cliff and Lew. "Because by this time he had a track record. He had other productions going on. He was doing the Cheap Trick live *At Budokan* and he did Mother's Finest and he kind of lost interest in Ted. I mean, at that point, we were obviously on the decline. The honeymoon was over. Pretty much after *Cat Scratch Fever*, Tom pretty much faded away. He would drop in every now and again and he was still on the credits, but yeah, he wasn't very involved. He would drop in on a mix session just to see how we were doing and stuff. Mostly, I did the mixes, in New York, after we finished the album. Tom and Lew would go on vacation and they would leave me in New York to do the mixes, with Tim Geelan. Now that engineer, Tim Geelan, he was another secret weapon, in New York, who helped record *Cat Scratch Fever*; he was a tremendous engineer. I've known him a long time, because I had been working in New York in the early '70s, and he taught me a lot. But he's another one you should write up. Both Tim Geelan and Tony Reale had a lot of input into the sound and in fact, on the first album, Ted Nugent even put, 'A special thank you above and beyond the call of duty to Cliff Davis and Tony Reale' or something like that. But both those engineers were hot shots."

"This boy's got this playing on *Need You Bad*. Fuckin' Les Paul's gonna poop!" said Ted at the time, plugging his new golden boy at the mic, Charlie Huhn. "You'll see him on the *Midnight Special* playing harmony guitar. I did it on the album, as I wrote the music and the arrangement and I like to play alone. But Charlie's from Grand Rapids and is just in-fuckin'-credible. One of the guys in my crew knew him and knew he was playing with a bar band in Grand Rapids. I had a couple nights off so I got in my plane and flew in to hear him. This guy blew my mind. I said, 'Prick, you are in the band. Come to see me tomorrow. Quick!' I gave him five songs and told him to learn them overnight. Perfect! It was kind of a test. He came the next night and played it better than Derek *ever* played it, sang it better than Derek *ever* sang it. I'm trying to act really nonchalant: 'Yeah, that's *pretty* good.' Inside I'm going, 'Oh no! He's a motherfucker! Give him lots of money and send him to the ranch'."

"Derek and Rob did a fine job for me," continues Ted. 'It's just that they were getting too lackadaisical. They figure the big-time hit, now was the time to lay back. Bull fuck! The way I see it is, the big time has come and now's the time to drop the hammer even further. I have to tell Charlie, 'Whoa! Hold on a second!' With Derek, it was 'Come on! Come on!' Fuck that, I will not have it. I realize I'm very obstinate and very one-directional. But I just can't think any other way. Certain aspects of music and the rock 'n' roll life must be that way. If you don't dig it then you gotta get the fuck out 'cos you're not really doing the job. You know what I mean? Everyone around me is well aware of my desires and I ain't gonna fuckin' budge. You gotta have discipline. It's either 'Yes, let's do it' or 'No, get the fuck out.' I'm allowed to say that; nobody else has that right. So right now, everything is perfect! Everything about my career. Something's bound to happen. I'm bound to lose a hand or something because it's so perfect now."

"Charlie is a great guy," continues Davies, with respect to Huhn, the new hire who would last through four records, still stomping the floorboards today as front man with Foghat. "Charlie was a blonde. Like, I mean, he was a diz-brain. Like, no brain, no headache, sort of thing. But he was an absolutely fucking wonderful, kind, guy. Really, really nice, got along well, good voice, took the direction well. I can't say too much about his guitar playing, but he held his end up with Ted. For the second parts, but he certainly wasn't any Derek St. Holmes on guitar. He was pretty much an average guitar player. But yeah, Charlie was great fun. We had a lot of laughs."

With Derek gone and as surmised earlier, one wonders if Meat Loaf could have got the gig. An amusing prospect, but pretty unlikely if only for the fact that Marvin was on the way to becoming a big star himself with his smash *Bat Out Of Hell* album. His work on much of *Free For All*, "definitely had put him a lot closer to being able to get a record deal," notes Cliff, Davies adding that, "Meat Loaf was fat, so Ted wouldn't have had anything to do with that. Yeah, Ted was into the rock 'n' roll image thing, the long hair and the clothes. I mean, we've butted heads. Because I'm not a hairy guy. I'm almost bald now. Back then I didn't have much hair. It was short, but Ted wanted me to keep it long; you don't look right. He's very much into the look, he's very much into image, he very much understood the business. I'm not talking about percentages and stuff like that, but he seemed to understand how the music world worked. He'd been around long enough; he had one hit with Amboy Dukes. He was a very savvy guy. All those magazines like *Creem*, Ted would read those things back to front, every single one of them, so he knew who was saying what and what the hip word was and this and that. This is in the early days now, but coming up to '79, it was more like cruising along with the breeze, pretty much."

Cliff confirms what so many have said before about Ted's aversion to boozing. "Yes, I mean, I actually saw him drink alcohol twice. Once was when he took the whole band out to Benihana's. I think this was like in 1975, when we were recording the album and we went to Benihana's in Atlanta, and Ted drank one of those tropical drinks with an umbrella and proceeded to just run around the room, run over people's tables, jump up and down doing fucking cart wheels. The other time was on the bus, we were on the road, maybe about '78 or something like that and for some reason he drank a beer and the same thing happened. He started doing cartwheels. But other than those two times, I've never, ever seen him do any kind of substance at all. Unless he was doing something we didn't know about. But I was around Ted for years and I never, ever saw him do any kind of stuff."

"I'm sort of an inbred," laughs Huhn, by way of introduction, meaning he wasn't exactly a born and bred Detroiter. "I came from the western part of the state, Grand Rapids and then went to college in Lansing and then onto Detroit with my wife Holly, which was the main reason we moved here, which was that she was working for the governor and I was working with Ted. So I needed kind of a major airport to get in and out of. That was in the late '70s. It was a good time to catch the last diminishing edges of the Detroit sound.

Because I was only about 18 in 1969 and that's when I was given permission to leave the city, you know, in the parents' car and I went immediately to Detroit and Ann Arbor and watched rock bands. That was the scene—Ann Arbor, Detroit, Elektra Records, the MC5, Iggy at the same time."

As for working with Ted, "As time went on, I got more adept at recording and performing at the level of a professional headliner, which is something I had to learn about. You know, I could sing and play and stuff when I was in a bar band, but I really had no clue until I got in the studio with Cliff Davies, what it took to make yourself sound good on record. So, I think the first album I did with them, *Weekend Warriors*, was a real awakening. But I was put under restrictions and so I had to kind of develop a sound. So that one was sort of work by rote."

But for reasons we shall see later, *Weekend Warriors* contains some of Charlie's finest memories with respect to getting to sing. "Yes, well, as vocal showcase, you know, *Weekend Warriors*, *Need You Bad*, *One Woman*, those songs on that first album, those were strong songs. But the performance really wasn't there unfortunately, because I was just starting out, and I was on restrictions, like I told you and kind of didn't know what I was doing. You know, being classically trained, you put yourself under a microscope. You're not sort of rough around the edges and brash and just going for it. So I kind of had a foot in the hole to start out with, as far as developing a style. But I sang eight out of ten on *Weekend Warriors*."

As for Charlie's views on the production of *Weekend Warriors*, "Actually, Tom was minimal in terms of input, the production of that. He had other things on the stove, so he was really busy doing those. Cliff and Rick Brodie took over; Rick is a friend of Cliff's from New York, who later was his partner in the Pronto Brothers production company and Rick is how I got into my band Victory in Germany in the '80s. It's kind of fun reminiscing about the history of all this. That album was done at Criteria in Miami, which is a beautiful studio and they tried all these cool little amps and stuff, but Cliff's recording style... you've got to remember, Cliff comes from a jazz background and he's really a proficient musician. Ted and Cliff clashed; let's just be honest. So from that standpoint, Cliff was trying to introduce Ted to different ways of recording. Ted was amicable about it, but it was difficult for him. So that's why you're getting some strange sounds. We used to collect... like everything was put under a microscope and it just wasn't big and ballsy like Werman used to get. Werman got that really warm sound on the first four Ted albums and then when Cliff took over, there was a change. It's hard to put a finger on it. As far as hits and stuff, I don't know if the hits were really there either. So there was a big change when Derek left and I came in."

Huhn disagrees with my assertion that *Cat Scratch Fever* isn't exactly big-sounding either. "You don't like it? Personally, I think it's really ballsy and rough and captures the band. That was the big hit." As for Tom's self-assessment that he tends to be much more about guitars at the expense of drums and bass, Charlie says, "Well, I don't know about that. But I understand. Tom is a producer that doesn't mind playing with the faders, you know what I mean? I worry about a guy who sets everything on zero and then just lets you work it out. I'd rather have someone just making... driving the sound. If he's going with a guitar sound, I can really appreciate it."

Ask about Ted being credited with bass guitar on the album as well, Charlie says, "Ted may have played bass on one or two songs, but actually it was John Sauter. It was interesting watching all that go down, but it was Cliff pulling the reins on that album. But we did a lot of live dates and John was on those; in fact he's in that big live shot on the inner sleeve of *Weekend Warriors*. We were at the headlining level when I joined, so it was like going from the bars to the stars for me. There were quite a few acts we played with that went on to huge success, like Van Halen, AC/DC, Scorpions, Journey, Cheap Trick. The list goes on and on; it was such an experience. I just wish I would've got autographed pictures of everybody back then (laughs)."

Uneasily, with these late '70s concert billings there's a bit of a changing of the guard. The Ted Nugent band with all the lineup changes, with ties to an older era stylistically... was the band ever at threat of being upstaged?

"Oh sure. Van Halen was so hot out of the box, they only lasted for like two or three shows and then they had to go. AC/DC was just on such an upward roll, that they were with us only for about six dates and then they went to headlining status. Scorpions, we ended up doing a lot of dates where they opened up for us. There were quite a few festivals. In fact, in '79, we started out the summer just doing weekends, the major festivals and that was such a shock after doing these grueling US tours plus the UK and Japan and all of a sudden being in the peak of the touring season and just flying to weekend dates and coming home during the week."

Weekend Warriors as an album was a bit of a let-down, especially given the fact that it failed to hatch a hit single. Indeed, as it stood, despite a tidy and growing batch of songs that were becoming FM radio staples, *Cat Scratch Fever* would be Ted's only clear hit song now four records in, on top of only one single amongst the tangled forest of Amboy Dukes albums. Not only did *Weekend Warriors* not hatch a single, basically nothing from the record became, over the years, any sort of slow-burn FM track, nor did much of the songs stay part of Ted's set list for long.

Still, the album reached No.24 on the Billboard chart and went platinum faster than any of his albums to date. By March of 1979, it had become the cap on five platinum albums in a row, with *Cat Scratch Fever* about to tick over into double platinum. Yet again, the band was shut out of single success this time around, despite being so big that Ted even having a pinball machine launched for his latest record. Trademark modern boogie construct *Need You Bad* was indeed gamely launched as a single (backed *with I Got The Feelin'*), but it rose only to No.84. Strong songs on the record include the proto-speed metal of *Cruisin'*, the hard-charging *Name Your Poison* and the full-on fantasy metal of *Venom Soup*, a song said to have been penned as far back as 1965, although nothing about it, from the evil lyric to the proto-power metal riffing, sounds remotely garage rock.

Describing the *Venom Soup* guitar solo to *Circus*, Ted said, "I wrote this really melodic line which comes in over the arpeggios (sings it). After a minute and a half of this elaborate intro, the guitar goes gaaahhhh and comes busting into this rhythm pattern in E minor 7th, with an occasional diminished... I put a little extra phase on the guitar to do this excruciating solo." Adding a love note to his choice of guitar, Ted explains, "They're all hand-made, these Byrdlands; they have an arched top for acoustic effect, a three-quarter neck that's a bit shorter and smaller than most. It just screams, so I get the kind of feedback I like." Live, he says he gives them, "a serious sweat bath to get a real thick sound. When I get off stage at the end of the night, you can turn the guitar over and pour water out of it just like a pitcher."

Elsewhere, Ted mines a field very much of his own elaborate construction, this insistence of writing and re-writing frenetic boogie music, James Brown-ish heavy metal if there is such a thing, sort of southern rock juiced with a little more guitar than usual. One would have to say that *Need You Bad, I Got The Feelin'* and *Weekend Warriors* fit this mould (there would be more, especially come *Scream Dream*), while *Good Friends And A Bottle Of Wine* and *Tight Spots* not so much, although with both of those, there's nonetheless a dopey roots feel to the hard rock riffing enclosed.

But it's all hampered and dampened by the production. Some of the above are somehow written heavy, but then rendered modest. The rhythm section is to blame as well—bass duties are shared by David Hull (from Dirty Angels and later part of The Joe Perry Project) and John Sauter—Cliff Davies in particular playing uninspired and simple, again, perhaps at the behest of Ted.

"*Weekend Warriors* was, I think, the weakest of the five I did with Ted," reflects Werman. "Because of the material, really. But I remember making albums and listening to FM stereo radio on headphones. I'd listened to the records on the radio and I'd say, man, these sound so good. There's something I still hadn't learned about making records and it ate me up. Then I finally heard one of my records and it was Ted. I think it was *Stranglehold* on FM radio and I almost fell over. It sounded so incredible and the answer was compression. Almost anything… they squashed sound so much in those days that… the compression really took care of any inconsistencies in the recording at that time because everything low came up and everything loud went down and it all kind of was squeezed out of your car seat. It's made more uniform. They were using a ton of compression. I mean sometimes you could hear… you could literally hear the DJ… the sound around him, the air around him, breathing. You'd hear it; it was hugely compressed. It was great. We loved it. We didn't know what it was but we loved it."

Is there nothing then that you could do as a producer to make your record sound better on radio?

"Well sure, you master it well. You disperse… you deliver the frequencies in a nice full range, you know? Like the bass drum is not the bottom of the record. The bass guitar is the bottom of the record. The bass drum goes above that, and then… if you played a record that was poorly engineered or mixed, and you turned it up, it would hurt. It would be unpleasant. If you played, for example, a Glyn Johns record like the Eagles' first album or *Who's Next*, you could turn it way up and it would just fill the room because there were no glaring peaks or there were no frequencies that leapt out at you. Upper middle range frequencies, upper mids, were really the most offensive, and that was what… if you turned the radio up, adults would block their ears because that's what they were hearing. But if you knew what you were doing, or you learned it eventually, you would manage to slot all the instruments into their own spaces. Then you'd fill the frequency range rather than having everything bunch up in the middle. Because all instruments and vocals have mid range, so you have to be careful in that frequency range and that's what made records sound better on the radio."

To these ears, this sounds like the exact problem both *Cat Scratch Fever* and *Weekend Warriors* suffered from—that they had much of the above done to them to have them sound good on the radio, but that in turn caused them to sound tinny, mid-rangey and all 'round anemic on a good stereo. No question, *Cat Scratch Fever* is the better production of the two, but more disconcertingly, the sum total of the songs on *Weekend Warriors* demonstrated a diminishment of levity, of gravitas, as if Ted's bristling image, his persona, was receiving more of his Gonzo grooming than the riffs themselves.

Rolling Stone's review of the album captured perfectly both the impatience the industry had with metal in 1979 (little did they know metal would rule all of the next decade!), while also playing up the idea that Nugent's particular strain was uncommonly and necessarily rootsy, given his long run in the business.

Wrote Michael Schneider, "Though Nugent's rock 'n' roll is certainly old hat—the guitarist unabashedly peddles such late '60s/early '70s technoraunch techniques as distortion, feedback and sledgehammer riffs—it hardly ever comes off as if stuffed with moth balls. Owing as much to Muddy Waters as to Bethlehem Steel, Nugent makes heavy metal sound exactly like it's supposed to: like a motorcycle gang who's come to take your daughter away. Undoubtedly, the artist's principal mission here is to celebrate the painful pleasure of high voltage. While this can surely be an aesthetic dead end, Nugent and his new band still play with fluency and passion. You've got to hand it to him for refusing to submit to what generally guarantees hard rock musicians plenty of airplay these days: Nutty Squirrels harmonies (Boston), clean-shaven squareness (Foreigner) and gooey sweetness (Heart). As abrasive as *Weekend Warriors'* whiplash rock 'n' roll may be, the songs themselves are never subversive or harrowing. Instead they're conventional (*Need You Bad, I Got The Feelin'*), thunderously optimistic (*Good Friends And A Bottle Of Wine*) or just plain goofy (*Venom Soup*). This is disappointing. Nugent could benefit from some conceptual audacity to really forklift his music. Though we are rapidly approaching the '80s, Nugent continues to cling to the '70s as if he were single-handedly responsible for keeping the heavy metal tradition alive. Fortunately, the best moments on *Weekend Warriors* suggest that this veteran still has a real future ahead of him. His ferocious zeal seems as instinctive and unforced as ever. For all I know, we might have to listen to this stuff until the year 2001 rocks and rolls around."

But still, there was the pinball machine! "Cute, huh?" says Ted. "Just think: America playing with my balls every night before I go to bed. What a beautiful vision. Again, nothing is sacred. Why not? If you manned my phone today, for an hour, you'd have to turn down 20 offers of commercial ideas or invites to speak or invites to partake in an event. I take most of the charity offers that I get, because I love to do charities for the military and for the kids, and for needy causes, but my staff turns down dozens of requests every week for product endorsements, for events, for involvement in different projects. But that one, I thought, was cute. I don't know if Kiss had a pinball machine before I did. They probably did. But I wasn't a pinball wizard, I wasn't a pinball player. But when they showed me that *Weekend Warriors* cover with the fully automatic guitar, I mean how cool is that? I mean I would have put that on a Holstein as a milk aficionado. Again, nothing is sacred. I have a simple screening system. Is it going to be fun? Let's do it. Will I be fairly compensated and will it be fun? I'm in and that was a gimme. That was so much fun, it was stupid."

Turning something like that down on principle doesn't really enter Ted's thought process.

"I don't think, no. That would be like saying Jimi Hendrix sold out because *Foxey Lady* was a hit record. You've gotta be kidding me. I mean my music is pure, Jimi Hendrix's music was pure, The Who's music is pure, ZZ Top when they made their biggest selling record, they didn't go in the studio… Billy Gibbons did not sit down and go, 'All right, how can we sell a lot of records?' No, he was in a room jamming and *Sharp Dressed Man* came out of his guitar. I guarantee you. He didn't contemplate the commercial considerations of his musical inspiration for the day. I believe this. I never sit down and go, I wonder what the public would like to hear. Never. I don't want to sound selfish, but I am. I make music for me, but I'm a music-craver. I crave this stuff and because I happen to know that everybody I know and I believe that every human being, craves a musical moment that represents something in their life's experience or dreams, that I'm just like them but I get to create it. I have a funny feeling that if I just keep doing it, that when you share it with people they might want to buy it. But that's not a cop-out; that's not a deluding of the purity of your music for commercial considerations. It's just how the world works. I'll take you back to the apple orchard guy. Does he love perfect apples? Well so do you. I had to buy this land, I had to put in these trees, I've been busting my ass all year to grow these apples and it costs X amount to get them and if you want one, you're going to have to pay one variation of that cost and you can have this apple for a buck. Do you want it or don't you? There's nothing wrong with that. In fact it's perfect. Capitalism is perfect because we're all consumers and consumers are going to demand the best for the best deal, and that's music or apples, man."

Amboy Dukes record label promo shot circa 1970. Left to right: Ted Nugent, keyboardist Andy Solomon, bassist Greg Arama, drummer Dave Palmer.
© Polydor Records

Above: Ted Nugent, Derek St. Holmes, Rob Grange and short-lived drummer Brian Staffeld, who is also pictured on the back of the debut album, but did not drum on the record.

Left: Ted with his trusty Gibson Byrdland hollow-body at an outdoor show, 1975 in Tulsa, Oklahoma.© Richard Galbraith

The Whackmaster braces himself for a truckload of feedback.
© Richard Galbraith

Above: Ted's classic look circa the *Cat Scratch Fever* tour. Tulsa, Oklahoma, 1977. Support on the night came from Artful Dodger and Rush.

Right: With his soulful lead vocals and good looks, Derek had a prominence within the Ted Nugent live show that positioned him in the eyes of some concert-goers as the leader of the band, or at least an equal to Ted.
© Richard Galbraith

Deadly Tedly hits a high note while Derek takes cover.
© Richard Galbraith

A rare shot featuring both Ted and classic-era drummer Cliff Davies.
© Richard Galbraith

Greatest Ted Nugent photograph of all-time,
a natural choice for the front cover of this book.
© Richard Galbraith

Both shots here are from a show on 29 July 1978 at the Cape Cod Coliseum, South Yarmouth, Massachusetts.
© Rudy Childs

Ted in full caveman mode.
August 18, 1979, Capitol Centre, Landover, Maryland.
© Rudy Childs

Above: Ted with his surprise hit hair metal project Damn Yankees.
© Tom Wallace

Below: The happy warrior circa 2000.
© Tom Wallace

State Of Shock

"We went back to tricks and little black boxes"

C ome 1979, and the big hard rockers of the day all seemed to be looking at a steep commercial decline all at once. The Cars and The Knack and The Police were what was happening, post-punk of a most behaved nature. Blue Oyster Cult shrunk their career with *Mirrors*, Kiss had a disco hit from the hard rock-lite *Dynasty*, Aerosmith was caught between a bad live album and a long night in the ruts, and even Van Halen's *II* browned the band out temporarily after the white hot fun of a self-titled debut so good they had to name it twice.

Ted sits in a funny place here, well, not funny for him, as he faced the double whammy of being ripped off by management and most hard on him, a divorce from Sandra, who died three years later in a car accident while driving over the legal alcohol limit. Sandra and Ted, married since January 31, 1971, divorced on December 31 of '79 and by all insider accounts at least, the failure of his marriage (they had two children together) affected his enthusiasm for music-making downward. I say that somewhat drolly, because in this writer's estimation, *State Of Shock* and *Scream Dream* are Ted's two best records, given a run for their money, for completely different reasons, by *Free For All*, and dastardly duo *Craveman* and *Love Grenade*, a pair of paralyzing, Tedinating, Whackmastered comebacks so molten, they manage to obliterate the memory of the man's horrid '80s and '90s output with a bloodletting efficiency that is as inspiring as it is deafening.

"As a manager, what you discover, which is really I think what is true about everybody, is that your ability to get a project started is very much a product of what's happening in your personal life," muses David Krebs. "So when we look at Aerosmith and we see that their downfall was because of drug usage, my own analysis of Ted's career, is that when he got a divorce from his first wife, his whole persona, lyrically, changed. Because he covered the Beatles, *I Want To Tell You*, which is so the antithesis of *Stranglehold* and *Cat Scratch Fever*, that instead of projecting from between his legs, he was projecting from his heart (laughs). It's a totally different sensibility. I saw Aerosmith undo their career for a number years from drugs and I saw Ted Nugent's career undermined by his divorce. I saw, to some degree, AC/DC's career undermined because of Bon's death from alcohol and whatever that whole thing was. So I was seeing one after another, where you can look at each band and maybe it's hard to really, from the outside, understand what superstardom is and what that means every day and what its effect on you is, ultimately. It gets around and you invite people around who are yes people, the whole thing changes. It's like songwriters, for the most part, write based on what's happening to them. We do not need Einstein to figure that out."

Recapping, Krebs says, "So Ted Nugent went through a very traumatic divorce and never wrote another great rock tune since... maybe one or two. Coming through the door at that time were AC/DC, Scorpions, Def Leppard—there was another set of bands who were writing great songs. If you look at the Aerosmith albums after *Rocks*, they go down in quality. There are less great songs each album after each album. If you listen to Ted Nugent after maybe *Weekend Warriors*, I think you see the same thing."

"David nailed it, absolutely," says Ted, cited this quote. "Because I'm a man who is genuinely, sincerely, emotionally and spiritually connected to my life, my family first and foremost and the people in my life. I want to make sure that my musicians, my crew, my management, my team, my hunting guides, but primarily my family, is taken care of. My divorce from Sasha and Toby's mother was devastating. It was an emotional and spiritual train-wreck for me. David Krebs nailed it. But, with all due respect for David Krebs, who I admire and consider a friend, a great manager would have... he knew it at the time. I didn't know it at the time. I'm owned by my quest to take care of my children during a very ugly, offensive and criminal American injustice system. The court system in this country is vile, there is no justice, it's not a justice system, it's a lawyer, judge... pay-off system. It's really ugly.

It's criminal. So I immediately circled my emotional wagons to take care of my children. A good manager would have said, wow, this is ugly. Wow, this is anti-rock 'n' roll, and certainly not Ted Nugent's perfect delivery of defiant music. Let's not record."

"But I'm so possessed by the music, I figure—being this rugged individual and defiant independent guy—that I could separate my personal duties to family from this outrageous musical statement. Plus I gotta tell you, I loved the song *I Want To Tell You*; I loved George Harrison's guitar playing (sings it). I love his stuff. It was what I was weaned on. So my inclination was, hey, I'm going to indulge and play some of this stuff. But a great manager would have said, you know what? This is not... certainly there is no limit to what you can do and what you want to pursue musically. But you know what? You need to take care of this. We've sold 20 million records. You don't have to record right now. Go take care of your family stuff and when you've really got that nailed down, then let's start the rock 'n' roll machine again."

Summing up his music from this period, Ted says that, "Tom Werman was a master of pure audio reverence for the original noisy rock 'n' roll. Noisy by the... the noisiness of Chuck Berry's guitar and the noisiness of Keith Richards' and Brian Jones' guitar. The clang of The Who drums/bass/guitar intensity. But he also knew that—and again, I reference the clang factor—you can make clangy noises, but if it's not in tune, the general clang listener is not going to accept it. But while you're in the studio making all these clangy noises, you're celebrating the outrageousness of it all to the point where you're not even paying attention to whether you're in tune or not. Well Tom Werman and Tony Reale, my engineer at that time... Lew Futterman played some role, but mostly Tom Werman and Tony Reale, as far as authentic rock 'n' roll-loving, demanding ears. They got that Gibson Byrdland and Fender amplifier that I had created this incredible tone and sound live onstage, which is what caused Tom to sign me to Epic Records. He heard it live and went, my God, I've never heard anything like this in my life, because there'd never been anything like this in the world of rock 'n' roll. A jazz, hollow-body spruce guitar through a clean but voluminous Fender twin amplifier creates a sonic, unprecedented... and they went to extreme meticulous demanding details and scrutiny, how to translate that through a microphone onto tape."

"Which is no easy task. I mean they literally got in front of these amps, almost blowing their brains out, finding the spot on the speaker, the sweet spot on the speaker that delivered what you heard in the room. It's so demanding, so meticulous, that I don't think anybody really realized this except the guys listening to this interview now who makes records and go, 'Yeah, we always have to do that.' So Tom and Tony went in and did that kind of scrutiny, because I'm in the room drunk on my playing. I love my playing, I love my sound. In the room, I'm hearing this whole room. But the microphone doesn't hear that. Microphone's gotta hear something right on the speaker that delivers what's turning me on. So they went to that great detail. Now by the time of *Scream Dream*, even—even though it was really good—it wasn't the thickness and the incredible unique tone of the *Ted Nugent*, the *Free For All*, the *Cat Scratch Fever*, and in many ways *Double Live Gonzo!*. Because once again, even during those recordings I'm inebriated by the performance, the playing and the sounds in the room, but those guys had to translate that onto tape. Nobody went to that length to listen for that sweet spot and to demand a very time-demanding scrutiny of audio delivery that actually translated on tape, like it did in this room during the mayhem during the jamming while we're recording. So we let our guard down. I think it's because too much too fast. If I had to do it all over again, even though I love the songs on *Scream Dream*, I love *Wango Tango*, one of my greatest songs... one of the greatest songs in the history of the world..."

Arguably, however, both *State Of Shock* and *Scream Dream* "sound" better and yes, are even more powerful and pure and electric than the reedy, paper-thin sounds from *Cat Scratch Fever* and *Weekend Warriors*. At least musically speaking, *I Want To Tell You* and *Alone* aside, *State Of Shock* is the walloping, heavy, grinding, groovy record that *Weekend Warriors* can nary aspire toward. Which brings up the disconcerting thought that Ted and his tight army of ears barely have a clue which of his records are good productions and which aren't. Now, maybe Ted is being high-concept artistic here and is talking about the songs. It seems that David is. In any event, we could have that debate, but to this writer's ears, pretty much everything is better on these two records than the ones before, save perhaps for *Free For All* which is an oddball of high fidelity high-mindedness, three distinct singers in Ted, Derek and Meat, but ferocious riffs a plenty, represented most pertly by *Hammerdown, Street Rats* and *Dog Eat Dog*.

Cliff Davies speaks the party line as well and you have to wonder if all parties are clouded by the fact that the record was the first of the catalogue to stall at gold. "*State Of Shock* was one of those albums where we kind of lost our way a bit, actually. You know, it was pretty obvious to me and Futterman as well, that we had to do something, change up. Ted's material was getting worse and not better and he was getting more adamant about it all being his. So, with *State Of Shock*, we went back to tricks and little black boxes. We got more into the production thing and made it more hi-fi. It was just at that point, we were on the road. We were never a recording band; we were a touring band. All the time we were touring, we were recording *State Of Shock*, in and out of the studio and on and off the road, in and out of the studio, on and off the road. It was a bit of a blur, really."

Had the band's writing chemistry changed with the arrival of Charlie? "Charlie never wrote anything, and Ted did all the writing on everything. Especially after Derek left. He didn't want to hear about anybody else writing songs. On *State Of Shock*, I think we did a Beatles cover. Again that was my attempt to get us more radio play. Except the version we did didn't turn out very well. Ted wasn't into it anyway. It could've been a great song, but Ted just didn't have his heart and soul into it. I think if we would've done a good job with that, which we didn't, we would have got a lot of airplay."

"I'll tell you, Ted was going through a change of life with his divorce and stuff and it was really a tough time for him," explains Charlie. "When he wrote the song *Paralyzed*, he was writing it about himself and I said, okay, why don't you just turn it around and make it about her, instead of being about you? He took that advice and it worked. Because that was Ted anyway. Even though he was hurt at that moment and was writing about how hurt he was, he still had this image to portray and maintain. That was kind of what I was reading into the situation and that's how the song got turned around to being lyrically about someone else, instead of being about himself."

Paralyzed is indeed one of Ted's crowning moments in terms of sheer electricity and heft. Those screams, the bulging power chords… it's a late period classic and the centrepiece of the album, perfect for a side one lead-off. Pretty much the second heaviest song, *Snake Charmer*, is emboldened by the guitar lick being played in unison with Charlie's powerful vocal, a sophisticated heavy metal touch. "That was pretty much straightforward all Ted," says Huhn. "Everything was right out in the open—a fun song to play and sing. The rest of them are all pretty much that way. But I really didn't have much influence on any of that material."

Asked if anything had pedigree going back a year or two, Charlie says, "No, because actually Ted is quite prolific. He works hard and he can do his homework and come up with the songs. They're not all hits, but still, it takes a lot of work to complete one work of music and then another one and then ten and 12, plus maintaining everything else he had going on."

As regards the controversial George Harrison-penned Beatles cover, *I Want To Tell You*, Huhn figures, "Ted was a '60s guy and he always loved that riff. We were riding high so he could do what he wanted, so he did that cover."

"Walt Monahan is a bass player from England who is a friend of Cliff Davies," says Huhn, on the band's latest switch in fat-stringers. "He replaced John Sauter, after John had a couple of relapses with diabetes and couldn't be depended on to play anymore. Plus there was a little conflict with John's bass style, although he had these beautiful basses; he was such a proficient player that he wanted to feed more into the part than Cliff thought should be there, so there was a little clash there. John is a great bass player from the Detroit area. He used to be in Detroit Wheels, the band with Mitch Ryder, ex-player with Jim McCarty. Sauter was a mainstay in the Detroit music scene in the early '70s. Just a great player. There was also another bass player, Greg Arama, who I auditioned with, with Ted—he was in the Amboy Dukes."

"Those songs were just more or less songs as they are," continues Charlie. "They weren't really important as to the sequence on the album or importance. More like album tracks. In terms of a single, I think they put *I Want To Tell You* out as a single and that did okay, but *Paralyzed*, that was the album track, first track, side one and the industry at the time wasn't conducive to releasing heavy songs as singles."

Did anybody try to float the ballad, *Alone*, o'er to radio? "No, I'm not aware of that, but we used to do that live, which is kind of weird. Being a hard rocking heavy act, you don't want a lull in the set." Walt Monaghan, bassist on the record, would not tour with the band. In turn, there was Dave Kiswiney. "He replaced John Sauter on tour," explains Charlie. "He was from Detroit, but I don't remember how he was recommended, perhaps from the crew guys. But he was just a perfect, solid, backing bass player, nothing flashy like Sauter, who wanted to be the lead bass player. Walt was an interim to finish recording the album. Walt wouldn't work out live, because he was handicapped and that wouldn't have worked out at the time."

"You know, the songs and the performances by the band were way better than the production," Ted told me, in 2007. "I don't think it was mixed very good. I don't think it was an accurate sonic representation of our bombast. Charlie Huhn, just a terrific A-list vocalist. He's got tons of soul. Again he's influenced by all those people I mentioned. But I thought we had fun recording it. There are some fun moments on it, but I don't think the sonic quality was able to deliver the heart and soul of the songwriting or the performances. I'm proud of it, but it doesn't qualify with my new stuff."

Was the inclusion of the Beatles cover a deliberate attempt at a hit single? "No, I never think of those concerns. *I Want To Tell You*, I just played it for me. Everybody loved the song and a great guitar lick. It's one of the guitar licks that I was weaned on. And *Alone* was a direct honest emotion about, you know, I was still lamenting the loss of my wife."

Paralyzed was somewhat the same story. "Yeah (laughs). That was the other side of the emotion. That was the, 'Yeah, I love you baby, but fuck you!' (laughs). That was a great song. I'm glad you mentioned *Paralyzed*, because we still play that song all the time. Did you see it on *Full Bluntal Nugity*? Because it's way better there. There's that sonic quality I was talking about. It's bigger and fatter and nastier. It was a little too clean on *State Of Shock*."

As for Cliff Davies (credited as producer, along with Lew), "I don't think he is a producer. I think he's a brilliant musician, a very gifted musician, not just on drums but musicality-wise. He has a great sense of... and again had that great R&B delivery. He literally guided and nurtured the *Stranglehold* performance out of Derek. I gave him great credit for that. But I don't see any evidence that he would qualify as a producer. Again, I think that his hand, with others that shouldn't have qualified as a producer, Lew Futterman, with all due respect and he's a great man and I love him dearly, but I don't believe they understand the fuck you middle finger grindmaster beast of what a big drum, guitar and bass sound is supposed to sound like. You can give credit to the *Ted Nugent* album, *Free For All* and *Cat Scratch Fever*, directly, to Tom Werman and myself and to Cliff, Derek and Rob for getting those authentic real world authority sounds. In other words, when you listen to Rob de la Grange play the bass in a room, you go, motherfuck, that's fuckin' perfect. Now capture that with the right microphone in the right placement in the right speaker on the right tape, that's the son of a bitch. That's where I think Lew Futterman and Cliff fell a little bit short."

Saddle Sore, *Satisfied*, *Snake Charmer*… "Those are all… they're just masterful guitar licks if I say so myself. I love those guitar licks. You know, *Saddle Sore*, that's because I'm a breeder. Sometimes I have to give my dick a rest. I don't know how else I can tell you that. I'm a man—someone shoot me. *State Of Shock*, what a great pattern that is. I mean they're just all great guitar patterns."

Back on the press trail for the *State Of Shock* album, Ted spoke of *Satisfied*, beginning with a comment on his practice of recording a track of feedback to be massaged into songs where needed. "These poor guys on the mixing board—when I put the thing down, there's this constant minute of squeal and they're going, 'What is he going to do with that?' When I stop playing my solo, they fade in that sound and it really makes a difference. On the *State Of Shock* album, there's a song called *Satisfied* where I do something that's just the reverse of that. I take the solo and work another part along with it, feeding back and then we put a backwards guitar on it playing the song theme and it comes out in reverse—the backwards part is mixed with the forwards part. It's a song that's in the thrust of *Stranglehold*."

"My turf is the stage; it has always been the stage," continued Ted, on his frustrating relationship with the studio, proven too many times by stiff, humourless productions afforded Ted Nugent albums. "My recording process is merely a vehicle for the continuing Ted Nugent saga to perpetuate itself, unendingly. Boy, that's eloquent. Anyway, in doing so, I find myself continuing my rock 'n' roll stage attitude in the studio. However, in the studio, you are playing for microphones and tape recorders. My music is designed for the human ear and the uninhibited appreciation thereof. But I go into the studio and they start slapping on a whole array of different microphones—it looks like somebody's on an international newscast deciding whether they're going to push the atomic war button. The microphones cannot absorb what the human ear can absorb, and vice versa. My stuff is designed for the live human ear. I'll go in and play a guitar sound that is biting and thick-sounding, and the microphone just goes, 'Sorry, does not compute, reject, try something else.'"

"I encourage people hanging out," says Ted, with regard to getting his creative juices flowing in this un-Tedly environment. "You know, a lot of young chicks are always conducive to blasting. That's how all the songs really get written too—just by plugging in and blasting. When I get in the studio and we've got a given composition that we're working on, I go in and I just start blasting out on it and just the whole rhythm of the song will inspire a solo or a nice progression. There's this relentless drive going on. As soon as I put a guitar in my hands, I have no control. I mean, I just go nuts."

David Fricke, from *Rolling Stone* has a point when he takes issue with the production of *State Of Shock*, except that he vehemently asserts that the knob job on *Weekend Warriors* is clearly superior. After relating a story about being played the track *Satisfied* down the phone line by Ted, then hearing the vinyl and declaring the audio on the phone call better, he writes, "Of course, it depends what you mean by better. What originally sounded like Terrible Ted's amplified growl turned out to be long-distance static obscuring a surprisingly clean production that isn't his usual style. The substance is identical: belligerent riffing, a subterranean bass, laughable lyrics about life as a rock 'n' roll stud and an impressive triple-tracked display of guitar feedback. Yet the surface, polished by producers Lew Futterman and Cliff Davies, is too shiny, too deliberately commercial, to be the work of the same maniac who split ear drums the world over with *Name Your Poison* on *Weekend Warriors* and the flagrantly misogynist *Wang Dang Sweet Poontang* on *Cat Scratch Fever*. As improbable as it may seem, the original heavy metal heathen appears to be flying the flag of compromise on *State Of Shock*, tempering his raw, rapacious sound with a pop sensibility designed to add to his denimed legions those disbelievers who think Ted Nugent isn't much more than a guitar-toting Neanderthal. Ted Nugent, for all his egotistic ranting, is no fire-breathing fool. He knows that FM radio won't play his records because it's not aesthetically sound to segue heavy metal hymns into the comparatively sedate likes of Fleetwood Mac or Heart. So he forges a few catchy riffs, tones down the Teutonic roar a smidgen and reins in more fans without losing sight of his artistic goal: to make Saturday night six-pack rock that will shake even the entrance to the airwaves."

Read the rest of the review and the opinion expressed, like many others on this album, is as much based on the inclusion of *I Want To Tell You* and *Alone* as it is on splitting hairs over Ted's near entire catalogue of middling productions. I'm reminded of all those Rainbow fans and critics who think *Down To Earth* is all about *Since You Been Gone* and *All Night Long*, ignoring the medieval metal clang of the rest of the record. In the same manner, *State Of Shock* is a murky, metal, minor masterpiece, all too overlooked in the catalogue, as under-rated as *Cat Scratch* is over-rated or at least "properly" rated.

While Ted was soldiering on with new folks (for this record, a new bass player in Walter Monaghan, paralyzed from the waist down), making what are arguably his best and heaviest albums, Derek St. Holmes, Rob Grange, and ex-Montrose drummer Denny Carmassi were building themselves a hopeful supergroup called St. Paradise.

Explains St. Holmes, "My mission for that band was to have a three-piece power trio that... we had a chance to do an American version of Led Zeppelin. So we tried that. We'd get a lot of shows with Ronnie Montrose. I had a chance to become really close with Denny Carmassi, the drummer and Rob always liked my style of playing and writing and always liked the Zeppelin-y big thug rock sound. So he wanted to come with me. I'm not sure it was the best idea for him, but we had two great albums, one of which is still on the shelf. That's St. Paradise *2*, which is still at Warner Bros., on the shelf. The first one came out and didn't do that great, because that year, that's when disco hit and they started to drop 30 acts from the label. Of course, we were one of the first new acts signed, at the beginning of the year prior, so they just went down the list and got rid of everybody that couldn't make money for them and we were one of the first bands to go."

The *St. Paradise* album was a raw construct, oddly similar in unhewn, sort of non-committal nature to a future Derek project, Whitford St. Holmes and while we're at it, Hughes Thrall. A detailed look at this period may seem excessive, but it reveals much about the personalities of Derek and Rob and their relationship with the Ted Nugent band, plus there's other Nuge connections aplenty. The story of St. Paradise is included as well because it's an obscure slice of Ted band history that has only sparingly been revealed...

"Again, we were just trying to be sort of Led Zeppelin-esque," explains Derek, addressing the style of the album. "We were just into those big heavy slow grooves and those sort of out-of-the-box guitar parts. So that's where we kind of came up with *Beside The Sea*. At the same time I was reading the trilogy and I was checking out the Hobbits and doing the whole deal that Robert Plant was. I thought well gosh, he's stolen from all of this, it can't hurt if I steal maybe two songs. So I think I stole *Beside The Sea* from *The Hobbit*, and I think *The Gates Of Hades*, which I think on the album is just called *Hades*. That's where those ideas came from. We were always into magical mystical things back then. We were all pretty much goofy, crazy."

"I probably am closest to, a cross between Eric Clapton and Robert Cray," says Derek, asked about his nature and character as a guitarist. "Even, you know, very Jimmy Page. I can do all of that stuff. I can hang with any of those people, in a heartbeat. Favourite solos... *Miami Slide* was a good one; I enjoyed that. But you know, I used so many effects back then that I didn't get a chance to get the prowess of my playing to the forefront. But that was the way back then. That was the way of the world and recording and sounds. So now, if you hear some of my music, I'm up front with soloing. I've always fancied myself as one of the better rhythm/solo players, like Pete Townshend, who's able to just keep it going and solo around playing a chord and getting to that before anybody even knows you've dropped the ball. I've had many people come up to me and see my three-piece band and say, 'You sound like you guys are five pieces!' I'm so proud when people say that, but it's a lot of hard work. Ask any of those guys in Rush, they will tell you how hard it is, to make a three-piece full. They're the kings of it."

As for Rob Grange's take on the motivation to put together St. Paradise,

"We used to go on the road a lot with the original Montrose: Sammy Hagar, Denny, Ronnie and Bill Church. They would open for us and we really liked the way Denny played drums One little thing lead to another and I think when Derek got the opportunity to leave Ted and do an album on Warner Bros., I think at that time, Montrose had split up. So Denny was looking for a gig. Derek and I pretty much got our pink slips, so we kind of put it all together and went off to Bearsville and did some demos, at Todd Rundgren's upstate New York studio and actually they came out really good. It probably would've been the next Ted Nugent album. I would think a lot of the stuff that went on the *St. Paradise* album, but there was a lot of conflict in our band, the Ted Nugent band, and actually it made up for some really good chemistry. You know (laughs), when you get inner turmoil in a band, it creates good stuff. As weird as that is, it creates a little bit of magic and chemistry because you've got a competition going on. They had the same thing happening in Fleetwood Mac; they were all husbands and wives and it made for some good songs. I think the thing that was cool about our band was that Cliff and Derek and I made for a really good nucleus on stage, so that Ted could play in and out of it, run around and do his deal while we set the foundation. I think that we inspired each other, including Ted, in the writing."

"We lived on the road," continues Rob. "All we did was concerts and sound checks and Holiday Inns and limousines and then get up the next day and do it again. A lot of the songs we wrote on the road at sound checks. We wrote the entire first Ted Nugent album a year before we got in the studio to do it. We wrote it at sound checks. Even the *Free For All* album, we all wrote stuff together and we all had our own ideas. Even though a lot of it went to the credit of Ted. As for his publishing and money, out of the four of us, he's the only millionaire, you know, multimillionaire. So even then, we weren't making any money and that caused a lot of friction in the band. We were told we were going to make a lot of money and we had contracts to make a lot of money, but in the end, we didn't make any money. Not to speak of. But I mean, (laughs), I want to stop myself and not get into it."

Asked if any of these particular songs were ever proposed as actual Ted Nugent songs, Rob says, "Well, no, by the time those songs were written, there was a lot of conflict in the band. What really should've happened, you know, now after all the water's under the bridge, Derek should've gone out and done his solo album with the guys from St. Paradise and then come back to the Ted Nugent band. But the problem was, Ted wasn't comfortable with that. That's the impression that we all got. So there was a lot of conflict. We couldn't get in the mix on the live shows. Our girlfriends would come back and say, 'Gosh, we couldn't even hear you out front. It was all Ted Nugent.' We wrote a song called *Dancing In The Shadows*, because we didn't get any spots or anything. Pretty much our side of the stage was dark (laughs). So what happened was, we all thought we were in a band. We thought it was the Ted Nugent band, and we were going in a great direction and it was great. But all of a sudden somebody switches gears and says, well, it says Ted Nugent and it's not so important for him to have a band and you guys, we're not going to put you guys in *Creem* or in the magazines. We're not going to let you be interviewed by anybody. Just Ted Nugent. On the albums, there's only going to be pictures of Ted Nugent and not the band. We're going, God, we worked all these years getting to this point and here we are, not making any money, it's just a drag. We're playing in front of thousands and thousands of people. Cal Jam was like 350,000 people and it was crazy. We never actually saw the money that we were promised. We weren't into it for just the money, but we'd been on the road for seven years at that point."

"But St. Paradise was a short-lived project," sighs Rob, "because it was really hard coming out of the Ted Nugent band into St. Paradise. All of a sudden we're back in the Hertz rental cars and opening up for other bands and stuff. In fact we went on the road and opened up for Van Halen in Europe. That was a difficult tour because everybody just wanted to see Van Halen. They were big, so it was difficult for us—we had 12 inches on the stage and one spotlight. But the band was fun and we had a great time. But I don't think the album was produced as well or as heavy as it could've been. We had the same manager as Ted Nugent, so there was kind of a conflict of interest there. It just really never got a shot at going. But the tunes we wrote, Derek and I pretty much wrote most of those tunes while we were still with Ted Nugent. It was mainly Derek and I who would write together. We would go to his place or my place and we wrote a lot of stuff together; even back before we had hits, we would write together."

More on Van Halen, Rob says, "Eddie would hang with us quite a bit and we would go drinking in bars and stuff and hang out. Also the bass player, Michael Anthony, he's a really nice guy. He's a real car guy like I am. He likes hot rods and stuff. But they were really cool to tour with. They were on their way up and doing really good. In fact I remember, when I first met David Lee Roth, I thought he's a lot like Ted; he's amazing. You talked to him offstage and it's just like talking to Ted."

Derek agrees that the St. Paradise record didn't sound all that great. As for producer Mike Flicker and his particular skills... "When anybody mentions Mike Flicker, I just think, he spent all my money. I don't know, we should've had a different producer than him. That was a power play which I had to go with. I thought the sound was muffled and just a lot of starting and stopping. It took a long time to make that album. We spent a lot of money sitting in different places in Seattle and waiting for Mike Flicker. Because he was working with Heart and whenever he worked with Heart, we had to be on hold. There were times where we wouldn't work for three days and it was eating up my money. Because I had everybody in hotel rooms for three days doing nothing, waiting for the producer to come back from working with Heart, so we could start working on the album again. It was killer. I don't have a whole lot of good things to say about that guy."

"I think when it came time to find a producer," adds Rob, "Krebs encouraged us to go with Mike Flicker, because he was in Seattle and he had had a lot of success with Heart. But we went in because it's what Krebs wanted us to do. But we didn't like the sounds he was pulling out of the studio and we thought the final cut of the album wasn't heavy enough. It wasn't as heavy as we wanted it to be. We didn't get a good connection there and we felt the project wasn't successful mainly because of his soft hand. Like the bass sounded really light and I'm a heavy bass player."

It didn't help that sitting in the racks, the album looked, ironically, like a disco record. "That's what everybody says!" laughs Derek. "You know what's funny, we never did get that. I guess we... I don't know, we just never got that. But yes, I've heard that over and over again. St. Paradise, well, we came up with the title of the band. We want to call the band Paradise. We were just so glad to be out of Ted Nugent's band and in control of our own lives, it was paradise. So we wanted to call it Paradise. Well, Warner Bros. had already had Leon Russell, who had a record label called Paradise Records. So he put a cease and desist on us and we just went, well, how about St. Paradise? Because nobody's got that. That's the beginning of my last name, and we'll still call it Paradise. The cover artwork, that was a clever man out of New York, who was a photographer. We saw some of his work and he had this light bulb in this girl's mouth. She was generating so much electricity that it would light up the minute she put it in her mouth. We thought, oh my, how erotic is that?!'"

"*Jesse James* was Rob's idea," continues Derek, asked for some stories about specific tracks on the *St. Paradise* album. "He's a big western fan. He was reading a book on Jesse James and that's where he came up with, I'm going to write a song about Jesse. I said okay. 'Jesse rode down from the mountain;' how does that go? I don't know. If I was playing my guitar I could finish the lyric. So he came up with that and I said let me help you write the music. I pretty much wrote the music and he wrote the story line. *Tighten The Knot*, that was about, strangely enough, a longtime friend of mine, Brian Staffeld, who used to be the drummer in Ted Nugent, before we got Cliff. He's actually on the back of the *Ted Nugent* album, at the Electric Ballroom— that's Brian up there on the drums. But Brian got hooked up with this person who started to take his life over. You know, she was slowly kind of tightening the knot on his life. We just sat back and watched how that kind of unfurled. I just decided to write about it. He was so tight into the family and then all of a sudden her dad is running his life, telling him to get out of music. I just kind of rescued him and said, 'Look, we need a drummer now in Ted Nugent. You're coming with me.' He said, 'What am I going to do with this girlfriend?' I said, 'You know what? Is this working for you? No. Is that situation working for you? No. Come on.' I just wrote that song about slowly tightening the knot around his neck, you know? (laughs)."

"*Gambling Man*, I just loved Bonnie Raitt and still do and had a chance to meet her last summer. That was fricking incredible and I thought maybe I could do something with that. She covered that song. I heard it and thought, gosh, I've never recorded a song by anybody else. But she touched me so, I thought, I've got to do this song, 'Rambling man, rambling, gambling man.'

What's it called? *Gambling Man*. It's two writers, two young little writers out in California who wrote that song. You know, I do remember somebody saying, 'Well, look, it's not written by her; it's written by these two guys and we've got to sign up to pay these guys.' So I said yes, okay. One day in 1997, I think I'm in LA with Ted, at the Hollywood Bowl and these two guys come in the dressing room, 'Hey, we're the guys who wrote that song.' I freaked out! It was so cool and we just sat down and chatted for a while."

"Bonnie Raitt has always been a favourite of mine," adds Rob, aligning with Derek. "That's a great song, *Gambling Man* and it really kind of fits the whole persona of St. Paradise, because we were out there flying by the seat of our pants, with a nickel in our pocket, hoping this thing was going to take off. That song is the real heart of St. Paradise, because, 'There's no food for the kids and there's no rent to be paid.' In fact we heard it on the radio one time in Atlanta and we all went nuts. *Miami Slide* was cool too, a really well-written song. There were a lot of cuts that never made it to that album that Derek had, that were really cool songs. They're probably in the can someplace. In fact, I sometimes go back and listen to the original tapes we did in Bearsville and they are better than the album. That's nothing to take from John Corey, a great talented guy, toured with the Eagles, but it was really Denny, Derek and I who wrote most of those songs. By the time John came along, we needed an extra guy, to do piano."

"*Jesse James*, I think I wrote that on the road at a Holiday Inn someplace, writing that on my bass, and showed that to Derek. I wrote the lyrics to it. You know, I think music passes from someplace else through you. It's like, it's either there or not there. It was just something I wrote. I gave up on the music business. To me it was a rip-off and after Nugent and I said man, I'm done, I don't want to do this anymore, living out of a suitcase. But even today, I still love to play and I play all the time. If these guys called up and said hey, let's go to some gigs, I'd do it."

Rob and Derek also put the funky, party-rocking, slo-mo Bo Diddley-ish Ted Nugent song *Live It Up* on the album, "because I really wrote *Live It Up*," notes Derek, "and just let Ted put some lyrics on it, because I wouldn't have been able to get it on the album had he not put his hand to it. I had to give him half of it."

"*Jackie* was Rob Grange," continues Derek. "That was kind of one of his girlfriends, which Jackie is actually Johnny Winter's ex-wife (laughs) – that's all another story. Johnny was hanging out with us and Rob Grange... another story. *Straight To You*, that's just a song about, you know, our intentions of how we really cared about what we were playing and wanted to get it to the people. Wanted them to know that we appreciated the audience. There were many times as time went on with the Ted band, where, you know, you can become complacent. After awhile, you don't even have to play good. You just kind of slog through it and they love you; the throngs of crowds loved you anyway. We kind of got jaded by that after a while. We thought you know what? We've got to get this back and give them good stuff. Not give them *Stranglehold* two speeds quicker, or some other form of *Free For All* with different lyrics to it. So we decided to tighten it up."

As for St. Paradise getting out and playing live, "We toured first in Europe opening up for Van Halen," reiterates Derek. "That was fine, then we came back and toured the states with AC/DC and Journey." As for Nugent songs in the set, "We did *Live It Up* and that's about it. What a silly thing to do. Because had we been smart, I would've done the whole *Ted Nugent* album, and everything that I wrote. We were so mad, Martin, at each other; I was so angry that any time I heard those songs it would just send me into a rage. It didn't make sense. But it was a very poor decision not to do those songs. The same thing with Whitford St. Holmes, which we toured with Blue Oyster Cult and Foghat, actually. We got together and what we should have done is all the Aerosmith songs that Brad co-wrote and produced and we should've done all the Ted Nugent stuff and we didn't. A couple of dumb kids."

"You know, really in retrospect, I think it was really Derek that got the band to break up," reflects Rob. "Because he was going in one direction and Ted was going in another direction. I think it was something that would have happened anyway, so you can't really fault Derek. It's cool that they got back together and have done some concerts and things together, but still I think it would be better with the actual original band. Because it just seems to click. There's just some kind of magic there. Maybe that's how it is when you become an older rocker. You are always thinking that the guys are going to get back together (laughs). But St. Paradise, yeah... Derek said, you are welcome to come along and I would like to have you do this project with me, so I said yeah, cool. In retrospect, he should've stayed in the band and done a solo album. But that's the way it rolls, you know?"

As for the fabled shelved second record, says Derek, "The second album was a four-piece band, with an added pianist/guitar player, John Corey. He was in the band that tour in Europe with Van Halen and then he got asked to join Rod Stewart's band. From that he joined Don Henley's band. That one I produced. Well, we had an English producer. I thought we were going to get Tom Lord-Alge, but then we got some English guy who worked with Queen. That one was a bit more poppy. Because we started to listen to bands like The Knack and then all of a sudden we thought, gosh, we've got to get a hit single out somewhere. We started to go the wrong way. We started to write for radio and it just didn't work out. But there were some pretty clever things on there. I co-wrote a couple of those with John, who was quite a writer, so we had some good stuff. But we kept that one under budget. I learned my lesson on the first one, watching everybody spend my money. So I kept a tight rein and we brought it in under budget. It never did come out."

And this was without Rob Grange. "No, I left," explains Rob. "I got married and my wife got pregnant, when I lived in Atlanta and she wanted to move to San Diego. Krebs said—and unbeknownst to me—you can't have Rob in the band anymore because it's not in the budget to fly him in and out of San Diego. Even though we were flying Denny in and out of Sausalito to Atlanta. But there just wasn't enough cash to do it. So Derek and I split."

Scream Dream

"Make sure we don't destroy anything, just barely."

It was reported in the Toronto Star, "In a surprise divorce settlement of a case involving sex and drugs, Nugent was granted custody of his two young children earlier this month. The 30-year-old superstar, who, according to court testimony made between $4 million and $5 million last year, hustled his daughter, Sasha, six and his son, Toby, three, aboard his private Learjet to Michigan, shortly after the trial. Outside the courthouse, Nugent said: 'I am completely concerned with the wholesome upbringing of my children. I'll be spending a lot more time with them. Even though I face a broader concert schedule, my jet enables me to get home to my farm often. I'll be a darned good father. You could add up the hours I am at home and it would make someone like a linoleum salesman or an insurance salesman look weak, by comparison. I will be a devoted father. It wasn't my hard rock singing that caused my divorce. People change, that's all. I do not attribute my divorce to my professional activities. But I'll never marry again'."

"It's more than just visitation rights," said Ted, openly discussing his divorce from Sandy with *Hit Parader*. "I have equal custody of Toby and Sasha. I stayed in court to win the battle and that I did. I mean you fuck with the baker and you get a bun: you fuck with Ted you get none (laughs). I went in there and I stood my ground. I basically refused to budge from my demands to fulfill and apply my fundamental paternal responsibilities and instincts to my offspring and that no way, conclusively, determinately, no way anyone could deny me that. I went in there and I did it. So I got equal custody. The children live in a Michigan residence until they're 18 or until they escape (laughs) and my ex-wife, the children's mother and myself rotate every other month. Perfect."

"So that way all of what I consider to be the children's needs—their maternal and paternal relationships—especially at this tender age, will be fulfilled. In other words, there is a consistency in their relationship, the interplay between themselves and their mother and themselves and their father. I feel the children's needs are met in their relationship with their parents and equally as important, in the establishment of their security, their roots in a consistent environment. I can't impress upon you enough what I've seen, how the children need to stay 'home'. 'When are we going home?,' 'Let's go home,' 'This is my room,' 'Put your toys away,' 'This is my closet,' 'This is my bed.' I think there's this urgency there."

Looking back on what set up this painful life event, Ted told *Rolling Stone's* Fred Schruers, "From 1963 through 1973, I was overwhelmed by and a victim of rock 'n' roll. Day, night, rock 'n' roll—gigs, amps, cars, jammin', jammin', jammin', writing, new strings, new speakers, new musicians, rehearsals, additions, tours, pussy, new songs, louder amps, more pussy. All the things that are essential to rock 'n' roll. Then in 1970, I got married. That was a major thing in my life. Another person that I would give vast consideration to prior to any decision of mine. Though that person, my wife, knew who she was marrying and what I was already deep, deep into. She was this naughty little gorgeous brunette who would have nothing to do with me and I wasn't used to that. She was just so beautiful, I really wanted her badly."

Apparently things went south pretty quickly once Ted had returned from an Alaskan hunting trip in '77, and then Ted, enthusiastic explainer that he is, began talking about it without reservation. Ted's relentless womanizing had been a factor, but then accusations of drug use on Sandra's part widened the rift. In any event, it sounds very much that touring, for the time being, had been curtailed. Hence Charlie's previous comments about ratcheting back on the touring, doing weekends and such, possibly another reason Ted's career was losing momentum.

Still, the band was turning in a barnstormer of a record, the irrepressible *Scream Dream*, issued in June of 1980, flyin' high off of a jokey, jammy, underwritten rocker of charming monotony called *Wango Tango*, one of a few "silly" songs on the album amidst some of Ted's most grinding metal rockers ever.

"I returned to some of the more rock 'n' roll aspects, recalling the initial experimentation of my recording career," mused Ted at the time. "In other words, when I first began, I knew nothing about nothing. *They* set the mics up, *they* said what was a good tape and what was a bad tape. But I've learned to know instinctively what is a good feel on a tape. We recorded the whole fucking thing in 16 days. This is amazing nowadays."

"It's rawer," continues Ted, wrong again about characterizing one of his productions and really, neglecting the opportunity to reflect on the types of songs he was writing. "I told my producers that production is a creative function and the creativity begins to inevitably overshadow the content. This recording technique can be improved upon, they say and the sound can be enhanced, they say. Sorry. Can't be. Sorry, you don't dare. Sorry, Chuck Berry's original honky-tonk sound is what I want, buddy. A little bit nastier, a little bit more present. I want to use that aspect of technical advances, but I don't want to technically advance my recording technique to the point where it cleans things up. It's easy to fall into that. I get a lot of arguments. They say, 'I think we can get this a little better' and I say, 'Bullshit! I'll be the judge of that. You turn the fucking dials, you fucking make sure we don't destroy anything, just barely and I'll tell you what's good.' I mean, I make a lot of enemies these days (laughs)."

Fortunately, years later, some of the love for these times still persisted, Ted telling me, "*Scream Dream*, I love that. *Wango Tango*, I defy you to come up with more of an insane, intense, funny song in the history of music; it's so over-the-top. It comes on my radio all the time here in Michigan; radio stations play it all the time. In fact, I was in Phoenix recently and it came on the radio and my rent-a-car all of a sudden went really fast. The songs *Scream Dream*, *Wango Tango*, *State Of Shock* and *Bite Down Hard*, moments like that... I love them all. The song *Weekend Warriors*—man, what a roustabout son of a bitch that one is. I love that album. But there were moments that were less than perfect. But then, it's a roll of the dice, ain't it boobie?"

In a rare music-centric interview, admirably coaxed out of him by *Melody Maker's* Steve Gett, Ted explains that, "We recorded *Scream Dream* featuring *Wango Tango* in February and March 1980, at CBS Studios NYC on 52nd Street, which is a converted cathedral. We used that for the sound, the loudness and the ricochet resulting from the tall ceiling configuration. We also did some of it at A-Square Studios in Michigan and at Quadradial Cinema Studios in North Miami. But the whole thing took just three weeks! We just went in there and went a yankin' and a crankin' and minimal thankin'. It went so smoothly because everything was planned out beforehand. I had already written the material by late '79 and we spent time on the last tour playing the songs. That general free-for-all approach has added to the spontaneity of the sound. Ted produced this one as I have produced them all, but I have a number of people turn knobs for me and the production credits go to the producers of old—Cliff Davies and Lew Futterman and Lew's production team. But when you go into the studio with the boy you have your meal written out for you."

Ted reveals to Steve the detailed notes set out for the album, aiding in getting it done so quickly and efficiently. "Everybody in our organization gets a copy of this and it tells the recording procedure, keys of songs, chord changes, general direction of the song etc. So there's no guesswork."

The manifesto begins with, "I will attempt all lead vocals and we can experiment with everyone's version. Vocal performance and delivery is most important," moving on to track by track instructions, for example, these for *Terminus Eldorado*: "Rhythm guitar: black. Solo guitar: very black (slightly drugged). Bass and drums: The Temptations on a binge. Vocal: black on black delivered by a Masai warrior in a black '57 Cadillac on a full-scale eclipse of the moon with a blind girlfriend and her black cat followed by a coal truck and a black velvet billboard in the background with your eyes closed. Chick vocals: judged by the colour of their skin and the company they keep. Must sing upwind of board."

"I have always done things this way," explains Ted, "and it immediately gives everyone an idea of what I am after with each individual track. Like there's one on here for the song, *Spit It Out*, which says Led Zep meets Gunga Din – heavy on the Din. So there you have basic train wreck meets glass metal!"

"The album is the most intense rock 'n' roll thing I've ever written," says Ted, as he does every time, with variation and with gusto. "It's the finest rock 'n' roll I've ever bestowed upon my fellow white rock 'n' rollers."

Offering a bit of gratuitous tech talk, Ted unwittingly lets on just how important he is to the production of his records. Happily this time around, there's no really issues with the sound. Sure, the delivery by the rhythm section is typically rigid (witness *Spit It Out* or *Come And Get It*, which sound like they're drummed in a matchbox), but for once, there's warmth, robust bass, high-fidelity appointments.

"I was using the Byrdlands almost exclusively, but I did also use a Les Paul on some of the tracks. I doubled the rhythm to *Scream Dream* and *Wango Tango*, one track using the Byrdland and a loud amp and another using a Les Paul and a not-so-loud amp. That way I got a vaster frequency range by experimenting with a multitude of mics as well, in order to capture that frequency stretch. What you accomplish through a multitude of speakers and amps live is the use of volume to obtain best impact. So where you can't rely and volume into a mic to be recorded, you have to compensate by getting the thickness of sound through frequency spread and that's why I use the different instruments."

"As we progressed, I sort of developed a sound," recalls Charlie, on his vocal prowess, left only to *Don't Cry (I'll Be Back Before You Know It Baby)* and *I Gotta Move*, both frantic belters in the singing department, both somewhat amusing boogie rockers offsetting the metal elsewhere found. "So by the third album, *Scream Dream*, I did record all the vocals. Then Ted ended up singing most of the songs, using the influence of my vocal as backing, or a guide track. Still, that's where I started really coming of age as a singer and guitar player. You know, I only had two of the vocals on it, but that is where I felt the freest."

Do tapes exist of you singing those *Scream Dream* songs?

"No, I did that in the studio and then he decided he wanted to sing them, so he used my vocals as a guide track. But it was his gig and that was the benefit of being a solo artist. You know, hey, I don't blame him a bit. I had a kind of sore spot for a while about that but heck, I got two good albums before that. Still, it was his band and he called the shots. I was a sideman and I had to deal with what I was offered and what I had to work with. I was handed my homework. I'm looking at that more like, unfortunately, not the strong upward momentum album he could have done—if he wasn't in the situation he was in domestically. That influenced him to no end, so I think that comes out. But he did his best to maintain his level of what you might call animalism (laughs). But sales fell off a little bit, and I don't think the strong follow-up singles are there."

An immediate, first impression that has been hard to shake after all these years is that the album is one of extremes, Ted's best metal at one end, cracking jokes at the other.

"Yeah, so you get a mixed signal unfortunately. But that's how difficult it is when you're in the business, you have to produce and you're under pressure, but you have to have a family life too. You've got all this stuff and how do you maintain and not let it influence you, or at least make it sound like you aren't influenced by it? It's difficult for me to say. I was just a sideman and glad to be there. It was awesome but I could see it was waning. I look at other bands who had peaks and valleys too, from Led Zeppelin to The Who, Ronnie Montrose and Sammy Hagar, with that smoking early stuff and then they get a little out there, stretching out. The artist has to have that leeway. But at the same time, you're a fan and you want to enjoy it and want to hear that stuff, but you don't know why they change."

But man, *Flesh & Blood*, *Scream Dream*, *Hard As Nails*... "You know, I respect your opinion on this. Because that's how I felt about that. I didn't personally enjoy the novelty stuff like *Wango Tango*, you know, being a Immaculate Wangette. Although I enjoyed *Terminus Eldorado*, because I play guitar on that. I got to put in and suggest chords on that one (laughs) and I got to play this sweet '50s Strat. But as far as singles and strong songs, it's sad when you can't get your album sequenced the way you want or you've got to listen to other stuff on there that just doesn't fit." An interesting one on the album, heavy, albeit in that jokey boogie realm is *Come And Get It*, on which Cliff handles lead vocals, sounding amusingly like a cross between Charlie and Ted, although less full-throttle convincing than either. Still, a commendable effort.

As for Lew Futterman's role, "he oversaw all the recording and I got the pleasure of working with him on *Weekend Warriors* and *State Of Shock*, but then I think he was kind of out of it by *Scream Dream*. He had the sixth sense of knowing how to oversee and make little problems disappear and resolve issues to make a complete picture. From that standpoint, he knew what was an album track and what was the hit. I guess he worked in the '60s with major acts who got him to where he was. He also had real estate and stuff and he lived in the Dakota, which is where John Lennon used to live. But yeah, Lew was a real overseer and could make those big decisions."

But it was very much Ted's show by this point, even more so than before—overtly, right there in the credits, it is drawn to our attention by implication that Charlie supplies guitar on one track. "We didn't really co-write," notes Charlie. "We would offer little titbits here and there, but he would get the final say. You have to give him credit there again for providing the opportunity to everybody to have work. Obviously, there are bigger political moves in the story of how Ted got his solo career. Yet then again, he did launch it and he was successful, so he was calling the shots."

"I was still hands on," figures Futterman, "but... my name's on there and was I there at all the sessions? Yeah. But by that time was I sort of worn-out with the whole process? Yeah. Was I, to a certain degree—with the exception of a couple of songs per album—getting enthused about it? Was I a little bit, 'Hey, whatever, whatever you want.' Honestly, I mean, there'd be a couple of songs on each album that I would get enthused about and I would really get my head into them and make my comments and so on, but the latter stuff, the last three or four albums prior to the end of the relationship, I was going through the motions. I was worn out with it because it was hard, hard work. Much of what I did was drudgery. Just trying to get the most out of everybody. Secondly I'd made a lot of money already to a certain degree, moved into the world of real estate development and I was really... I mean after the Ted relationship I did maybe another three albums with different acts and then just walked away from it."

"Funny story about Charlie," laughs Cliff. "We were doing a video in Omaha. We had a gig there and they rented the arena three days in advance, three days before the gig, to shoot a video. The first video we ever shot was for *Scream Dream*, actually. Yes, just one song. It wasn't going to be live or anything; they just used the arena to shoot the video in. Of course, it's a pretty awful video. So we were always in different places. Like, Charlie lived in Detroit, I lived in Florida Keys and we all gathered there. So we're ready on the first day to do the video and we get a message from Charlie Huhn, can't make it. We figure what happened was, he's in the Detroit airport and he's got his ticket and he's ready to get on the plane. He decides to go outside and smoke a joint. So he gets too high. Instead of throwing out the part of the ticket he should have, he threw the boarding pass away. He gets to the plane, they won't let him on the fuckin' plane without a boarding pass. So he calls David Krebs in New York who rents him a Learjet to fly him from Detroit to Omaha and it costs $5,000. Charlie at the time was making 500 bucks a week. Actually, after Rob and Derek left, Ted never gave anybody points. Once Rob and Derek left, it was just me and Ted and everybody else was a hired gun. He was paying Charlie Huhn and Louis 500 bucks a week, while he's got multimillion selling albums. So anyway, the Learjet cost $5,000 and Ted Nugent took it out of his salary."

With the UK in the throes of the New Wave Of British Heavy Metal at the turn of the decade, it was fortunate for Ted that influential writers like Malcolm Dome were on board, the metal sage writing that, "When Ted Nugent put out *State Of Shock* last year, I wasn't alone in wondering if the legendary Motor City Loudman had lost his appetite for high-volume histrionics. Indeed, at times, SOS was almost laid-back and The Nuge seemed to have renounced his predilection for blood-red meat in favour of a more frugal vegetarian diet. Well, *Scream Dream* happily knocks all those sacrilegious thoughts into the nearest garbage bin, because Nugent is back at his tooth, fang and claw best. With his troubled and much-publicized divorce behind him, he's put together one of the finest offerings of his Amboy Dukes/solo career to date, taking the music, once again, right to the edge of insane mayhem and leaving the listener in a state of gonzoid shock. Taken as a whole, *Scream Dream* is a monster-sized success that reaffirms the man's right to sit right on top of the US metal pile and of course it has the masterpiece of *Wango Tango* to add to his vast canon of greats. An advert for a Nugent album (*Weekend Warriors*, I think) once proclaimed that he would never tap you on the shoulder when he could hit you in the face. That just about sums up *Scream Dream*."

Seconds the influential Phil Sutcliffe from Sounds, "*Ted Nugent* would easily rate in my favourite five heavy albums of all time and after days ear-bashing with *Scream Dream*, I reckon this is the best work he's turned in since then. He's run wild again and he's playing faster and rougher. I hope Ted can survive the less savoury developments this album implies—the savagery which his wife's departure obviously set seething in him. Apart from *Terminus Eldorado*, in which he gloats (humorously?!) about a woman killed in a car crash, the album is full of orangutan grunts and squeals which are kind of silly/funny but also edgy. Perhaps Nugent is a Neanderthal manqué— at least he wouldn't have to bother with love back in the Stone Age."

But as much as Ted was embraced by the NWOBHM fans, as one of the forefathers of the genre of heavy metal (despite Ted's famous rants against the English, second only to his opinions on the French), Nugent has always been uncomfortable with the idea of folks labelling him metal. "No, no. Too many boys in denim and leather. No, not heavy metal. I am rhythm and blues. I think heavy metal's cute. I mean, I'm a big fan of defiance, but I see an awful lot of cookie-cutter sheepness in the world of heavy metal, particularly over in Europe—I know this is going to piss some of those guys off, like I need to try—but when you all wear the same thing and you all got the same chained truck driver wallet and you all got the same pierced body parts and the same tattoos and you all got the same patches and all the same jackets, I hate that shit. It is so not individual. It is so sheep-like. Now Metallica, that's heavy metal, and I love that shit. I suppose Judas Priest delved into the heavy metal, though I consider that just grinding rock 'n' roll. I don't consider myself heavy metal at all. I consider myself an American rhythm and blues, rock 'n' roll guy."

"Metallica would be the ultimate poster child for rock 'n' roll becoming heavy metal, because of the overwhelming focus of the chug factor and tuning down to make it bigger and fatter and heavier. I'm a big fan of that stuff," continues The Nuge, somewhat unconvincingly, albeit probably cognizant of how much the Metallica boys have been influenced by Ted. "I love it when it's done with spirit and with soul. When it sounds like machines and guys are (screams), I mean there are moments when we can capitulate and there are moments of maximum intensity, that we all can get into the final Wilson Pickett at the end of *Hey Jude* scream, you know that song? Wilson Pickett singing *Hey Jude* and where he howls like an escaped beast. I know that is so inspiring that a lot of those artists took those black moments of howling escaped beast-ness and made their entire song like that, which I think is cute and cool, but it's about execution. Aerosmith is not heavy metal. They are rock 'n' roll, rhythm and blues. ZZ Top is not heavy metal, they are rock 'n' roll, rhythm and blues. All my favourite bands from the Beatles to the Yardbirds to the Stones to Green Day, that's not heavy metal, that's rock 'n' roll, rhythm and blues, even though Green Day might not know it. I'm a celebrant of Chuck Berry's dream and Bo Diddley's creation. I continue to this day, but it's my baby. We all have our own statement, we all have our own musical dreams and aspirations, and once again I just cannot gush adequately about the gift from God of the virtuosos I've been surrounded by all my life. No Ted Nugent music has meant squat just because of Ted Nugent. It's always about my incredible musical geniuses that somehow find me and make my music that much better."

Intensities In 10 Cities

"All the songs were in A, but don't tell anybody"

A lready, while ranting and raving about the qualities of *Scream Dream* to any overwhelmed journo that would listen, Ted had it in his sights to record, unusually, an album of all new original material, but like a regular live album.

"I write so much I never have time to stop," Ted told *Melody Maker*. "I've already written nine new songs and the one I played you earlier on is just one of them. It's always difficult to know what to put on an album. I just gotta beat my skull against a brick to cool my brain and to comprehend the fact that an album will only absorb 40 minutes of my material. I write hundreds of minutes, hours and hours and I just gotta accept that I'm beyond my own wildest dreams. I'll never get all my material recorded."

Executing his vision was an act of logical beauty. Ted knew that these songs would swim and swing best after being road-tested throughout the trunk of a tour, so when it came time to record them, he waited until the last ten dates. "See, the trick that I was pulling here, which ain't really a trick at all, is that if you start with some new material at the beginning of the tour—and we had about 20 new songs at the beginning of our tour—and you play it every night, boy, do you get a feel of what has impact. Boy, can you get it tight. So after playing the new songs in concert from April through August, we came up with the ten best ones and recorded them live to get that magic, that flame. It's the best son of a bitch I've done since the first Ted Nugent album. We're all a-rompin' and a-stompin' and a-chompin' at the bit. Of course, I'm not saying that *Wango Tango* was any slump!"

Entitled, brilliantly, *Intensities In 10 Cities*, that wasn't always the plan. Said Ted, "Originally this album was going to be called *You Can't Keep A*

Good Dog Off Your Leg and we had a picture of about 20 chicks literally climbing up my leg. It was right after I got off stage and I was all sweaty, so it was like they were climbing a greased pole. What I'm gonna do now is use that title for the next album."

Next album? Didn't happen. "Things fell apart in the '80s because of financial reasons," mentions Cliff, alluding to another huge issue seldom discussed at this time, the disappearance of a stack of Ted's cash, let alone proper payment for the peons. "Ted had a new guy working the finances, and he just rubbed everyone the wrong way, fucked everything up and I said hey, I've had enough of this. I just left in 1980 after producing *Scream Dream*," an odd coda for Cliff, who perhaps is erasing from his memory his performance and co-production credit (with Rick Browde) on the *Intensities* record.

"*Intensities In 10 Cities*, that's when I really started to let loose," notes vocalist Charlie Huhn on a more optimistic tack. Now onto his fourth record with the band, call that testimony to Charlie's ability to keep up with Ted and to keep within the boss's good books as well. "Especially with the falsetto screams and stuff like that. Ted was a major influence on my vocal creativity as far as getting a range and discovering a falsetto and just getting into this whole metal thing, and getting articulation and enunciation down, developing a style. So it was all a learning process."

Logistically, "We only did a couple of the songs live at each show," says Charlie. "What we did is we played a couple of different tracks at each show and that way the album was put together as being live, but it was often different cities. That's how they got the title. Ironically, all the songs are in A, but don't tell anybody (laughs). Everyone has their opinion about that album. It didn't do that well, unfortunately. You know, times were changing and being a live album with all original songs, it was tough to try to make it work. There wasn't really a radio song on it and how do you put a live song on the radio, especially in 1981?"

But songs do occasionally hang around, Ted mentioning this record's *Jailbait* all the way in 1977, as a song that might potentially show up on the next studio album. "Once they're written, I will not allow them to be altered because they are now my lyrics and they definitely say something. But all my songs are written the same way. When I write a song, I go into the dressing room and plug in and the first thing that comes out is a new song. I won't let that first lick be altered because it just jumped out. It's what makes it rock 'n' roll. The moment you start thinking about a lick, it's lost all hope as being a rock 'n' roll lick. Once I get the rhythm pattern, I open my little book and I choose a title according to how the song sounds. Now in *Jailbait*, I talk about cars with keys in the ignition and young girls. I think when you listen to a song, you don't give a shit what it says. It's the whole feel. Then once you have liked the song, you want to continue the enhancement of the appreciation by listening in fact, to what he is talking about. It doesn't really matter as long as it's rock 'n' roll. As long as it's about some form of good clean fun."

Jailbait, a groovy hard rocker with a malevolent chord sequence, was issued as a single, rising to No.56 on Billboard, helping the album limp to a No.51 placement. Retro-cover *Land Of A Thousand Dances* and the frantic, flippant boogie rocker *Flying Lip-Lock* were also semi-single material. Elsewhere, well, highlights were few and far between. *Spontaneous Combustion* had fire, as did the briskly punky *My Love Is Like A Tire Iron*. But *Put Up Or Shut Up* was ill-fit metal for metal's sake and *I Am A Predator*, nothing but a barely written boogie jam. Over to side two, *Heads Will Roll* fit uninspiringly right in-between those two solitudes. Late in the sequence, *The TNT Overture* is a mere hard-headed instrumental jam, leading to the last track on the album, a fairly nasty and convincing punk metal rocker called *I Take No Prisoners*.

Despite the sum total of the songs coming across, weirdly, as too heavy (as if that's not what we, as fans, can't get enough of, in theory), it must be said that the experiment of cranking them out live triumphs over Ted and his tough luck in the studio with Cliff. The sound is crunchy, raucous and electric and so are the performances, with Cliff even turning in an ass-kicking drum performance, one we knew was hiding there somewhere, because we last heard him roar all over *Double Live Gonzo!*.

According to Charlie, it doesn't sound like any of the *Intensities* rave-ups ever got proper studio treatment along the way either. "I'd have to look back, but no, we didn't go into the studio and record any of that. That was all live; we had a mobile recording unit out of Texas; Chet Himes, he and his wife Debbie were out and he did it. But no, it was just Ted in his glory years, going out and doing what he wanted. You know, *Land Of A Thousand Dances*, just Ted being Ted. You've got to hand it to him, somebody that made it up there headlining arenas and coliseums, they just deserve to do what they want."

Doing what he wanted, *Intensities* continued Ted's tendency to wrest control, most notably, taking the singing away from Charlie. "Yeah, well, I sang eight out of ten on *State Of Shock* and then that's when Ted decided that he wanted to do the lead singing, so he sung eight out of ten on *Scream Dream* and then the same on *Intensities*. There was a little animosity about that. But heck, like I said before, it wasn't my group. It was his call, so I had to honour that."

The cover of the album features Ted typically bug-eyed and delirious, literally basking in the arms of his fans. He's wearing nothing but his loincloth. Which in Ted's world, isn't just a loincloth, but a philosophy.

"Why not the loincloth? I was writing songs and again, I'm a reflection of my life's experience. I'm a hunter. I'm a killer. I kill my own food, I kill my own clothes, I kill my own lamps. I got lamps made out of dead shit over there, how cool is that? The term killer, you know why killer is a great compliment? Because in order to bring life to your family you need to kill shit and who's the best guy in that camp? The killer. Nobody ever told you that before, did they? That's why that's the supreme compliment. Who's the best guy in the village? The guy that brings us fucking food. That would be the killer. You all owe me. You never fucking heard that before. You didn't know that. I had to tell you that, because I am the only killer in the fucking entertainment world and I know where life comes from. It's a grizzly, beautiful ballet of tooth, fang and claw. So when I was writing music because every hunting season I killed shit to feed my family, the purest protein gift from God available to human kind. It's a spiritual experience, especially with the bow and arrow. So this was a deep, spiritual, driving force in my life, as a hunter, a fisherman, a trapper, a genuine hands-on conservationist. This is the primal scream. It's not a song. I am the primal scream."

"When I wrote *Living In The Woods*, *Great White Buffalo*, *Hibernation*,

Migration, Tooth, Fang And Claw and *Fred Bear*, when I'm writing these songs that celebrate my hunting lifestyle, I realize, wow, not only do I kill my own food and kill my own guitar picks—literally made guitar picks out of antlers and bones, much like the original man. How perfect, how pure. There's nothing more pure than me. So I go, you know, the girls really like the physicality of it all. I'll give them some fucking physicality. I'll wear a fucking dead rabbit onstage. This is priceless shit. You guys gotta enjoy uncle Ted shitting a coyote onstage, but a lot of people think I wear a tail. I'm actually shitting a coyote. But I started to integrate the celebration of my pure, primal scream hunting lifestyle, in song, in lyrics, certainly in guitar, animal licks. I figured why not?"

"Originally I wore those moccasins. I killed the pheasants, I killed the elk. I killed the animals that I made my stage clothes with, the vests and the feathers and the teeth and the claws and the eyeballs. I figured I'm a pretty trim, fit guy. I just figured one night playing, I think it was *Living In The Woods* or some damn song, I decided—I killed a rabbit that weekend—and I had actually cured the skin with the brains, it's an old aboriginal system by which you process leather using the brains of the animal. This is serious stuff. I mean I know I'm a little giddy right now because it's really fun and it's exciting and it's so outrageously different, I can't hardly stand myself. If I wasn't me, I'd really enjoy me. So I just decided one night, I took some rabbit skins that I had killed recently, I put some leather laces around them and I wore them onstage and there was nothing holding me in. My balls were swinging in the fucking breeze."

"That's all I wore, and I got on top of the fucking amplifiers and I'm up there jamming with my nuts hanging. I didn't realize it until Dave Palmer said, 'You know when you're up there I can see your balls.' I went, cool! I jumped down at fucking Grande Ballroom and I'd be jamming like a man possessed. Some black chick reached up and got a handful and I realized I needed some new loincloths. We need a loincloth that is more encompassing, shall we say. So the loincloth was just a total knee-jerk reaction to my primal scream purity, that if I'm going to kill shit, I'm going to wear it onstage, but I should probably get something that's a little bit more containing, shall we say. But you have a smile on your face. That's what I bring to people. That's some funny shit, and it was just so knee-jerk and so natural and so organic, I'm singing these cool-ass grinding songs, why not wear some dead shit I just killed? So over the years I saw people really got a kick out of that and I got a kick out of it. The drummer certainly got a kick out of it, so if you're getting a kick out of something, that's a good apple. People will buy that delicious apple, so let's make sure all the apples are as delicious and red and juicy as possible. Is that a great fucking answer? I want a copy of that one. It's fucking awesome."

Ted's run with Epic Records would coincide with the complete dissolution of any semblance of his semi-permanent and semi-celebrated band concept, essentially forevermore.

To recap, with respect to the Epic catalogue, The Nuge's manic run ended with two strong records in *State Of Shock* and *Scream Dream* that reached gold, followed by live oddity *Intensities In 10 Cities* in March of '81, discussed in the current chapter, an album that did not reach gold, nor was it all that appreciated or discussed at the time. In other words, it was barely a blip on the radar. What followed marked a sort of bright spot however, in November of '81, Epic issuing *Great Gonzos! The Best Of Ted Nugent*, which eventually went an astounding double platinum (of note, the '99 reissue includes three bonus tracks, anchor of which is a corking, melodic, speedy new original called *Give Me Just A Little*). Now, a diehard fan like myself barely notices anybody's hits pack, but it's an interesting phenomenon, this concept that a career is so much more than the art, that there's an undercurrent of gathered new casual fans that can send a post-contract compilation to such sales heights. The parallel phenomenon—and this existed with Ted, surely, as it did with Kiss and Alice Cooper—is this idea that ticket sales for concerts remain strong well past the droop in record sales. It stands to reason then, in summation, the heady sales figures for *Great Gonzos!*, coupled with continued strong concert receipts beyond the only "hit" album (*Cat Scratch Fever*), proved that Ted Nugent, as a reward for all his hard work, his 10,000 hours so to speak, had indeed become a part of the fabric of American pop culture.

Epic-logue 1: Adrift In The Atlantic

To reiterate a point alluded to in this book's introduction, I called the 2012 version of this book *Epic Ted Nugent* because I wanted it to be an examination of Ted's catalogue on Epic Records, which comprehensively and neatly encompasses all the albums that are near and dear to my heart. These also being the hit records and the ones pretty much all of us care about with passion and intensity. In a nutshell, the ones that are both critically and commercially acclaimed. This updated edition sticks to that original thought, although we've changed the title to reflect the fact that we've got quite a bit of new material in here.

In any event, I've retained those compartments used in the original book. This partitioning works out neatly as well because the subsequent years in the book of Ted, weirdly work out to a good news/bad news story as far as I'm concerned, with Ted's records on Atlantic, an imprint of Warner Bros., being mostly barren of good music, and then his three studio records thus far on the associated Spitfire and Eagle imprints, *Craveman* and *Love Grenade*, plus *Shut Up & Jam!* on Frontiers, being huntin', gruntin' rock 'n' roll grenades that I crave.

Ergo, in the spirit of my mandate, these three periods will be dealt with as codas, epilogues (Epic-logues, actually!), i.e. in less detail than those Tedly times and magical musical crimes that are stuck way down in my DNA, the records of the late '70s (plus *Scream Dream*–yeah, baby!). So let's proceed, shall we? First with the pain and then with the pleasure, a gosh-darn happier ending to the story I cannot imagine.

"I'm auditioning some young blood. I found this band in Detroit called the DC Hawks. These three brothers, all in their early 20s, play guitar, and my God, can they crank! Even though I haven't made the final decision, I'm leaning toward hiring the whole band, which also includes a bass player and a drummer. That would be the ultimate assault." These are the somewhat desperate-sounding words of Ted post-career collapse, nothing winding up happening on that front, as a wounded Nuge limped towards his first album on his deal with Atlantic.

Nugent, recorded in Hollywood and Ann Arbor in the spring of '82 and issued in August, to be sure, would feature "the DC Hawks" on two tracks, *Good And Ready* and *No, No, No*. But the official lineup, which could have been a corker but wasn't, featured Ted along with Dave Kiswiney, a returning Derek St. Holmes, and Carmine Appice on drums.

"Isn't that a great record?" enthused Ted years later. "Dave Kiswiney, Carmine Appice and Derek St. Holmes—what a great fucking band that was. *No, No, No*, *Bound And Gagged* and *Habitual Offender* are great, great songs. *Tailgunner* is great as well. Those are those guitar licks I was talking about. They are incredible, signature guitar theme lines—I love that stuff. I love the cover too. Did you ever look close and see the brass knuckles I am holding?"

After (consistently) extolling to me the virtues of *No, No, No* and *Bound And Gagged*—inexplicably, for they are dullard, dated Kiss songs at best—Ted, also consistently, adds that, "*Habitual Offender and Out Of Control*, on *Cat Scratch Fever*, are two of my favourite songs of all time. *Habitual Offender*—that is a stone cold son of a bitch. Again, I never, ever, ever gauge any of my personal appreciation based on commercial success. It's a nice manoeuvre and it's enjoyable and I certainly spend the money, but my personal moments have nothing to do with anything commercial. The drive of my life comes from moments with my son in a fishing boat or with my wife on a mountaintop hunting goats in Hawaii. These are the moments that drive the quality of my life. I certainly appreciate with all my heart and soul all those people that have supported my career and bought my music and celebrated the intensity and the touch that it represents. But some of my favourite moments recording-wise never made me a penny."

The *Nugent* album is certainly in that category, but worse than its immediate commercial ineptitude, the record's self-production is unimaginative, simple, weak, wholly lacking in dynamics. In tandem, Carmine, one of the world's grooviest drummers when given the chance, plays it as straight and lifeless as Cliff did, once more, the curse of behaved drumming and behaved knob-jobs dooming songs that might have struggled to a semblance of life.

Staying pretty much out of it, Carmine noted to me that, "On the first one, just called *Nugent*, I did all the drums and I helped him produce it. On the second one, I really didn't do much on that. I've been getting miscredited on that. All I did was some background vocals for him. I like Ted. Ted's a good guy. He's a rocker and he believes in what he does and when he gets onstage he gives his all. He's into it, you know?"

Why on earth was Derek back in the deadly Tedly fold? "For the money. That and because I wondered if we could retrieve that sound again. We just never could because he would never put together the right combination. It was 50/50 between doing it for the money and hoping we could get the sound back. We got Carmine Appice for the '82 album and tour. He is an excellent drummer but does he fit with Ted Nugent? No, he does not. The bass player, Dave Kiswiney, was almost the guy. But were they Cliff and Rob? No."

Generally speaking, the *Nugent* album played up Ted's tendencies to play unremarkable roots rock, verging on southern rock, boogie, the most pedestrian of radio-potential hard rocks... if only it wasn't so dated all the way back to 1974.

In conversation with *Kerrang!'s* Laura Canyon, Ted put his usual mega-positive spin on what from the outside, at this point, looked very much like the implosion of his career. "It's not a new beginning but it's definitely a fresh and renewed and upgraded chapter in the continuing saga because I have applied and improved and certainly increased the demand on myself for eliminating any compromise in my life, my music and my career. I took a long, hard look—harder than long—at my music and the delivery thereof over the last year and a half and on three fronts decided unequivocally that I could improve the functions and upgrade certain elements—in management, in production and in the record itself. I now manage myself 100%, I now produce myself 100% and I decided to go with new fresh blood to a new label. It was one of the most gambling-est rolls of the dice I've ever made—but we all know I lack no confidence. I went in and recorded the album with no label, I financed the whole project myself and produced it myself, so even though it's not a debut, certainly it is as producer-manager-totalitarian dictator of the project."

"Anything that smelled of compromise, I shot in the kneecap and sent home to mama," continues the ever-quotable Ted. "I wasn't standing for any shit whatsoever. You see, I've got a big heart—you've got to realize that. When guys make recommendations I've always given them some credibility and consideration, and many times the benefit of the doubt. So the last couple of years my recording projects have had elements of compromise. While I was fighting major battles over individual instrumentation—yes the snare drum can sound like a fucking cannon, yes the guitar can be abrasive and blend with the instruments—I was losing the war of overall production. I don't think the last few albums have been consistent in their production beyond passable. I think *Intensities In 10 Cities* as a production was embarrassing."

"The Ted Nugent album, *Free For All* and *Cat Scratch Fever* were all so fucking fantastic production-wise that I got comfortable," continues Ted, seemingly oblivious that he had just produced an album far worse than anything yet issued under his studly name, or at least since the Dukes. "They went so well, they sounded so fucking good that I went, 'Goddamn, the process is down, we've got it figured out, it doesn't need the attention I gave it on *Ted Nugent, Free For All* and *Cat Scratch Fever.*' False! I didn't recognize it at first. I just did not identify it. When I should have identified it, all of a sudden my personal life exploded with the divorce and my attention was completely diverted. My attention was completely on the other side of town. So needless to say, it's water under the bridge; and I am blaming my producers, but above all I'm blaming myself for spreading myself thin. I never get lazy. The threat of having my children taken away—the albums be damned! But if the manager was on the fucking ball, he would've said, 'Don't record.' If I would have been Superman, I would've been able to say to myself, 'Hey fucker, you're not rocking your dick off; back off for a minute, take care of those personal things and then when you've got the flames shooting out of your eyes and feel back, jump into it!'

When Canyon, rightly, tries to articulate that the record's got an, ahem, more musical contour to it, Ted responds by saying, "I've always told you, you know goddamn well, that my major inspiration in the world was the

Rolling Stones. So maybe those elements are resurfacing again as they did on *Stranglehold* and *Dog Eat Dog*. Because you've got to remember, those songs did have all those elements; there was real melodies and real ensemble vocal parts to them. You know what I think?—my album career should have gone *Ted Nugent, Free For All, Cat Scratch Fever, Nugent.* That's a harsh sample, because I wouldn't want to eliminate some of my favourite fucking songs. I mean, *Wango Tango* is as good as any *Stranglehold* and *Paralyzed* is as good as any *Cat Scratch Fever* and *Scream Dream* is as good as any *Motor City Madhouse.* But overall, as a manager speaking now, I believe that would have made more sense."

"Production means listenability," muses Ted Nugent's new producer, Ted Nugent. "In producing this record, I want those fucking drums to pound your spine, I want those guitars to crash and reverberate and I believe on this album they do just that. I don't believe by any stretch of the imagination this album is guitar-shy. You fucking listen to it again and that fucking guitar is dangerous. Every instrument is in the right proportion as I want them. In fact to this day, I listen to this new record and I still don't understand how the drums can be so loud and the guitar can be so loud but you can hear every damn line the bass player plays and the voice is still on top of that. I fucking did an outstanding job. A goddamn miracle worker!"

Unfortunately, making everything that "represented"... well, one necessarily has to compromise. But worst problem, aside from the lifeless songs, one can imagine Carmine being told to just stay out of the way. As for his own six-string performance on the record, sez Ted, "I listen to this new album and I listen to the fucking solo on *Ebony*, which happens to be a beautiful song with a well-thought-out lyric and the patterns are just fantastic. I listen and go, 'Oh my God, that's the best thing I've ever done.' It's absolutely breathtaking if I can get goosebumps when I'm listening to my songs after I play them and play them and still go nuts on them. You could play *Bound And Gagged* from this album and I'd be covered from head to toe with goosebumps, guaranfuckingteed! That's the true test for me, because rock 'n' roll was meant to excite me. I'm trying to develop this album in suppository form so I can stick that baby up my ass and go everywhere with it!"

But at least he had Derek back. "I think that some of your best vocal performances today on some of your vocal-oriented records are merely versions and renditions of the style that Derek St. Holmes initiated on the *Ted Nugent* album. I think he's got the best voice in rock 'n' roll for my music. So I called him up and said, 'Come on home, boy.'"

"It's a pain in the goddamn ass!" obliges Ted, on his habit of switching out band members all the time. "But it's worth it to keep that energy there. It's worth putting up with mountains of bullshit to deliver what I believe is the best. I believed at the time that The Hawks were the best. This has all been very difficult because Carmine is a major talent and a major ego and Derek is a major talent and a major ego and I'm a major talent and an outrageous ego and that's pretty difficult and energy-consuming. But it's worth it. These bands that stick it out—I sometimes wonder if there is really enough friction to keep them exciting. How the Stones have done it, I don't know."

Nugent tracks that made the set list come the tour time included *We're Gonna Rock Tonight*, *Good And Ready* and *Bound And Gagged*, the first of a growing number of overtly political songs from the mind of the Tedinator. "I like to think of it as extremely patriotic rather than having a political connotation. There's American red blood bubbling in every boy's veins in this country and when you hear this abuse of Americans and this flag being burned and this hostage you get pissed off. I would never in my life attempt to censor myself in any way, shape or form—especially through my music. If this attitude on my part surfaces in my music, I'm not going to try and quell it. If the patriotic flag-waving part surfaces—these are the things I believe in. I believe this is the best country in the world and I think you should be willing to kill for it."

Nugent peaked at No.51 on the charts, with its follow-up, *Penetrator*, issued in January of '84, faring no better, rising to No.56. The theme for *Penetrator* was to try to get Ted into some of that hair metal money. The Ashley Howe-produced album featured Ted collaborating with a number of song doctors (Ted had written every song on *Nugent*), with keyboards all over the place, and featuring a St. Holmes-styled belter in one Brian Howe. Again, there was an entire sacking and reconfiguring of Ted's band.

But first there's the cover art, which sent a message more metal than the music. "The reason it's called *Penetrator* is because I think it has a nice ring to it," Ted told *Kerrang!'s* Dave Dickson. "What other reason is there to call an album anything? No, I think *Penetrator* sounds kinda rock 'n' roll, don't you? It can be interpreted via ballistic considerations, via sexual procedure, even via decibel approaches, yeah? I thought it sounded good, you know, plus the artwork I chose for it was very penetrator-oriented. It's a picture of a great muscle-bound arm on some faggot and on the arm, there's a very elaborate tattoo—a kind of oriental dragon. The forward section of the dragon has become animated and is biting into the guy's arm! I saw it in a magazine and I remembered it as I was preparing the album. I thought of the name *Penetrator* and remembered there was an element of penetration in that piece of artwork. It's very graphic! Besides, I didn't want my picture on the cover again. I forget the artist's name, but it's a really good drawing... Looks just like my arm, actually, not that I'm a faggot or anything, but sometimes you have to defend yourself against those sort of people."

"I was listening to all kinds of tapes of both outside material and potential vocalists for the album," continued Ted, asked about the acquisition of unknown Englishman Brian Howe. "I was certain of three things: that I was gonna use Cliff Davies and Mark Boals for live work; that I wanted to use Billy Squier's band on the record, and that I was on the lookout for a killer vocalist. After listening to literally hundreds of tapes, I heard this voice come out and I said: 'Find me this guy! I've gotta have him!' That's how I found him."

"I was a struggling male model for Mothercare about two years ago, still learning my craft!" counters a wisecracking Howe, in conversation with Malcolm Dome. "No, seriously, I'd been in a few local bands, although nothing special. Anyway, I put together a demo tape and sent it to Atlantic Records. Needless to say, I heard nothing for about six months and completely forgot about the tape. One day though, someone from the company rang up and said they liked the songs very much but felt there was nothing to be done with me as a solo artist—however, how would I fancy becoming Ted Nugent's new vocalist? At first I was a bit dubious, but eventually agreed to fly out to New York and listen to the numbers being put together for the new album. I thought they were great and… the rest is history!"

"I felt under intense pressure when I first joined the band," continues Howe, after all these years, now more famous as the replacement for Paul Rodgers in Bad Company. "After all, let's face it, Ted Nugent is the greatest showman in the world; no one ever upstages him. Ted is a complete lunatic, yet is still rather sane if that makes sense. He's an incredibly shrewd businessman, but when were on the road, the things that happened are just unbelievable. If I told you some of the things we got up to, I doubt if you'd regard them as factual. The motto for the tour was, 'Are you sure?!' I tell you, it's a miracle I'm still alive. For instance, in Germany, Ted raced his Mercedes 80 miles an hour down the autobahn—backwards! Needless to say, the gearbox blew up on us. Then, in New York, Ted and I had a race through Manhattan in our separate Mercs. We managed to literally hit the Brooklyn Bridge and then he went smack into the side of a bus! Now Ted is an amazing driver, but I'm certainly not. When I look back on incidents such as these, I can't help but shake a little with fright. By the end of the trek, we'd managed to wreck so many hired cars from Hertz, I'm sure they'll never rent us another vehicle; we must be on their blacklist now!"

As for all the outside songwriters on *Penetrator*, Nugent figures, "Well, the huntin' season went on a little longer last year and I didn't get out of the woods! No, I'm just looking to expand the horizons of my musical endeavour. Don't let anybody tell you I'm gettin' lazy! I listened to all these tapes that other people had submitted, because I'm constantly getting a truck-load of tapes in the mail. I go through some of them and my assistants go through others, looking for different things, even if it's just a title. *Tied Up In Love* was a title and a great chorus: 'You got me tied up in love/You got me tied up in love.' I had a vision of a urine-coated barbed wire bullwhip! But for the common man to consume the concept, I went with the general flow of the chorus and put all my own music to it. I had to give the person who wrote the chorus a credit, though I forgot who it was. Whoever it was, I've never even met this person, I just took their music and Nugentised it! And for *Knockin' At Your Door*, written by Andy Fraser, I just thought it was a great song. I think Brian sings the livin' shit out of it. Same with *(Where Do You) Draw The Line* by Bryan Adams and Jim Vallance. Brian sings the livin' shit out of that one too. I think Bryan Adams has come up with some of the best songs ever written!"

"What kind of question is that?!" pounces Ted, chided by Dickson over the use of so much keyboards. "Where's the equation saying keyboards equal safe ground?! I think there are some keyboards that sound like giant boulders being shoved up your ass with no lubricant—and I think that's a desirable sound."

Ted also conceded the commercial failure of *Nugent*. "I've never had a second's doubt about myself. I felt that if I just kept yankin' and crankin' people would get hip to what I was doing. The last album was great—I don't give a pound of penguin crap about what anybody else thinks. There were some guitar sounds on there that were extraterrestrial, just incredible. That millions of people didn't get into it didn't really bother me. I know that people who did will never have their braincase fit the same way again."

As for winding up now on Atlantic, Ted rationalized it thusly. "I felt that my record label didn't believe in me the way they had done a few years earlier. I think they were more interested in promoting Boy George than working for me. That's when I knew it was time to take the Nugent rock 'n' roll show someplace else."

"I love every album I do, but this one is special," continues Ted. "This one expands my music. I just put all my years of knowledge and general rock 'n' roll know-how to work and came out with an album that is, undeniably, a classic. Rock 'n' roll's back and it's stronger than ever. I'm right there crankin' up the most rockin' music around. I rock 'n' roll because I love it. I've got enough money to last me the rest of my life. But then I'd be depriving everyone of my talents as a rock 'n' roller and that wouldn't be fair. I can promise that will never happen. As long as there's rock 'n' roll, young Ted will be there crankin' out the best."

Years later, when I asked Ted about the record from his entire catalogue that was fraught with the most friction and bad vibes, he figured, "Probably *Penetrator* on Atlantic, '83 or so. Everybody was talking about music trends and influences and looking for different angles and things, where I should have been like AC/DC—I should have gone in there and just made the most blatant Ted Nugent record I could have possibly made. But I'm a team player and when people on my team who I respect recommend things that might be discomforting to me, I'm a giving and open person and of course it was the stupidest thing I could have ever done (laughs). So in my old age I'm less giving and I'm less tolerant (laughs)."

And yet *Penetrator*, for all its negatives on paper, is actually a pretty decent album, the songs possessive of, yes, some of that hair band energy, with Brian Howe providing the critical mass and even charm with his Paul Rodgers-like delivery and clarion pipes. Even Ted responds, at least from a soloing standpoint, with lyrical harmonics, melodic licks, carrying on a monologue or dialogue over and around riffs that sound nothing like his from the past. The keyboards are both loud and now dated, but they somewhat fit the vibe of the record, adding texture within a sonic spectrum that actually does sound expensively achieved and quite big, unlike the craft shop lack of ambition that killed the *Nugent* album. With respect to hiring on Ashley Howe to produce (Nugent had been under the impression early on that it would be a co-production), Ted had done so because he had been impressed by the sound Howe had gotten on the *Abominog* and *Head First* albums from Uriah Heep. There's definitely some congruity there, especially with respect to making keyboards play and bray loud with guitars.

But yes, *Tied Up In Love, Blame It On The Night, (Where Do You) Draw The Line, Don't You Want My Love* (all incidentally, in the *Penetrator* tour's set list)... these are fairly intense songs within the melodic rock realm, not a realm we are used to seeing Ted operate in, but here he is nonetheless and he does a pretty good job of it.

Ted's guitar is still quite pervasive. Nugent, being the boss, crams in a lick wherever and whenever he feels like it, which is everywhere and often. "Listen to some of those note patterns on the *Penetrator* album—some of those note flurries are not meant to be. Take the intro on *Tied Up In Love*— where did that come from? What kind of fucking run was that? That's fucking amazing. Listen to the solo on *Tailgunner* on the *Nugent* album. I listen to that and I go, 'Who is this guy?' The speed, the dexterity, the weird note configurations—you won't find these anywhere else. I'm moved by my playing. Listen to the solo on *Go Down Fighting*. Oh my God. I'm bending notes where the good Lord did not intend us to bend them; dissonant, upside-down patterns. I find that so many people don't come to grips with the stuff I play or that Eddie Van Halen plays or Andy Summers plays. They're listening to the song. Go *beyond* the song. Listen to what's *in* the song. There's one run in *Don't You Want My Love...* Duane Eddy would just give his left nut to get the twang that the solo starts off with. Then it goes into this Afro-American blues line, then the solo goes (sings it) and the last bit is the fastest thing ever recorded. I don't feel at all restricted by the rock framework. In fact I don't even feel I've begun. *Stranglehold* has jazz, rock and blues in it; *Take Me Home* has some of the most bluesy jazz patterns that have ever been played anywhere, anytime. I mean, really listen to that shit. I'm not just raving because I think I'm hot; I'm raving because I am hot."

"Worldwide, *Penetrator* has sold about twice as many copies as its Atlantic predecessor, *Nugent*," noted Brian Howe. "We've actually achieved what many thought was impossible and turned Ted's career around. He'd been on the slide for some little while, but now he's reestablished a solid base. We were very disappointed, though, with sales of the LP in Britain. I think it's done about 2000 copies, which is less than *Nugent*. I can't explain the problem."

Malcolm plausibly notes that maybe it's because Ted's summarily ignored the UK, literally playing one Hammersmith show and that's it, for each of the last three albums...

"I'm trying to persuade Ted to come over again very soon and this time bring the full American show and take it across the country," replies Howe. "I tell you, our US stage set was the most spectacular out on the road in recent months and it was so loud! We had iron mesh covering the amps, not just for effect but also to stop them being blown all over the place by the sheer volume they were being forced to deliver. I had to anchor myself to the stage every night or else risk the possibility of ending up in the audience, such was the instrumental force behind me. As for the kids, those in the front rows would go home with their hair frizzed. Our show encapsulated every parent's nightmare in two and a half hours. I'll be honest, if I wasn't involved in the business and had a 15-17-year-old daughter, there's no way I'd want her to go anywhere near this band. We are frightening!"

"The American tour was very successful," continued Howe. "We played six shows a week for four months. Of course, there were periods in the tour when business was slack, but then you've got to remember that on many occasions we were following Van Halen and the Scorpions into cities. Both of those acts had hit albums/singles and a very high-profile and we had neither. At the end of the day, though, we drew very large numbers, which is great for a guy like Ted who has been going for two decades; I wonder how many acts capable of selling out 15,000 seaters today will still be pulling good crowds during the 1990s?!"

Ted's next salvo for Atlantic, *Little Miss Dangerous* (with Brian Howe nowhere in sight!) was issued in March 1986. The album is more of the same "'70s rocker makes hair metal" as *Penetrator*, but even better. "I agree with *Little Miss Dangerous*!" says Ted, after I chide him about the low quality of all these albums, adding that this would be my favourite between *Scream Dream* and *Craveman*. "Killer sex monster supreme! I also tend to agree that the records twixt those two were inconsistent as all hell, as I had made the terrible error of compromising with management and record companies to try some new things. Never again. I mean, I love them all, even though some of them sold squat. There are three songs on *Little Miss Dangerous* to this day that I just can't get enough of. The song *Little Miss Dangerous* has the sexiest sounds in the history of noise. I just can hardly stand the song, it's so intense. There was a song called *Angry Young Man* which was the theme song on the *Miami Vice* episode I was on back in the old days. Then the *Painkiller* song, I just, I mean, that is another song that should be illegal to play in a moving vehicle because it's so compelling, it's so intense. I just love those songs."

In fact the title track was used in an episode of *Miami Vice* as well, the slow-burn of a song also become Ted's biggest hit since *Wango Tango* and in fact, his biggest hit ever since that novelty track and his time on Epic Records. This song of "sexual inspiration exploding in a firestorm of spiritual orgasm" is sung by Ted, purposefully lowdown on the energy spectrum and thus, a bit wobbly, which I'm sure wasn't intended (although he did once hire Meat Loaf!). It is one of the few not sung by the album's erstwhile lead singer, Dave Amato, another stylist in the mode of Derek, Charlie and Brian Howe from the last record. Additionally the song lives and breathes on a loping, funky bass line, while Ted indulges his new solo an' lick stylings, from grind to lots of pinging, pinches and pull-off-type effects. Elsewhere, essentially reminding us of the controversy around the *I Want To Tell You* cover, there's Burt Bacharach's *Little Red Book*, known to us through treatments by Love and Manfred Mann. What's most remarkable about the track (besides more of Ted's pinched harmonics) is that one really notices how radically electronic the album's production is, particularly the treatment of bass drum and snare drum. All told, *Little Miss Dangerous* becomes the more successful record to the paired *Penetrator* in large part because of its daring production, as well as the peaks and valleys stylistically, amplified by closer *Painkiller*, a brisk Ted-sung metal item bolstered by a strong pre-chorus and even gnarlier chorus.

Finally, on the positive side, Nugent is the sole writer of most the tracks. But on the negative, there really is no band to speak of: officially it's Ted and the basically unknown Dave Amato, along with three drummers, two bassists, three keyboard players and three producers! And that cover shot? Well, that's actually Ted and his daughter, while on the back, quite amusingly, that's Ted and his Mohawk.

"At first I wanted to call this album *Assume The Position* because that's what I've been doing a great deal of lately," said Ted back on the press trail in 1986, talking with *Hit Parader's* Andy Secher. "We started recording this record in California, and there's just so much fine leg out there that a man can't help but want to assume the position virtually all the time. After that urge left me momentarily, I thought about calling it *Radical*, because that's what the music is. Then I thought about calling it *Assume The Radical Position*, which I figured would cover everything. Then I proceeded with the song, *Little Miss Dangerous* and it just became a higher and higher priority until it emerged as the title track. I try to let the music tell me what the title of an album should be, and while *Assume The Position* cover all the bases and more, *Little Miss Dangerous* has a real street vibe to it. After working with the people on *Miami Vice*, I liked that title a lot."

Surveying the diminished appetite for his music in the hair band mid-'80s, Ted commented that, "I've never been shy in the image department, but I've always had the guitar licks to back it up. That's one of the reasons I want *Little Miss Dangerous* to be a hit. I want people to listen to it and go, 'Holy shit, how did he make his guitar sound like it was falling off a cliff and landing on my grandmother?' There's still a place for the kind of rock 'n' roll I'm playing. If there isn't, we're all in a whole heap of trouble. I'm a big rock 'n' roll fan. I love playing it, but I still get a big kick out of listening to it, which is why I'm pissed that radio doesn't play enough of my music. But I'm happy that people like Bryan Adams, Tina Turner, Heart and ZZ Top are on the radio. They're mega-successful and they deserve to be. People like Dokken and Ratt are doing some good things too. They're making accessible music that still has that rock 'n' roll edge. I'm out to prove I'm as diversified a musician as anyone. People think of me only as this over-amplified guitar madman, but I've always written songs that have a lot of melody and substance. I don't care if they're talking about *Workin' Hard, Playin' Hard*, *Cat Scratch Fever*, or the stuff of the new record, the music has evolved. The simple fact is Ted Nugent can still rock with the best of them."

"The band consists of Dave Kiswiney, Cliff Davies and Dave Amato, with Amato and myself handling the singing chores," continued Ted. "It's a band that really kicks ass. At this very moment, I have Davies chained in a cave with a quad-bass drum just begging to be let loose so he can inflict some damage on everyone's eardrums. We're ready to hit the road and play at least two hours every night."

Indeed it's very interesting that for both of the past two records, Ted went with a whole band of strangers for the recording, and then toured these revolving door collaborations with Dave Kiswiney on bass and more shockingly, Cliff Davies on drums (after *Penetrator*, granted, Billy Squier needed his band back to work on what would become the platinum-selling *Signs Of Life*). But putting aside how odd it is that Davies would consent to return, it's even stranger Ted would include a drummer that was even more of a throwback to the '70s than Ted himself is, especially one here in the hair era that is notably as follicly-challenged as Cliff was.

Addressing the ousting of Brian Howe after just one album, Ted told Howard Johnson that, "Brian Howe does have one of the finest voices I've ever heard. It's the kind of style that's unique to English vocalists and he gave a good effort. But he had reservations about the Nugent style in terms of furthering his own career, so I sent the Limey back to his Commie island with a rose up his butt."

But forget trifles like lead singers come and gone, the reason, apparently, that *Little Miss Dangerous* shines so brightly is all that sunshine. "I've been so fuckin' wound up and excited on this one it's outrageous!" continues The Nuge. "I know what you're going to say: 'Is this because of the fact that I've been recording in California?' I say of course it is! I'm glad that all these fuckin' degenerates are here and not at my ranch, but it provides a certain rarefied atmosphere in which to work. There's so much concrete and homosexual activity here that it can produce an overwhelming negative vibe for the young white boy from Detroit, but there's also a fire that exists in extreme metropolitan areas that is highly conducive to rock 'n' roll! This is the place for professional rock 'n' roll manoeuvres; its electric tensions are ideal in arousing the spontaneity my music needs. Of course the leg quotient on the West Coast is intense. It has aroused the animal sexuality in my songs. Oh, the *Wang Dang Sweet Poontang* is featuring heavily in old Ted's equation and this has proved one volatile habitat for this puppy to be cruising in! This is the high point of my rock 'n' roll career; I am moved by the guitar sounds I'm making!"

"I can't even begin to tell you how good some of the songs are!" says Ted, but begin he does. "*Crazy Ladies* gives hope to the whole planet, *Little Miss Dangerous* will probably cure AIDS single high-handed and *Savage Dancer* will have Colonel Gaddafi 'round at my ranch begging to sweep my dog kennels! I mean, this album is so good, I've had Indians in my bed for the last coupla months 'cos it looks like a tepee! I've had a boner through the whole project! When I pick up my guitar all that shit just bounces off my cranium. I want abuse, I want barbaric gut-level offerings. I want to be a nasty-streaked slime master and on *Penetrator* some band members wanted to do radio-type songs. It was less than wholly Nugent. Well, on this one I pulled my ass up and pleased Ted first and foremost. There are keyboards on the new album but they're there to embrace my guitar, to make Nugent impacting! Look how ZZ Top do it, how well they do it, and you'll see how I'm approaching things."

The way Ted would be approaching things would change yet again come *If You Can't Lick 'Em... Lick 'Em*. Weirdly, Ted would hang on to Dave

Amato, but in what was a near repeat of his relationship with Charlie Huhn, he'd take over the vocal duties, in this case, all of them, allowing Dave backing vocals and some rhythm guitar. Tom Werman would return to the fold as producer, but even though the keyboards were all but gone and the guitars were more hard-charging, there's an ear-fatiguing hardness to the sound and not in a good way, like hair metal in a boomy concrete venue made for hockey.

"After the last collaboration on *Weekend Warriors*, Tom got into a lot of drinking," says Nugent. "When I worked with him on albums like *If You Can't Lick 'Em... Lick 'Em*, we just weren't effective. He just wasn't the mother hen, mother grizzly bear protecting her cubs like he was with my previous experience. I had such an immense respect for his musical touch, musical grasp and his musical vision that it was heartbreaking to see that compromised on my later collaborations. But I think Tom is like a Marine. He adapts, and even though he's made some mistakes like we all have, I think some of his most crude moments on things like even Mötley Crüe, were very poppy but sold them millions and millions of records."

From a positive perspective, the record was a return to more of a hard-rocking sound, even if the magic wasn't there from a song standpoint (i.e. *Funlover* was just *Painkiller*), as if Ted was grasping for songs, struggling too hard and without the instincts of youth to correct recent critically-mauled wrongs—very much like Alice Cooper on *Constrictor* and *Raise Your Fist And Yell*. Outliers on the album include a Stevie Ray Vaughan-style blues ballad, weirdly kicking off side two, called *Spread Your Wings*, and then at the end of the record something called *That's The Story Of Love* which sounds like a crappy Bon Jovi song... because it is.

"For years, Jon would come to my shows," explained Ted, to *Kerrang!'s* Sal Treppiedi, who skillfully coaxes a very good interview out of The Nuge. "He was a fan. We got to know each other better just before he became the hottest rock 'n' roller on the planet. When he came to Detroit, he invited me down to the show. I love jamming. Whenever Heart come to town, I get up and do *Rock And Roll* with them. Whenever Sammy Hagar comes to town I do the same. I did the same with John Waite when he came to Michigan. I love to jam. Jon called and asked me to come down and jam with him. He told me that they would learn one of my songs—he wanted to do *Cat Scratch Fever*. I went down there and his band played it note for note. The crowd went Gonzoid. We did that three times in Detroit and once in LA. He kept telling me how he couldn't believe that I was not still one of the top rock entities around. Now, he knows he's got power. He told me to come over and write a song with him and Richie. I thought that it was a great idea. I had a fucking riot. I worked with Charlie Sexton for a while, spent a little time with Holly Knight and Paul Stanley and came up with some licks. I spent time with Jon and Richie and *Story Of Love* just came flying out. Richie had a bass line, Jon started spitting out vocal parts and we all started spitting out lyrics."

"Now here's something that will blow your mind," continues Ted, who, incidentally, during the *Little Miss Dangerous* era, jammed with Stevie Ray Vaughan and Pat Travers in Detroit, both in the same night. "Everyone was excited that we were going to have a Jon Bon Jovi song on the record. They loved the way it was going, but nobody loved the title. I don't even like the title to this day. Johnny Cash could sing a song called *That's The Story Of Love*. I love Johnny, but I wouldn't play his music. There was no other title we could give it. We thought that the idea of Nugent doing a contemporary song with a contemporary giant had a nice touch to it. Do you know that in the final analysis, Werman begged me not to put it on the album? He thought that all the other songs on the record were tough with clever titles. They were all Nugent snag rock. But that title was not there. He figured that kids would hear the title and that I wrote it with Bon Jovi and know that it's not me. But I told him that I wrote it with him. Listen to the guitar. Who else could that be? I respect Tom's judgment, but after two months thinking about it, I realized that the song had to be on the record. The solo alone is worth its place. Yeah, it may not be like the others, but it is Nugent—it might be the second single. It was great work by Jon. He put his heart and soul into it and he did it for me."

"My new album is the killer," proclaims Ted, as usual, really believing at the time that he was speaking the truth. "It's back in the saddle. No one though can predict how well it will do. I'm not banking on squat. Only thing that I'm banking on is that I will tour all year and have the time of my life and see what happens. When September comes, I'm going to stop touring and go hunting. I think anyone that has any fucking rock 'n' roll brains cannot deny that this is Nugent returning to form. This album should've been the follow-up to *Cat Scratch Fever*. If I'd had ultimate control, I wouldn't have put out an album until 1980. It should have been this one."

Same thing, incredulously, that he said about the *Nugent* album and by the way, says Sal, what do you think of that record now after six years and three more records?

"I had no idea," answers Ted. "I never have a concept. My visions are song by song. A lot of times, the product itself is consistent and it looks like a single vision, but that's because of the time. On this album, every song belongs, and it's very consistent. It's conclusively Nugent. If you go beyond the production and listen to *Bound And Gagged*, *Tailgunner*, and *Fightin' Words*, that is definitely me. But the production doesn't present itself. I think that taking the production chores myself was a mistake. You know who my worst enemy is? Me! When I'm in the studio, my energy and my enthusiasm is so contagious that everything that I do is perfect. There is this excitement that permeates the studio. Werman, though, is too smart for that. For instance, some of the stuff I play will have the others thinking it is great. Werman, though, will say, 'It's a motherfucker, but it's out of tune.' You have to watch my ass. I'll make you think that my shit doesn't stink if you hang around too much."

"On this album there is a balance of uninhibited enthusiasm and controlled technology. For this record, I told myself that I would not record until Werman was available. What Werman had was an uninhibited enthusiasm for street-level rock 'n' roll. He's not just producing a record, he is making this music. The reason that I feel, and you would have to ask Tom why he stopped producing me, is that Lew Futterman started using Cliff Davies and Ric Browde a little bit more come *Weekend Warriors*, *State Of Shock* and *Intensities*. It was my death. If you sit down with those guys, they'll tell you that it was death because they produced it exactly how I asked them to produce it. Bullshit. These are not opinions either. These are conclusions. I'm too old to be opinionated. My enthusiasm can be interpreted in two ways: either you join me or it intimidates the shit out of you. Familiarity breeds contempt. I want my music to be big. I didn't make my earlier records sound the same way intentionally. That's it. I'm not looking for something. I already found it. Now I'm delivering it. Most artists aspire for growth and new exploration and diversion. I do too, but not in style—in content."

Like I say, could have been the theme of this whole book and indeed it recurs again and again, all of this blame game toward production, who was really producing, who thought they were, what went wrong at that specific stage of the process, even if the role of the producer in any band has always been contentious and decisively non-specific.

"We got into this big thing about change after the *Cat Scratch Fever* LP," says Ted, clearly ready to reassess his past during this chat. "I told them that we had to grow and develop but that if they wanted change to go and listen to somebody else. That's why there's all these different types of music. If you want to go horseback riding, you don't rent a car. If you want to rent a car, you don't go to the stables. That's why you have choices in life. I stood my ground, but they were producing me. I would go into the studio and guitars would sound different. They would tell me that I've had the same guitar sound for so long. I would say, 'Am I missing something? I don't have a different guitar sound. It's still me.' They fought me and fought me. It got to the point where if I said I needed more of this, they'd get pissed off. So the sound of those records got to be all fucked up. God damn them. That's why the inconsistency was there."

As has been examined, this supposed drop in quality circa *State Of Shock* and *Scream Dream*... well, divorce aside, there was the implosion of Ted's business affairs.

"That I made $40 million and had certain people running my life that lied cheated and destroyed such a huge empire when I just lead a simple life... If there was justice, I would have killed 40, 50 people. That's why the elements of my life are so intense. Not only is there joy, but there's also vicious hatred and anger in my blood when I need it. That's good, because you never lose touch."

"I know what you're getting at. It's happened so many times. A lot of people really think that I'm smart. I'm sure there are those who think I'm a dumb fuck, too. But I think I have a reputation as a smart and aware guy. I've been fucked in the ass too many times to be too smart. But again, you have to identify your priorities. If you become so scrutinizing so as to make sure that every step of your life is safe, the steps aren't as much fun. Run through the landmine field every once in a while and see if you touch one off. So without being too cautious, I paid the price in the '60s, '70s and most horribly, in the early '80s."

"I've always been a bit bewildered by the inconsistency that I was the number one grossing act in America in '76, '77, '78 and '79, and then all of a sudden... I know my products weren't as killer. I know that *State Of Shock* was not as good, and that the *Nugent* album was flawed, and I know that the *Penetrator* album was not my finest album, but I was amazed that I went from selling a million-and-a-half to selling 300,000 overnight."

Piled on to the wars over production, the divorce, embezzlement, there's also the all too familiar story about being over-worked, something that can lead to fatigue and lack of enthusiasm to be sure, but also over-exposure in the marketplace.

"I have my theories; I know why," reflects Ted, on a situation in which bands all too often find themselves embroiled. "I'm so enthusiastic about my music and about life, that give me an inch and I'll probably take a light year because I'm digging it. In so doing, my managers weren't gonna say, 'Well, we better not let Ted tour this year,' because I wanted it so bad I could taste it. But it would have been smart if I hadn't played San Antonio and every major city in America six times in four years. It would've been great if I hadn't put out a record every nine months for over ten years. So my managers were assholes and I was an asshole in some ways too. Again, you can't harness enthusiasm or it's not real enthusiasm. I couldn't wait to go into the studio to make a new record because I had so many ideas; I couldn't wait to go to San Antonio again and I couldn't wait to do this and that. My manager said, 'Well, he's willing, let's book him; he's willing, let's record him.' If I was smart, I would've gone, 'Well, we just finished playing every major city three times in two years. Fuck you. I'm going away for a year.'"

"I would like to get on top again," mused Ted, watching arch-American hard rock bands sell three and six times platinum without breaking a sweat as the late '80s came to a close. "I don't like opening. It's not painful, but it's not for me. If I had more room, I could cover more ground. As far as specific endeavours, I'm doing everything I want now. With my kids, I've done everything just right. I have a great home, I have great friends, good hunting dogs, fast cars and trucks, all the respect a guy could want. I'd love to hurt the cocksuckers who robbed me; I'd like to see those fuckers grovel."

Once more, Ted made a separation between the band that crafted the record and the one that toured it, key hire, or re-hire, being Derek St. Holmes. "Well, Derek isn't on the album, but with him on the tour, it's maintaining that reunion attitude. I hired Derek not for nostalgic reasons, but because of the respect I have for my style of material. We went to great pains to learn songs again. It took great effort to learn those songs just like the record."

It is refreshing to hear Ted talk about the ins and outs of maintaining a career, the story of that horrible Bon Jovi song, the debate over inclusion of it and even the title of it and that neither he nor the guy with the supposedly good ears, Tom Werman, could tell that it was crap. Ted by this point had swallowed some pride in admitting that, at least now and I suppose in the old days too, that he was second banana to Kiss and Aerosmith, having signed on as back-up act for both those old warhorse competitors, while for *Penetrator*, overseas, he supported Judas Priest! There he is, trying new things, hair metal, getting Derek and Cliff back periodically, re-teaming with Tom Werman who... again, as we've seen, everybody's got their own opinion with this band in terms of who carted around and disseminated the magic and nobody seemed at the end of the day to come to consensus on who that was, or for that matter, what music turned out good and what music turned out bad, whether we're talking material or whether we're talking tones.

At this point, having run out of ideas, there was nothing left to do but form a supergroup and call it Damn Yankees. And damn it if it didn't work. The self-titled debut, issued in February of 1990, rode the hair metal wave to double platinum and a No.13 placement. The band's second and last, *Don't Tread*, issued a year after happy hair hard rock was over, namely 1992, stalled at gold and No.22 on the charts, still much better than anything Ted had generated since his greatest hits album, the very best of all those Atlantic albums getting to no more than 300,000 pancakes and usually less.

The Damn Yankees consisted of Ted plus Tommy Shaw from Styx, the relatively unknown Michael Cartellone on drums (now with Skynyrd), and the irrepressible Jack Blades from Night Ranger, years later, producer of The Nuge's firecracker *Love Grenade* album.

Introducing the band to *Guitar World*, Ted explained that, "As a musician who's been able to do as he damn pleases all through my career, I suppose you could say I'm spoiled rotten when it comes to flexing my music muscle. I've run into a bunch of people throughout my career who I admire and who I find intriguing for their potential jamability. I always love the time Billy Gibbons and I spend together. I got to jam with Jimi Hendrix, BB King, Albert King and Freddie King, Bloomfield… so many different people. Believe it or not, I always knew that Tommy Shaw had an incredible rhythm and blues twang inside of him that he never really allowed himself to develop with Styx. Listen to some of his vocals, the rougher stuff that Styx did— Tommy's an ass-kicker, and a serious git-ar player. So I was in New York in November of '88 and Tommy and I were both on Atlantic Records. Tommy's manager Bud Prager, requested that I go kick around some ideas with Tommy, so I went out and we started playing. The music I heard that came out of Tommy and I just plain wanted it. It sounded so cool. It had such a non-Caucasian R&B groove thing happening that I just said, 'Hey, this is cool.' We developed a couple of tunes right there, man, bing, bing, bing, three or four songs that night and I'm going, wait a minute, I want more of this shit. So the rest is history. We called Jack Blades about whom we both had the same attitude—I think that *Don't Tell Me You Love Me* and *(You Can Still) Rock In America* by Night Ranger, which Jack wrote, are probably two of the rockiest rock 'n' roll songs ever. Jack had always expressed to me that he wanted to be in a guitar-strangler, ass-kickin' band. Y'know, 'cause I think that Night Ranger has fallen prey a bit to the ballad manoeuvres."

"Basically, it was really a knee-jerk manoeuvre," continues The Nuge. "I mean, we went in there and we were all friends; none of us felt we had to develop something. I went in to see if Tommy and Jack excited me. Tommy probably went in to see if Jack and Ted excited him. Jack went in to see if Ted and Tommy excited him, and drummer Michael Cartellone would've kicked all our asses anyhow. So it was really one of those historical garage band, show-me-your-shit-mister kind of things where if it wouldn't have been exciting, we'd have walked out of there just as fast as you could blink."

Asked how he differs as a guitar player from Tommy Shaw, Ted figures, "It differs greatly. Number one, he's one of the best slide players I've ever heard and I can't wait to pick up on some of that. I want to play slide real bad. Tommy Shaw is incredibly articulate on his guitar because he does have a vision. He has a clear vision of a rhythm and blues structure based on honky-tonk and boogie-woogie, just like my stuff is, but he is a bit more reserved player than I am. I'm the Whackmaster. I just go for it when I play the guitar. It's, 'Sorry, the bridge is up, nobody else is invited, this is Gonzo land.' I really lose my mind when I start playing my guitar. Where I think Tommy has more control over himself; at times I wish I did."

"Ted is just as crazy and insane as he's always been," laughs Jack, looking back. "I mean, Ted has been the head of Ted Nugent world for more years than I can care to comment on. I love Ted because Ted says what's on his mind. He doesn't try to be politically correct, he doesn't try to make everybody like him. He doesn't care. There's a lot to say for that. Tommy, I've known him for 20 years, and he's a great guy (laughs). He's a wonderful, fun guy. Tommy is a real true artist. I mean, Tommy is really that artiste, you know what I mean? I love people that... and I think sometimes he gets overloaded and I think between the two of us, we make one hell of an artist (laughs)."

Pure hair metal this band was (geez, and no, not even remotely non-Caucasian), as is evidenced by hit power ballad *High Enough*, plus the fact that a big shot producer was part of the fold to spend money and hopefully add his own stamp—with both records, that cliché position was filled by Ron Nevison.

"Well, Ron was great," continues Jack. "Ron was... the Damn Yankees. You know, a lot of people had issues with Ron Nevison because he was sort of like, Sir Ron from Beverly Hills. He was very sort of opinionated and very pompous but he needed to be that way. Ron was an incredible talent and with Damn Yankees, Ron, it was really fun working with him, because he can do anything. I mean, anything he asked Tommy and I, we would do it immediately and it would be done in an hour and a half. It didn't take four hours. Ron, I think, really appreciated that. So I never, ever had an issue like other people had with Ron. I know that one time I was talking to Mark Andes who played bass with Heart. We were halfway through the first Damn Yankees record and we ran into him in A&M Studios in LA. He said to me, 'Oh, you're working with Ron. Oh boy.' I said, 'What do you mean, oh boy?' And he says, 'Man, just you wait.' I go, 'What are you talking about?' He goes, 'Just you wait. Wait until you do your bass parts and you'll see what I'm talking about.' I looked at Tommy and Tommy looked at me and I said, 'I already did my bass parts and it went perfect,' you know what I mean? He looked at me and said, 'Oh,' and then walked away (laughs)."

"Maybe it was just individuals. You know, so many people said certain things about Ron. He did Kiss, I think he did Ozzy, then he did, you know, the Yanks. I mean Ron was on fire, and the guy did Led Zeppelin *Physical Graffiti* and he did *Quadrophenia*, all the Bad Company records, all the Babys records. I mean, I bow down at the altar of Ron Nevison; that guy is so talented."

And working with Ted? "Well, yeah, the reason everybody gets along with Ted is because Ted's never around. So it's really easy to get along with him. I mean, here's how it worked with Ted. It's like, okay, Ted, we need… You know, Tommy and I were there the whole time with Damn Yankees. Ted was like, okay, we need you this week to record. So he says, 'Okay, I'll be in that week.' What he would do is, that week meant he was flying in late Monday night and he would be ready to play Tuesday and he would leave sometime Thursday afternoon and that was Ted being there for a week. So he just went in and did his solos with Nevison and played his guitars. Ted is so on top of his game that you know, when he had to lay down the rhythms, they were perfect. When he had to lay down his solos, he just played a bunch of solos and put it all together, I mean, it was no problem. So no. When Nevison did a Night Ranger record, it was the same thing; it was very easy."

"It just wasn't who we were," says Jack, concerning *Bravo*, the legendary shelved third Damn Yankees album (a song from which Ted played for me on acoustic guitar backstage one day in Hamilton, Ontario!). "I mean, it was the wrong producer, it was the wrong time, it just wasn't right. There were too many things piled up against us and that's why we put a spike in it. There were a lot of good songs and over the years (laughs), those songs have appeared on a Styx record—*Cyclorama* had a song on there, *Yes I Can*, and

I think Ted used *Damned If You Do*, one of the riffs, on *Craveman* and I used one of the songs, *Shine On*, on my solo record. So the songs are popping up, you know? (laughs). Because a good song is a good song and every once in awhile another one of them pops up somewhere. But it just wasn't us; it wasn't Damned Yankees."

Explains Tommy about *Yes I Can*, from these 1999 sessions, "We recorded a version of that on the 'never ain't nobody ever gonna hear this album' Damn Yankees' third piece of shit album. Because it was really an awful album. Except for the music is good. The band was great, the music was good—the album was just dreadful. The reason the album was no good was because none of us were available. We tried doing it through a producer, but it turned out the producer wasn't a Damn Yankees fan. We found that out too late in the game. It just suffered because we weren't all there going, 'Yeah, no, yeah, no, yeah, that's great, no, don't do that.' We had somebody else doing that, that really shouldn't have been doing that, which is our own fault. But we loved the song *Yes I Can* and everybody was like, 'Yeah, get that song on a record.' Then Glen Burtnick wrote that instrumental part to it and that made it our own. In comparison to the original, instrumentally, quite a bit different; melodically, it's pretty straight down the pipe."

Out on tour, with the likes of Bad Company, Poison and Jackyl, the band threw in a little Styx (*Renegade*) and Night Ranger (*(You Can Still) Rock In America*), with the obligatory Ted selections being *Free For All* and *Cat Scratch Fever*. All through this time, Ted was getting more political (and by '93, sporting the longest, bushiest beard of his career!), the band's songs serving as patriotic anthems during a time in American history dominated by the Gulf War. As well, Ted appeared on Rock The Vote, in opposition, of course, to Bill Clinton and the Democrats.

Having run its course, Tommy Shaw and Jack Blades teamed up for a low-key project under the moniker Shaw Blades, leaving Ted to run off and make another solo album, to be called *Spirit Of The Wild*. Even during the career of Damn Yankees Ted was doing solo dates, most significant feature of that being his continued work with Derek St. Holmes, plus the working up of *Fred Bear*, a tribute to one of Ted's hunting mentors and soon to be on his next record, the pounding mid-paced jam metal of *Motor City Bad Boys*, a track unreleased to this day. Leading up to the *Spirit Of The Wild* sessions, there was also a bass guitar-dominated instrumental called *Sunrize* which Ted talked about going on his next record for sure and which didn't happen, as well as one called *I Wanna Go Hunting*, which turned out to be one of Ted's usual happy-go-lucky hard rocking boogie metal tunes, sort of punk rock meets southern rock. Both of the latter, plus *Fred Bear*, would emerge on Ted's bizarre and low-key *Hunt Music* concept album independently issued in 2004.

Spirit Of The Wild was generated through Ted's continuing contract with Atlantic, in May of 1995 (Damn Yankees were on Warner Bros. as well). Surely the success of Damn Yankees gave hope that the record would matter, as did the release of a 34 track Ted Nugent box set called *Out Of Control*. Issued by Epic/Legacy in June of 1993, the track list logically for the most part celebrated the glory years, although a nod to the Amboy Dukes was there, along with a token track from the barren Atlantic years, namely *Little Miss Dangerous*. Best bits for the super-fan however would be the inclusion of debut-era rarity *Magic Party*, a grinding, garage style alternative version of *Street Rats* with Derek singing, plus a top-notch classic era Ted rocker called *Walking Tall*, an anthem that represents one of the rare times the southern rock Ted and the metal Ted merged like Blackfoot on a tear.

"We hooked up in '87 and did a tour that went really well," explains St. Holmes, offering some of the ramp-up to the reunion with Ted. "By the end of '88, the band was sounding really, really good. We did the huge Kiss tour from '87-'88. Just as we were getting ready to do a new album and tour in '89, Ted's mother died, and that was pretty devastating to all of us. It slowed everything to a screeching halt. Just as he worked himself out of the sadness and depression, he was offered this project called Damn Yankees. So he completely changed directions and gears and started going with Tommy Shaw and Jack Blades, which became Damn Yankees. It was a good move for him, but who knows what might have been if that hadn't happened? I'd see him every New Year's Eve. I'd go up and play with him in Detroit."

The perennial track from *Spirit Of The Wild* is of course *Fred Bear*, a huge fave of the Nuge himself, and one that he almost always plays live. "Yes, there have been times that I can't sing it. I have to say, 'Nuge, hold it back and sing that damn song, would ya?' It is very emotional. It is about a man that I loved, who died right when my mom died. The song represents the loss of my mom, my dad and my friend, Fred Bear. I feel the pain and loss of millions of people that have latched onto that song. There are a bunch of states that have never played that song on the radio, but even when we play that song in those states, there are a bunch of people singing along to every word of that song, who are teary-eyed because everybody has a Fred Bear. The music is so uplifting and it is a positive memory and positive salute to my friend, Fred Bear and my mom and dad and to everyone's Fred Bear in their life. It is a positive force. One of my biggest battles in life is to discipline myself to not allow the lyrics to own me, but for me to own the lyrics."

From a production standpoint, *Spirit Of The Wild* sounded good and there's the odd snarling rocker on there, such as *Primitive Man*, *Just Do It Like This* and the Damn Yankees-like *Wrong Side Of Town*. But much of the rest was variously light in the loafers, jokey, hummable, basically humourous. *Tooth, Fang & Claw*, *Fred Bear*, *Lovejacker*, *Hot Or Cold*, *Kiss My Ass*, *Spirit Of The Wild*... all variations of the above, sorta of happy, bluesy, laid-back, a l'il southern rocking... you can hear that Stones influence, for sure, that Ted brings up to put a positive spin on these sorts of "miniature" songs.

"We got together to do *Spirit Of The Wild*," continues Derek. "I co-wrote eight of the 12 songs. We did all that, put the album out and it did nothing. It stiffed because Ted insisted on releasing his single first, called *Kiss My Ass*. That was fine for a live song, but not to put out as a single. MTV or VH1 wouldn't touch it. He wouldn't just play it safe and put out a regular song. But that was the demise of that album. Sometimes Ted is his own worst enemy. But he's getting smarter as he gets older."

"Hell, *Lovejacker* alone is worth the price of admission!" Ted told me back in '08, in defence of the record. "The mighty *Fred Bear* has no equal when performed in Missouri and Wisconsin where it has dominated radio requests since someone snuck the song onto rock stations in those states way back in 1990."

In conversation with Jeb Wright... "If you listen to *Lovejacker*–what a lick that is. I don't even know where that lick came from. I am driven way beyond musicality. I don't know why it works but it works. It is basically a bastardized horn section played on guitar. I am unlimited on my approach on the guitar."

As for the surprise return of Derek on vocals, this time on an actual album... "Ted called me up for *Spirit Of The Wild* and I knew he would not get the original guys back together so I wanted a hand in who we got. He picked the bass player. He picked a guy that I would not have picked. I picked Denny Carmassi because we played together in St. Paradise. You remember the song *Lovejacker*? That could have been the next single for Ted and Ted knew it but he could not handle having another single with Derek St. Holmes as the singer because then he would have to deal with Derek St. Holmes."

"Again, it's about dollars; it's about tour success," said Derek, speaking with Fuse. "We went out and toured *Spirit Of The Wild*, but not with the same band that we recorded it with. It was cutting costs. If you go out to play golf and you've got four killer players on your team and just when the biggest tournament comes up you figure, 'Well gosh, we can save a couple hundred bucks if we just take out this Joe Schmo as a third guy. We'll play the tournament and we'll win it;' well you're not gonna win it. So we didn't use Denny Carmassi who was the drummer from Heart who did the album. We used some young brand new kid. The enthusiasm just wasn't there."

Asked why Ted would keep shunting Derek aside and trying different— and lesser—singers, Derek throws up his hands. "It's crazy. I tell ya, two people that I respect have come up and told me the same doggone thing. One of them is Gene Simmons and one is Steven Tyler. They have both come up to me, taken me aside and said, 'Derek, I don't know why the guy can't figure out you're his singer and he's your guitar player. You guys made the best music he's ever done. Why he can't continue that, I have no idea.' Especially Tyler—it blows his mind that Ted is as dumb as he is. He can't figure. I said, 'Well I don't know. I can't figure it.' Those guys are smart. Look where they are. Look at how those guys have pulled it together. You think there's still some fighting going on and turmoil? Absolutely, but at the end of the day they go, 'Now wait a minute. This fighting and bickering can't go past this point anymore, because this deal is working.' I talk to Brad probably once a month. He has said, 'Sometimes I just go through the motions but at the end of the day I am making all that money, and pretty soon I'm gonna retire. We're still doing it.' I said, 'God bless ya. You're doing the right thing.' I think we might do another record. Listen to me—record! We might do another CD. He's got all these songs ready to go. We talked about it. We'll probably get the same Whitford/St. Holmes lineup."

It would be a long seven years before Ted would return with a new batch of songs, but when he did, boy all the doubts and mis-steps... they'd become obliterated in a frenzied electric storm. Not many of these codgers win back the respect they once sweat blood to achieve, but Deadly Tedly would get all of it back and more come the dastardly duo of delicious rock platters known as *Craveman* And *Love Grenade*. Hyperbole? Ridiculousness? Wishful thinking? Play them loud an' proud start to finish and get back to me...

Epic-logue 2: Eagle Spits Fire

Post-*Spirit Of The Wild*, Ted continued to tour, hunt, talk guns, freedom, all that stuff, writing, demonstrating the energy of ten men, now he's in Michigan, now he's set up his survival camp in Waco... but there were no new records forthcoming, marking the biggest gap between Gonzos since '67.

But then there he was with a manic historical live spread, *Live At Hammersmith '79*, issued in the spring of '97, followed by more of a deal, *Full Bluntal Nugity*, four years hence, June 5th of 2001, Deadly Tedly doing the dirty dog for a modest mid-sized label called Spitfire, Ted most definitely still spitting fire.

"Well Martin, there is nothing in the realm of little that can begin to describe it," chuckles Ted, asked if he could tell me a "little" about this new powered proposal for Ted as torrid trio. "Basically, I can hardly stand myself so God knows what the paying customer must be going through. The fact that I have Tommy Aldridge on the drums, who is without question the world's greatest living drummer and Marco Mendoza on the bass guitar, whose name might not be known. But there is no question that Marco Mendoza is the world class virtuoso bassist that Tommy is a drummer. To be surrounded by these kind of... you know, I'll let you know what planet they are from when I find out. These guys are so dedicated, so heart and soul, so dedicated to their musical vision and when they apply that musical vision to my musical vision, white people shit blood, which is my goal. Just a second. There's a cat climbing on my wife's computer. I've got the answer on my right hip. Anyway, the intensity, Martin, when you hear it. I'm sorry, there is nothing that will prepare you for it."

"*Double Live Gonzo!* pretty much set the benchmark for over-the-top intense energized rhythm and blues from semi-Caucasian idiots and this new one, it kills *Double Live Gonzo!*. The fact that we had done hundreds and hundreds and hundreds of concerts together and culminating in all places at a private campfire in Detroit with 35,000 of my closest friends, my closest hunting buddies, the unified energy level is just stupefying. Yes, it's mostly classic Nugent stuff that I've played a gazillion times but I'm a real lucky fuck in that I escape the sonic bombast naked dance every year, all my life, and put down the flame-throwing guitar and I pick up a bow and arrow and I vanish and become silent, peaceful, spiritual, solitary and immobilized— that's really what my bowhunting represents. Although I climb mountains and breaststroke beaver ponds, I nevertheless shut down, shut up and vanish. So when it is time to play the guitar—literally at the age of 52, it's as if I'm 9-year-old Ted grabbing the guitar in the garage, 1958—it's rebirth every year because there's nothing like sonic bombast and feedbacked guitars and illegally pummeling rhythms to satisfy the cravings of a man who has been quiet and sitting still for four months. You know what I'm saying?"

"So when you sleep good, you're energized and my hunting is basically a battery-recharging orgy," continues Ted, clearly, once again, on a roll. "So what we've got here on record is a guy who, every year my hunting season gets longer, more intense, but intense in opposite manifestations, i.e. silence. So after all those months of solitary immobilized silence, I want to rip people's heads clean off and poop down their neck! Tommy and Marco love that attitude and love that energy and love that outrage and so they absolutely invest every ounce of piss, vinegar, heart and soul and blood and guts into it and we recorded it, we actually captured it. I could hardly function in the studio mixing this stuff because number one, there are no overdubs, no repairs, no alterations. We merely balanced the instrumentation for sheer outrage. It's a race and we all crossed the finish line neck-and-neck, photo finish. I am just so beside myself and enjoying my company, that I captured this outrage. There is one new song called *Clusterfuck*; it's a love song, spelled *Klstrphk*, a military term for, 'Damn it, we're going to get this right one of these days.' It's just a magic moment for me and my trusty Gibson guitar."

As for a set list and now track list, fortunately, the album isn't full up with only the obvious. "Well, we do some of the master-blasters, *Cat Scratch Fever* and *Yank Me Crank Me* and *Hey Baby* and *Stranglehold* and *Great*

White Buffalo, *Fred Bear* acoustic, which is just ridiculous; it's so intense, the way the acoustic guitar was meant to be. No wonder the guy from the Mamas And Papas died. He probably heard this, no offence of course. It just goes on and on. There's a version of *Motor City Madhouse* that I don't think should be legal to play in a vehicle while the motor's running. It's just ridiculous. I listen to it and I go, 'Oh my God! What's that!? Who does he think he is!?' I mean, I've just never heard anything like it. *Cat Scratch Fever* and *Stranglehold*... when you hear the performances of both of those, on this new *Full Bluntal Nugity*, the fire has not waned once spit. I just get... it's just hysterical."

"The fact that this new *Full Bluntal Nugity* is a live record, I have to tell you what transpired that night," continues Ted. "My manager Doug Banker, who I've worked with now for over 20 years, is also a musical genius and a creative master of understanding the essentiality of spontaneity. If you're not just letting it rip from your guts with no inhibitions and no consideration for the outcome, you're not really playing rock 'n' roll. Here's the beauty of it. My bloodbrother manager Doug Banker, set up a state-of-the-art digital recording mobile unit for our New Year's Eve Ted Nugent Whiplash Bash No.13, in the Motor City and recorded us without telling us. How beautiful is that? What it means is that we just went for the jugular and sucked blood. It was absolutely over-the-top. We didn't fix or edit or overdub anything. The spontaneity is miraculous. That recording stands alone because I didn't know I was recording! How beautiful is that?!"

"But I think, as I'm finishing up some of the basic tracks for my next studio recording, that will be out on Spitfire this next winter, I don't really see anything different. I think what I've learned is that there is a retro demand when you acknowledge honestly what makes the best record. I could reiterate with what Joe Perry and Steven Tyler just said recently that the name of the game is just shut up and do it. I learned from—or at least was reassured—by people like Sting who says there is just way too much technical preparation and technical scrutiny, when in fact some of our favourite records of all time were made before any of this modern technology was available. They not only stand up today but they kill most of the stuff out today. So we're going for the grunt factor, we're going for the hump factor, we're going for the bash clang boom crunch explosion that makes my music the best there is and just get the heart and soul greasy performances. That's the name of the game. So if you spend too much time on technicalities and scrutinizing the procedure on which you record, the songs start to lose their erect fibre. I'm leaving the technology to the technicians, but they better stay at my pace, because I want it spontaneous. What I've heard from Joe and Steven—because I'm collaborating with them on new songs for my next record—that every guitar solo and every vocal on their new album was all first runs and that's how you get the spontaneity. Those two guys are involved plus Kid Rock, Sheryl Crow, Shelby Lynne, James Hetfield and Sammy Hagar; I mean just some of the greatest collaborators... it's like a creative whitewater juice flow orgy, man, I'm having the time of my life. If it was the campfire, we'd all have tankers of rocket fuel just poured on us and you'd see the marshmallows cooking for a half mile. I certainly expect to be on Kid Rock's next record and I wouldn't be surprised if the energy of the Ted Nugent Sheryl Crow collaboration doesn't spawn some stuff from both camps. That Shelby Lynne's a bitch— she needs me. I think she's Ted Nugent with a pussy (laughs)."

As amusing as that is, once *Craveman* would go into production, these collaborations wouldn't be there. Nor would Tommy Aldridge, who would be replaced by up and coming Detroit firecracker Tommy Clufetos.

"I suppose I can share some of them," said Ted, with respect to songs planned for the record. "I've got one song that's an instrumental called *Earthtones* and one of my favourite songs ever written called *Crave*. I've got another song that pretty much sums up my life, *I Won't Go Away* and I've got a beautiful love song called *You Can't Be What You Eat Or I'd Be Your Daughter*."

This last one didn't happen, or perhaps the title got changed, but that was neither here nor there, as Ted put aside the new record for a spell and did some more road work. In what had become modus operandi for Camp Nuge, Ted was rocking big stages as part of packages with other legendary classic rock acts, right about now, those co-conspirators being Purple and Skynyrd.

"With Deep Purple and Skynyrd, time is restricted because there are three of us and I'm never afraid to open the show," noted Ted, slightly competitive as usual. "People say well, you should be the headliner; well guess what? When it's all said and done I think I am the headliner; it doesn't matter what time I go on (laughs). I'm going to deliver various new licks and play as many of my classics as I can. I wouldn't doubt if my set list is the *Full Bluntal Nugity* album."

I asked Ted if he figured he'd be doing all the vocals on the next record. I mean, I knew that Marco Mendoza could sing, but in totality, we were looking at Ted's first power trio here. "Well, even on this new live album, Derek's vocal on *Hey Baby* is almost impossible, but guess what, Martin, Marco Mendoza's performance of *Hey Baby* is better than most of Derek's! Now Derek, in his finest moment, is untouchable, but that's why Derek is not in my band. There weren't enough finest moments. But Marco's version of *Hey Baby* is just perfect and he will be performing that one on this tour. But, as to the studio album, you know what!? Who knows? I bet I'm going to do a double vocal with Kid Rock and I expect on this one song called *Naked*, I will do a collaborative vocal with Sheryl Crow. I bet the song that James Hetfield and I are writing, I bet we'll sing that together. It's quite possible the way that Sheryl and Shelby Lynne sing together, I'm writing a song that I would like to just hear them sing. So that's always a possibility."

At least Ted does concede that the Aerosmith cameo wasn't exactly a done deal. "I think they're gonna. I think they're going to at least sing the chorus with me. Joe and I will probably do a double guitar line."

Count this fan perfectly satisfied that none of that bells-and-whistles stuff is present on *Craveman*. If the record sucked, well, maybe it would have been a nice diversion. But fact is, *Craveman*, issued 24th September 2002, would be a white-hot corker of a record, Ted making good on his fire-spitting live shows in the handful of years leading up to it by putting up without shutting up, completing the circuit: icon status methodically, relentlessly intensified and solidified, first doe to the towering terrific-ness of his recent trio-ness, but now he had a studio album that... stay with me, people, objectively, in a blind taste test, might have been the nest of his whole damn Gonzoid career.

Like the equally molten *Love Grenade* which we'll talk about later, granted, fully a third of the album has its pants down, matching, frankly, all of the others for less than stellar material–one third at most on the best records, two-thirds or even over two-thirds on the worst of them. But man, even the lesser tracks here—and it's always the jokey ones—are actually pretty damn locked down, disciplined, funky yet heavy, eventful. These would be *Cum N Gitya Sum-O-This*, *Pussywhipped* (actually a cool, punky stomper of a track), *Sexpot* and *My Baby Likes My Butter On Her Gritz*. Probably least of value would be *Earthtones*, merely because it's a mid-rock instrumental, and *Wang Dang Doodle*, which is more like a waste, a reconstitution of *Wang Dang Sweet Poontang* but not even a real song.

The boulderising balance is what makes *Craveman* arguably Ted's most vicious delicious album ever. *Klstrphnky* kicks it off with near thrash instrumental intensity before the new tri-partite Ted collapses into *Crave*, six guns blazing, unarguably demonstrative of the most electric and sonically powerful production job ever on a Ted spread. Next up is *Rawdogs & Warhogs*, maybe Ted's most carnal and metallic track ever in his life up to this point. A couple of solid rockers later in *Damned If Ya Do* and the slinky Marco-sung and bass-flung *At Home There* and impossibly, Ted is located at an even more metal-than-though place, *Change My Sex* featuring rhythm section on laser-stun while Ted riffs like his rhino depends on it. *I Won't Go Away* fills up the album with additional killer hard rock and gorgeous hard-ass guitar tones an' textures, while *Goin' Down Hard* offers more of the same heavy-for-Ted metal, each with Ted singing his balls off, putting in a vocal clinic bolstered by his various credos, widening arcs back to his personal philosophies, which lead and bleed throughout the record, mischievous growl and eye-wink included.

"I'm really proud of that album," muses consummate bass virtuoso, showman, singer, writer and post-Ted journeyman Marco Mendoza, who, let's face it, must have been a huge part of bringing Ted up to the quality levels The Nuge was now attacking up into the 2000s. "It's unfortunate that not a lot of people know about it, but I think *Craveman...* that came at the peak when I'd been working with Ted for three or four years, touring a lot. Tommy Aldridge gave me the call, actually—he brought me into the mix with Ted Nugent. He was slotted to support Kiss on that huge tour, '99, 2000. Tommy had some reservations about the existing bass player and he had prior commitments. I got a call, came in and again, you know, I got my hands on everything Ted Nugent and adapted some of the style, definitely the pick finger and did my homework."

Ted was about to get his first look in a long, long time at a potential co-worker that could be truly transformational to Ted's music. "Well, I came in, had the opportunity to meet Ted. He's checking this guy out, he's got tattoos, he's got piercings, he says, 'I don't know.' Then I pulled out this 1914 Luger that my dad had given me (laughs) and that was it. He goes, 'You're in, man.' So yeah, we've been working for a while, and let's just say that Ted had kind of given up on recording music and all that. But then he got inspired, you know?"

"Tommy and I— and this is Tommy Clufetos—we were laying it down," continues Marco. Despite Ted's swearing up and down to the contrary, there hadn't been that many rhythm sections that would be able to lay it down like these two cats—as evidenced by all the legends who have hired Marco and Tommy since. "He's so strong as a drummer. He and I had been working on some of these parts and were laying it down. He kinda like... he started getting inspired, man. He would pick up his guitar backstage and play with us, which was unheard of, with Ted. So we started to get these songs, started writing and then there were some songs that Derek St. Holmes had recorded. So I enjoyed the whole thing; the whole Ted Nugent run was great. To me, he represents rock 'n' roll to the max. For me, one way, I think he's misunderstood. He's right wing, whatever you want to say about him, but when you know him one-on-one, man, he's definitely a power to be dealt with in every way."

"He's a great human being. I've never been... to that point, I had never been treated that good. Ted really, there's a lot of mutual respect there and he kinda pushes you. Because he's so strong. Performance-wise, he's on it, he's just on, man. You go, you gotta be there. So yeah, we all got inspired, we started writing some stuff backstage, and we went into a studio, and *Craveman* came out. You know, it's unfortunate that the industry is what it is. It just didn't have the exposure that it deserved. But we started playing the songs live on stage and they were really well received. I had a blast with Ted. *Craveman* came around, and there was obviously *Full Bluntal Nugity*, the live album and the DVD—they're great, man; they're really well-made. So yeah, proud to be part of that, absolutely.

Recently, he actually called me. I'm just mentioning, he called me; his bass player, Greg Smith, got tied up in Europe, overbooked himself. Ted wanted to do some shows and he called, no rehearsing, no nothing, did my homework, showed up, did five shows and I had a blast, man. But that's how it is, given how great Ted is live, full-drive, forward, hitting hard—that's how he is. It was fun doing it, definitely."

Further on how Ted drove the band to excel live, Marco says, "He would talk to me and he would say, 'Marco, 100% is not enough. Think about it, man. 150. That's what I've got and that's what I'm bringing to it. You better be there–watch me.' Ted kind of adopted this, you know, the Mitch Ryder thing, James Brown thing, where he likes to direct the band on stage. So, yeah, little things like that. Which makes for a great performance, definitely when you're on a huge stage. Let's just say that he would kind of direct me, look at me, 'Are you following me?' kind of like the James Brown/Mitch Ryder thing. He was a big fan of that."

Pressed for more of an indication of how working with this new generation (two actually: Marco could be said to be from a whole previous generation to that of Clufetos), spurred Ted forward toward making such a kick-ass album, Mendoza figures, "It's hard to tell with Ted, man. Ted's got like frickin' 50 things cooking at any given moment. He's really involved. He doesn't believe in wasting any time. In that way he inspires me. He'll wake up in the morning, find something to do, very productive, write something. In that way he's misconstrued; he's so driven. To most people— and I'll include myself in that—I'm really passive, man. A couple hours, wake up, have my coffee and think about what I want to do. But he goes. But I think, yeah, when he found himself with cats who love to play music, yeah, a lot of us are jaded, man. You get to that point. Tommy and I had been doing so much work, that we were excited about the whole thing and let's just say that we pushed a couple of buttons, you know? Tommy, when he gets on stage, man, he's a frickin' machine. He just goes. Yeah, we kind of inspired him to grab his guitar backstage and his playing improved lots. That guy has a unique sound, man. He's got fire. From time to time, he relaxes like all of us, but he grabbed his guitar and started working. Unfortunately, Tommy Aldridge had an injury that had to get taken care of and we ended up with Tommy Clufetos, who's now working with Ozzy Osbourne. But the album *Craveman*, every so often I would play a couple of tracks and it's really, really good. The tracks—they can stand on their own, at any given moment."

As to getting in on the writing credits for *Earthtones* and *My Baby Likes My Butter On Her Gritz*, Marco says, "Well, backstage, you start grooving and getting some ideas out and if he likes them, you bounce them around. He develops them and starts writing lyrics and we throw it into the pot and surprisingly enough, because we had so many tracks, we went to the studio. I think we had 20 or something. He really liked those and that just shows, to me, the other side of Ted, that he really appreciated me being part of the mix, so he was including me on the writing and publishing and all that. That's what he does when he digs you, man—you work for him, he'll reciprocate. That's what it was. But again, he always writes. Everybody writes. We're always writing little ideas here and there, sketches and when the time comes to go into the studio, that's when you develop ideas."

"One thing I learned—believe it or not—is that a lot of those tracks are done by Ted," says Marco, asked about boning up on the bass parts within the catalogue classics. "Like, *Stranglehold* was recorded by Ted and not a lot of people know that. A different style. Having come from the southern rock thing, man, that influenced and inspired me. Berry Oakley, Allman Brothers, Grand Funk Railroad, Ted Nugent, Lynyrd Skynyrd, Leon Wilkeson, who I had the pleasure of meeting when Ted was supporting Lynyrd Skynyrd; it's unfortunate he's no longer with us. But all those guys had a different style of playing. But you listen, you play along, and then it becomes time for you to own those tracks."

At this point, Ted stayed semi-in touch with the guys from the classic Ted Nugent lineup, seeing them on and off. But it is also known that Derek, Cliff and Rob had reached out to him to whip a gig together, but that Ted essentially blew them off. Ted's comment on the situation: "They actually called and asked my permission. I told them that they didn't need my fucking permission. Here is a point: I love them all madly and I always salute them. They are perfect examples of what I have been blessed with. Those records mean what they mean because of Derek, Rob and Cliff—there is no question about it. However, a point to ponder, they quit because I was 'holding them back.' If I was holding them back then once I let them out of my grip, wouldn't they have accelerated beyond me? Maybe you can point to anything that any of them have done. They do nothing. I set attendance records in 2007 at the Oregon State Fair, the Alaska State Fair and the Washington State Fair. I set attendance records at the Ribfest in Chicago – 42,000 people."

So had Ted basically ruled out any chance of a reunion? "I would love to but it would be all nostalgia. We have looked into it and there is not a promoter in this country that puts one dime of value on Derek, Rob and Cliff doing anything with me. We have asked for years and been told that it doesn't mean anything. Here is another reality—you can tell that I am still as energized as a fucking teenager. Those guys grew up. I have grown up but I didn't let the music mellow. When you grow up you tend to have your music mellow but I don't want my music to mellow. If you play mellow then you can't be in my fucking band. I have a musical responsibility. My music deserves animals on drums, guitar and bass. I talk to Derek all the time. He is one of the greatest vocalist and guitarists that has ever lived. He came up last year and we played *Hey Baby*, *Stranglehold*, *Motor City Madhouse* and *Cat Scratch Fever* and it was awesome and the place went wild. But you know what? It didn't pay anything extra. I loved having him there and the people loved it but the promoter doesn't care. It is a big problem."

"Fifty fucking years later I am still travelling with a full headline production. I have a road manager, stage manager, sound man and lights. I have a professional headlining machine on the road with buses and trucks but I am not making the money that Aerosmith makes. I am working frantically to pay for all this world class talent I have around me. I still make unbelievable money but before we play the first note on the first stage it costs me over $300,000 just to fucking rehearse and get everything ready to go. Quite honestly, if you are coming on the Ted Nugent team then your presence needs to bring an income. I am not going out for charity. "

"Derek and I have been talking a lot lately about getting together and writing some songs. I would love to have him sing on my next record. He is busy and I am busy and I wish all of them nothing but the best. Rob came to a show but he didn't get up and play. I have not seen him play in 25 years. My music is just too sacred to just experiment with a guy I have not seen in a long time. Derek got up and jammed. I have not seen Cliff in years. They are good men and they are talented but I don't think they are quite the animals that my music deserves. You have to put a crowbar in your teeth and play *Wango Tango*. If you don't bite that crowbar in half then you are not my musician."

Mused a frustrated Derek at the time, "If we could play and it would be financially smart, then we would do it. Also, if anyone wants to pay us just to get back with each other and play again then we would do that as well. They are like brothers to me. We lived together for a long time and we did a lot of growing up together in our 20s. When we got back together we just picked up where we left off. My son is 19 and he asks me all the time, 'What is his deal? If you guys got back together and did one tour then we would be set for life.' (laughs). I am sure that means I could buy him some stuff—that is how a 19-year-old thinks. He asked me, 'Does he not get it? That guy can't sing as good as you. What is he doing?' I tell him that it is what it is. If Ted was smart enough to get Rob, Cliff and myself in a rehearsal space, then he would have a million-selling album on his hands but he is too selfish and egoistical. I am not sure it is either one of those words but I just can't describe it. Some people are chronically cheap and he is one of them. But if he sees a hunting safari for $7200 then he is ready to leave right now. But, hypothetically speaking, if he could spend $5000 to put his career back on track, he won't do that. I am just making up numbers to make a point. If you can plant the seed and make him think that it is his idea then it usually comes to fruition. It is just the way he is."

"Actually I think that would be good for Ted, because Ted really does need some material," figures Rob. "He writes good stuff and the stuff that he did with Damn Yankees was really good, but the tough part is, he can't stay in a band environment very long. Like he would come to town and he would have different guys with him now. Even with Damn Yankees, that was a great band, talented people and they did two albums and they dispersed. So Ted is a good guy, but he is a tough personality to be in a band with. It's too bad we can't all get together, because there is still some magic there. When Derek,

Cliff and I got together... I have a feeling we will, because we're all still alive and healthy. I went to see Ted in Hollywood this summer and it was the first time I saw him in 30 years. I felt bad because he really does have a hard time hearing out of one ear. It's really affected his hearing. But he didn't have much time to talk. We were at the show... like anything else, you're on the road and you get to see him for 15, 20 minutes backstage, then he was on his way. He always likes to see me. Gave me a big hug and everything. The hard part is sitting out in the audience listening to all the bass lines (laughs). Wait a minute, that's not how it's played!"

Noted Cliff on the situation, "Well, this guy I am doing this nonprofit organization with, Michael Krikorian, we're partners now, back then, Michael thought it would be a good idea to get the old band back together and we will do a video and try get the video company off the ground, at the same time rebooting Ted's career. But Ted really wasn't interested. I can't blame him, really. We're in much better shape and after a couple years and a few more years and a few more videos, we're getting ourselves better. But back then we were bush league."

"Frankly, I don't think Ted wants to work with anybody," continues Cliff. "I don't think it has anything to do with relations or patching up. Ted and I probably had the fiercest relationship, because I sued him quite aggressively after I left the band. He owed me a lot of money, which I didn't collect much of. So we went through the justice system like a couple or three times. The last time I met Ted, it was a buyout deal. I said, 'You know Ted, I'm wasting too much money on attorneys and so are you; it's not really worth it anymore. There's no money there; give me a check for 25 grand, we'll shake hands and I'll go away.' Which is exactly what we did. So we left friends. See the thing is, Ted Nugent, only wants to be there on his own on stage. For Ted Nugent, the bass player and the drummer are just stage props. They're only there because people expect them to be there. If he could be on stage all on his own... and I don't think he really cares. I don't think he necessarily cares about trying to put the old band back together or do a reunion tour. You know, Ted is only 25% a musician—he's 75% a professional hunter and naturalist. So unlike a lot of people in this business, he's got bigger fish to fry. I mean, the average guy of Ted's age, who's been through what Ted has been through, maybe on a lower level, probably has nothing else but his music and his guitar. That's simply not true with Ted and it never was. There was never this total dedication to this one thing. This is one of the things I do. The other thing I do is like rebuilding engines in my four-wheel drive and the other thing I like to do is to go and be the great white hunter. Musicians don't tend to have that many interests. It tends to just be music and that's it. So I don't think Ted even really thinks about it. I think if someone came to Ted and said, 'Hey Ted, we'll give you a million dollars to put the old band back together and do one last tour,' I'm sure he would say hell yeah. But at this point, it's much more of a financial issue than it is any other kind of issue. I haven't got a problem with it at all. I mean, I completely disagree with his political leanings on that front, but Derek and Ted get along well, and Rob and Derek and Ted get along well and we've been through rough times. But at this point, we're all in our late 50s. You've got to bury the hatchet some time (laughs). I mean, I think we could do a tour and get along fine, but I just don't see the necessity. I don't think anybody really wants Ted Nugent. I think it's just one of those things he's done."

"He's the kind of guy who makes more enemies than friends," muses Cliff. "Maybe it's his political stance. There are always people out to get him. There are a lot of people out there who hate Ted Nugent's guts. I mean, PETA would like to have him tarred and feathered and run out of town on a rail. All those sorts of organizations are dogging him all the time. Ted is a big hunter and a real right-winger. Well, I'm left of the New York Times, and I've been a vegetarian since I was 17. So there's a little bit of a disconnect there between us. But I respected him and he respected me for it, so was never a problem. Rob became one too. I don't remember exactly when, but it wasn't back on the road in those days."

Five long years would roll on before Ted—and fully triumphant without Derek—would see it in his soul to whip together another studio album. And on 4th September 2007, there it was, *Love Grenade*, not quite the stiff proposition that *Craveman* was, simply due to the math of a greater emphasis on the comedic.

But first there were months-in-advance warnings from longtime bud Jack Blades, who would wind up producing the album, as well as providing bass on three tracks. "We're trying to get Ted out of that hunting thing, out of that tree stand and to get some songs together, which he's doing now, which will be really fun. *Craveman* was great; that song *Crave* that Ted and I wrote, at the beginning of that record, that sort of set a bar for what needed to be done. That's the thing—Ted is really in a great space right now, so good stuff will come out of that. Ted will always have a lick in his heart, man. Ted will never abandon music. That's who he is."

Then once the album was done, it was time to talk to Ted himself, who, as usual was almost psychedelically proud of his new baby. But arguably for only the second time in a long time, it might be said that Ted was disseminating extreme praise with which we could all agree.

"Well, take a song like *Love Grenade*—it's a celebration of just defiance and irreverence and just uninhibitedness. Whereas on *Craveman*, the song *Crave* embodied my defiance: 'A simple life I will not have/It doesn't satisfy me/I don't believe in the status quo/It kind of leaves me weak.' Fuck you to standard operating procedures by soulless little emotion-less flat-lining compliant subservient fucks out there. So that's never changed (laughs); that's a great source of joy for my band out there, all of my teammates. So it's a matter of delivery, it's a matter of chord changes and guitar licks, and what *Craveman* represented, hell, what the first damn Amboy Dukes album represented, any album I ever made represented, is an accurate and completely honest musical unleashing of my current state of mind, my current celebration of life, good, bad and ugly. It manifests itself in the spontaneous guitar licks that leap off my fingers and off the fretboard every fucking time I pick it up."

"So, you know, never has there been a moment of contemplation, about, 'Geez, I wonder what music I should make today?' No, no, no, it's geez, I wonder if that girl's sexy. Let me check my penis and see if it's getting stiff. Fuck you! It's going to happen, baby! I think that music, as most good things in life, should be... once one absolutely commits himself to intelligent prioritization in life, intelligent accountability in life, as I've done for 59 years, then you just have an imminent absolute faith in what you do or say is going to be, not only okay, but me. This is what I believe. I don't have to think about the shit. I've been paying attention for a long time. Bo Diddley is still in my hands and even though I'm 59, because I spend half the year absolutely disconnected... well, that's not the right word either, I'm not making music per se. I'm literally in a swamp. I'm in a tree. I'm in a forest. I have a sharp stick. I'm going to kill some dinner. Martin!—I'm the last of the fucking Mohicans! I'm the only guy you'll ever talk to that plants his own fucking firewood and is still alive to harvest it and get heat from it! Are you with me? You're not going to have that conversation with anybody! I'm the only guy who takes care of myself in an absolutist, insisting, militantly mandatory self-sufficiency, rugged individualism, absolute independence."

"And yes, I'm eating some beautiful strawberries right now and some peaches that some fine Oregonian just brought up to me because they love Uncle Ted madly. I didn't plant that peach tree and I didn't harvest it. But in my own way... I did, because I've been performing; I've been an asset to earth. I've been an asset to mankind. I've never taken from mankind. I've put more in than I've ever consumed. I mean, the evidence is irrefutable. But some dipshit hippie so-called journalist fuck wouldn't even understand what I'm talking about... I pray that the sincerity in your voice and the brain that you indicate you have, understands this simplicity of what I do. So, *Craveman* and *Love Grenade*, I think this is a, well, I wouldn't say there's more uppityness in *Love Grenade* than *Craveman*, I'm not so sure. I mean *Craveman* and *Klstrphnky*, get out of here! *I Won't Go Away*, *Pussywhipped*, the song *Crave*, those are great fucking songs. But I happen to think the overall sound and the musicians, the musicality in the instruments and the sounds on *Love Grenade* is superior to *Craveman* and of that I'm very pleased."

Taking stock, Ted is right on the few counts which he chose to get in and distinguish the two records over. First, both albums sound fantastic, but true, *Love Grenade*, produced by Jack Blades, is even brighter and more electrocuted than *Craveman*, produced by Ted and Drew and Chris Peters. Second point, agreement as well, the song are quite interchangeable, given the subject matter and even the performances and singing thereof—all at an A+ level. Third, Ted (half) ascribes more "uppityness" to *Love Grenade*. No idea what he means, but if he means happiness or by extension, goofiness, yes, it's got more wisecracking.

"But it's just another notch in my rifle stock in a great, great hunting exhibition, for quality of life," continues Ted. "I happen to make ferocious rhythm and blues with a hyper-intensity that comes off very rock 'n' roll. Now have you heard the record? Then you know what the fuck I'm talking about. *Aborigine*, what the fuck kind of song is that?! That's a fantastic piece of music. The song *Love Grenade*, and *Girl Scout Cookies*, fuck me! If you can find something sexier than that, call me!"

Does the record perhaps get a little Rush-like conceptual at the gooey center? After all, there's *Geronimo & Me*, *EagleBrother*, *Spirit Of The Buffalo* and *Aborigine*, before a transition back to the scorching metal of *Stand* and *Broadside*, two of the man's grindingest, gruntingest rock onslaughts ever (if there's anyone left breathing after *Still Raising Hell* earlier in the trip).

"You know, it lends itself to that, because my life is a concept. It is the concept of no rules, except decency and goodwill. But no status quo regulations affect me at all. The world is a seat on a bus in Selma and I am a girl named Rosa Parks. I would love to meet the fucking human being that will attempt to tell me I can't put my black ass on that seat. Are you with me? Which, you Canadians… we ought to learn a little something from. Be that as it may, so when you say concept, I mean, *Geronimo & Me*, listen to the fucking lyrics of *Geronimo & Me* and then follow it with *EagleBrother*. Think of the song *Funk U*. Yeah, there's a concept here, the number one concept, let it rip. Play your heart and soul out. When you get Tommy Clufetos on drums, Martin, and Barry Sparks and Jack Blades as your rhythm section, God Almighty just shines on me. What a lucky guitar player I am. So no matter what musical creation I come up with, these guys maximize it. I'm just so blessed. I thank God every day."

Now that Ted has brought it up, Marco Mendoza is a hard act to follow.

"Well, stop and think, Martin. Let's analyse it briefly here. Or comprehensively. Now go ahead and examine every record, every rhythm section. Think who has been our rhythm section. Tommy Aldridge? Denny Carmassi? Cliff Davies? Carmine Appice? Get the fuck out of here. Think about that! All right, Carmine Appice and Tommy Clufetos and Mick Brown, Marco fucking Mendoza, and Barry fuckin' Sparks, Jack Blades, now there's Greg Smith. I can't… I've got quite an imagination, you might have noticed. I can't imagine in your worst nightmare, that's how creative my fuckin' brain is. But I am stymied to think that I could do better than Cliff Davies and Rob de la Grange. Then I got Carmine Appice and Dave Kiswiney and then I got Tommy fuckin'... then I got Denny Carmassi and then Tommy Aldridge... think of my musicians! They're the greatest talents that have ever walked the earth! For sure, I mean literally, every rhythm section I've ever had, qualifies as the top 1% of gifted rock 'n' roll virtuosos that have ever lived. Name someone better than Tommy Clufetos, Tommy Aldridge, Marco Mendoza... you can't name anybody."

"And every time I look to the heavens, I go, man, you're a wild motherfucker, because here I am, it's time to make the record, because I never plan it. It all falls into place and who is available? But these motherfuckers. So I'm glad that you are focusing on that, because I'm really looking for journalists who at least have a modicum of appreciation for heart and soul musicianship because I am just inundated with it. I've got to tell you, I wish you could have seen last night in Lynden, Washington. You know, I've been around the block a few times. I'm approaching my 6000th concert. Are you ready for this statement? Are you ready for this declaration? I don't think you're ready for it. Last night, August 15, 2007 in Washington, not only did we double the attendance record in 2007, we doubled the audience that REO had the night before. That's been going on for a dozen or so years. It wasn't 100,000 people. I played half a million people, but it was about 20,000 people a' way the fuck up in Lynden, Washington. They had to recruit ticket buyers from 200 miles away."

"But here's a declaration that is mind-boggling. I never—and remember, I'm from Detroit; remember, I played *Fred Bear* in Detroit—I never heard an audience so voluminous and intensely... just decibels, as I did last night after we finished *Cat Scratch Fever* and we were getting ready to do the *Great White Buffalo* encore. My son is changing the screen on my microphone. I'm putting my headdress on for *Great White Buffalo* and he's looking at me. He said, 'Dad, can you believe this?!' Because he's been watching me for 30 years and he's seen the mountaintops I've been to. I guarantee you, Martin, up to 6000 concerts, thousands of them would rival any audience anywhere. Last night was a new peak. That's insane. If I was a more emotional, if I wasn't so manly, I would cry. Instead, my scrotum just descends a little further. So I take it to heart that the music, remember, you probably don't know this, but *Rolling Stone* won't tell you, the rock 'n' roll publications won't tell you because I'm not on heroin, I guess. I'm on the Board Of Directors for the NRA and I'm not in rehab this week, so I don't qualify, but I set 11 attendance records in '06, California State Fair, Oregon State Fair, Washington State Fair, Alaska State Fair, Nebraska, Kansas, Florida... all across the country I'm setting these attendance records. Tens of thousands of people in 2007. I'm so humbled I can hardly stand myself. So the music you hear, the cockiness and the spirit and the electric middle finger running amok on *Love Grenade* is in no small part due to the genuine intensity and enthusiasm of the audiences every night."

"I mean, it's off the charts; it's off the charts. If you would've seen the first show in London, Ontario. It's off the fucking charts. I feel sorry for bands like Deep Purple, who are an amazing band with amazing musicians and amazing music, but you can't follow me up there! You can't go on after my ass! Or you're going to be playing music for people to walk to their cars by. I felt terrible for them. But if you want to follow me, have at it, fucker! This is the energy level. You know, I'm 59 and I should not have this kind of energy. I should be calming down. But I've got a bumper crop of fuck yous in my garden this year. I've got enough to go around for everybody. So I'm feeling mighty good, mighty spirited, and I think the songs you are identifying on *Love Grenade* are your credible evidence to that."

So is there a little more fooling around on this one versus *Craveman*?

"Oh, I don't know if you can fool around more than *Pussywhipped*," laughs Ted. "I don't know if you white boys know this up in Toronto, but *Wang Dang Doodle*—I'm embarrassed to tell you I can't tell you right now if it's Howlin' Wolf or Muddy Waters. I think it was Howlin' Wolf's first single; his first hit record was *Wang Dang Doodle*. So I ripped that title off, because it's such a cool title. Now, subliminally, I used the title *Wang Dang Sweet Poontang* because I knew I had heard that somewhere. But I forgot the actual existence of the song, *Wang Dang Doodle*. Obviously, it's a proper and sincere celebration of the finer sex. So on *Craveman* and all my records, I mean, how do you get more goofy and fun-loving than *Wango Tango*? Get the fuck out of here. Do you ever hear that on the radio in Toronto? Because when you do, your car has another 100 horsepower. It's just so fucking fun.

We play it every night and it's so fun. It's the only song like it in the history of music. It really is. I think *Funk U* is right up there with it. I think *Funk U* is a combination of *Wango Tango* and *Motor City Madhouse* on steroids. I mean, screaming... how the fuck do I scream like that?!"

Which brings up a point worth reiterating once again. Incredibly, however much you are ready to cop to this pair of pounders being Ted's best productions, some of his best and heaviest writing ever... I'd venture to say that *Craveman* and *Love Grenade* are also the crucibles of Ted's most forceful, strong, powerful, convincing lead vocals of his career. Only Ted will never put himself in the camp of his vocal bloodbrothers... "No, no, no, those guys, Charlie, Derek, can out-sing me, sing-wise. In fact, Derek jammed with us in Las Vegas last week and he still has great pipes. He's jamming with us in LA House Of Blues and Anaheim House Of Blues this coming week. I'm just giddy about it."

But the riffing on here, that's another matter. "You see, my life is guitar patterns, which you would see in its finest moment on *Broadside*, *Bridge Over Troubled Daughters*, fuckin' *Love Grenade*, fuckin' *Girl Scout Cookies*, *My Baby Likes My Butter On Her Gritz* on *Craveman*—get the fuck out of here! Those are... my God, Martin, put my discography in front of you and listen to it—every song has this beast of a guitar lick, which is why God had sent Les Paul to electrify the guitar."

"I'm always adventuresome and experimenting," continues Ted, as we pick up on his mention of gear. "With Damn Yankees I used the goddamn PRS exclusively, just because I love the touch and Paul makes such a masterful instrument. I'm always playing around, with a Paul Reid Smith for the occasional *Little Miss Dangerous*, or of course *Fred Bear* every night and *Painkiller*—goddamn, what a fucking song that is. Jesus Christ!"

There's no question that Ted had achieved a new plateau of tonal boner magic power in a studio environs come *Love Grenade*, not to mention the power coming off the live stage from these trio configurations of his in recent years. "I can tell you right now, on 16th August 2007, I'm going to beat it. My guitar tone right now with a Gibson Byrdland and a Les Paul and PRS through these Peavey amplifiers that we're customizing, I'm thinking I'm calling these new Nugent amps either Love Grenade amplifiers or possibly

C4s, for the plastic explosives. But I'm tweaking these Peavey amplifiers and God they are rich, they are fat, they are just sexier than hell and I love them."

As for the inclusion of a new recording of *Journey To The Center Of The Mind* on *Love Grenade*, Ted says simply that, "We were jamming in the studio and Jack says, 'Fuck, we oughta record this fucker, 'cos it sounds great!'" The writing of that one was of course carved in stoned stone years ago, but Ted was open to his band and their ideas for the rest of the album. Turns out that the boss prevailed.

"Well, I would like to think that just because of the incredible calibre of musicians I always surround ourselves with, because of the open communication that I can still demand and cultivate and appreciate, that no one ever hesitates to tell me when there's a booger coming out of my nose. That's called friendship. That's called an honest genuine loving relationship, especially motivated by a musical shared vision. So yeah, the guys would comment, but, I'm like a runaway freight train. I wrote every lick, every lyric, everything, it's all mine. In fact, it's rather... it's a source of extreme consternation that on the *Craveman* record, that it gives Tommy and Jack credit on a couple of songs that they didn't write one note, not one lyric, not one guitar change, nothing! They were mine, but because my original guitar pattern was used... like in *Pussywhipped*, I think it gives those guys credit (ed. actually not). They're not writing on that. But I came up with the *Pussywhipped* theme line. We recorded songs as Damn Yankees, where we have an agreement that whatever we write together will be shared. But if they did on the original *Pussywhipped*, they did write some stuff, but none of the stuff they ever brought to the table was ever used on *Craveman*. That's because of strange, weird, cosmic legalities, that I give them credit where they don't deserve the credit. It's just strange."

"No there wasn't," offers Ted, however, when asked if any songs from the shelved third Damn Yankees album was pulled forward for use on *Love Grenade*. "There are a bunch of songs that I am dying to record with the Yankees. Just magic pieces. I've got a song... once again, I came up with a theme line called *Can't Stop Dreaming*, and our original demo of that is just one of the finest pieces of music's that I've ever had the privilege of collaborating with. It's got a guitar passage to die for. But I've rewritten completely around my guitar lick—that is one of my favourite songs I've ever played in my life. I hope one day you and I can get in the same room and I can play it for you."

That title... in fact, I'm pretty sure that's the one Ted *did* play for me! "Could be. Martin, I've got to tell you, I am a tsunami, a white water rapids of songs (laughs) and guitar licks. Every time I pick up the guitar... I mean it, people dismiss my hyperbole, but it's my only attempt to get close to accuracy, this flow of my music. Every time I pick up the guitar, those *Broadside, Bridge Over Troubled Daughters, Love Grenade, Funk U, Don't Tread, Crave, Pussywhipped*—they just blow up! Tonight I'll go to the dressing room and I'll tune up and an incredible guitar passage will come out. Brand new, incredible guitar passages! That is fuckin' unbelievable. That's what happens when you are clean and sober. That's what happens when you even acknowledge that your gift from God is a sacred temple, and that you treat your life with reverence."

Talking about the fiery new album with Jeb Wright, Ted immediately gravitated to the title track. "I am so proud of that. You listen to that opening guitar lick and there is no question who the fuck that is. The *Girl Scout Cookies* lick is a masterpiece. If there was a music industry like back when there was a music industry... it used to be the people in the music stores loved the music. The people who promoted the concerts loved the music and the disc jockeys loved the music. The bands loved the music and the people loved the music. People celebrated the music like *Walk This Way* and *Cat Scratch Fever* and *You've Got Another Thing Comin'*–they liked that spirit. You can't find a disc jockey, a promoter and a record store in a town that have any idea what the other guy is thinking. Music doesn't bond like it did then. I think guys who made music in the '70s and '80s spoiled people because the music was so good. I think we burned everybody out. I don't know what the fuck to think anymore."

"I love the song," continues Ted, on the subject of bringing *Journey To The Center Of The Mind* forward as far as it could go (not far) just like Purple did with *Hush* (not far either). "We play it most nights. We were in the studio with Jack Blades. I was playing with Tommy Clufetos and Barry Sparks in the studio—I surround myself with virtuosos. Every time I grab a guitar, fire flies. You should conduct an interview with Tommy Clufetos and Jack Blade—they will tell you that every time I touch a guitar a grind happens, a magical guitar masterpiece just blows up. When I tune my guitar, I always play licks to tune it—my old stuff. I play *Cat Scratch Fever* or *Motor City Madhouse* to get tuned up and one day I just started playing *Journey To The Center Of The Mind* as we were getting ready to record a song for *Love Grenade*. Barry and Tommy just kicked right in and it sounded like the Amboy Dukes back in 1968. Jack goes, 'That sounds fucking great. We should record that. I said, 'You're goddamn right we should record that.' So we did."

And *Spirit Of The Buffalo*? "What a great fucking lick. It says everything in Uncle Ted's life." While *Geronimo & Me*... "is like *Baby Please Don't Go* meets *Motor City Madhouse* meets *Tooth, Fang & Claw*. It is a celebration of the aboriginal lifestyle. The real Native American pulse is a driving force in my life. I have a great relationship with the Indians in my life. I hang with the aboriginal people in the places I travel. I hunt with the villagers of Africa and I hunt with the different tribes in America and I find it really moving. I wrote the lyrics at my anger over the abuse of the red man in America. I wrote, 'You cannot put me on a reservation/My spirit is a beast you cannot kill/Trail of tears, evil manipulation/You will never stop my honour or my will.' That is a fucking red man on a mountain on horseback ready to charge up your ass. I love that spirit."

Jeb also hits Ted up for a few words on his strange excursion into reality TV, the usual kind, 'cos Ted's for a long time been filmed partaking of outdoorsy pursuits. No, VH1's *SuperGroup* had Ted as one cog in a band of semi-ill-matched but well-known rockers preparing for a concert, as well as presumably trying to knock together an album, which never happened. The band called themselves Damnocracy and the show ran for seven episodes.

"That was cute. Scott Ian is the real deal. I didn't know anything about him because I don't care for that real Caucasian music. Evan Seinfeld–I don't care for that heavy metal stuff. Both Evan and Scott turned out to be good guys. Sebastian Bach is a good man but he was totally in a tailspin. He finally hit rock bottom a few months ago and his family forced him into rehab. He called crying his eyes out apologizing to me. I wish him Godspeed and I hope he is well on his way to recovery. This is not a knock to those guys but rather a testament to my incredible musicians that God blesses me with every year: none of them would qualify to be in my band. Well, I suppose Jason could be but Jason is not as good a drummer as Tommy Clufetos or Mick Brown are. He is not as good a drummer as Tommy Aldridge either. My musician roster is the best that has ever lived. Right now my music has never been more throttling in all my 50 years."

Back to *Love Grenade*, I asked Jack Blades about producing The Nuge, Blades, as I've alluded to, achieving what is perhaps the best damn knob-job of any record from Ted's long career. "Well, you know, Ted trusts me, because we've known each other for so long. We've been such good friends for so many years, that Ted knows I don't have another agenda when it comes to Ted. All I want is the best I could possibly get out of Ted. When we did the *Love Grenade* record, I remember Ted was like, playing different parts of different songs and stuff like that and he came up with a title. He told me what the title was he wanted to call the album. I said, Ted, that's not... what does that mean? That's like, come on, you're the guy who came up with *Intensities In 10 Cities* and frickin' *Full Bluntal Nugity* and *Wango Tango*. I said, 'What's a better...' and the next thing you know, the next day there's a message from Ted on my cell phone, I listen to it, and it's like the lick for *Love Grenade* and he says (screams), 'Love grenade! Love grenade!' I said that's it, you know what I mean? (laughs)."

"In other words, I pushed him and when you push Ted, that's when you get the greatness out of Ted. Ted is so intense, it's very easy just to go, oh yeah, he's Ted Nugent and he plays a lick and it goes like this and you go, 'That's cool,' and everybody goes, 'That's Ted, that's great.' But when he plays a lick like that to me, I go, 'No, come on Ted, where's friggin' *Cat Scratch* lick, where's *Love Grenade* lick, where's *Wango Tango*?' (sings it–one, do, dree, fo!). You know, that's Ted Nugent, so when we went in the studio, the beauty about Ted is, Ted is the real deal, man. All I have to do is put a mic up against him and he just goes for it. You don't have to coax anything... it's like (sings crazy). It's like that, it's like holy shit! You just get the best out of Ted and I've always got the best. When he does his solos, when we're playing solos, I'll be, 'Yeah, that's cool, but it's a little meandering Ted—come on!' I want to hear a 'whhooooooo!' Give me one of those notes that just makes the hair on the back of my neck go up and lifts my spine up. I want to hear that dying rhino, you know what I mean? Then all of a sudden you hear a 'whooo' and that's what's so great about Ted, man—he's the real deal."

"Ted pretty much wrote all the stuff for the *Love Grenade* record," says Blade, cutting off any ideas that the likes of Barry or Marco or energetic young Tommy are in the muck building things uncredited. "I mean, it was all about Ted. Barry is a great bass player and that band is so easy, to have somebody like Barry, because Ted does a song and Barry can translate it just like that. Barry Sparks is like boom—he just jumped on it and played great. The drummer we had on, was Tommy C, who is Ozzy's drummer, and Tommy C is just a frickin' slammer. I just love Tommy and he and I are good buddies. You know, they know what Ted likes. Then they just play what Ted likes. But Ted was like, 'Here are my songs; here's what I've got going' and all I have to do is say, 'That one's good, that one is like so-so, we need another one like that one' and boom, the next day there would be another one like that one."

"Constantly, constantly," admits Jack, asked if there was any debate about the amount of comedy showing up on the record. "But you know, it's Ted's record. Like my solo record. Am I going to play... people would give me a debate saying, are you going to do a song like *Anything For You*? It's a little mellower than what I normally do and things like that. But you know what, it's my solo record and I'm going to do it. Yeah, I had a big debate on *Girl Scout Cookies* and that kind of stuff. All those kinds of things. That's not my cup of tea, but it's Ted, you know and it's Ted's solo record. I felt like there's enough... there's just some great rockin' tracks on the record. If he wants to have something like that, if he wants to shake it up with stuff like that, then he can shake it up with stuff like that. It's okay by me."

As for an actual production philosophy, Jack is one of those guys who stays out of the way and let's the artist be all he should be. "Yes, it's very important to be who that person needs to be. Ted is just a frickin' gonzo guitar player—it's massive, it's big guitars, Ted likes drums way back. He doesn't like drums loud. You know what I mean? This is the way Ted is. It's Ted

Nugent, it's the vocals and his guitar. That's the important thing. With me, I'm more like a Beatles kind of guy, so I want to make sure there's frickin' killer vocals, lots of harmonies, lots of vocals, things like that, with everything sort of in the mix, in the painting, really clear. So as a producer, you need to look at exactly what the record is all about and that record was all about Nuge."

Post *Love Grenade*, there would be two additional live albums, *Sweden Rocks* and *Motor City Mayhem*. As regards the former, Ted told me, "I haven't listened to this new CD since we recorded it, so all I can tell you is that it accurately represents the ferocious talents, energy and dedication of my amazing band mates. I am *always* surrounded by world class virtuosos that put their heart and soul into every minute of every song at every concert. The calibre of musical genius that I am forever surrounded by is every guitar player's dream, and this *Sweden Rocks* live CD is how I have always dreamed that my favourite music would sound and feel. Mick Brown and Barry Sparks are my *Motor City Madhouse* gods of thunder!"

Reacting to the surprise inclusion of fully four tracks from the *Ted Nugent* album on *Sweden Rocks*, Ted figures, "I so crave all my throttling music that it is a mind-dusting challenge every tour to choose which kids I toss out of the boat. Lately we have been cramming many masterpieces into elongated dance-a-thon medleys. This live CD just happens to include a list of songs I decided to celebrate then and there. I can't go wrong."

But now he has to play them as a power trio—how has that changed what happens up on Ted's stage? "I also crave tasks and challenges when it comes to milking blood from my amazing Gibson and PRS guitars. My instincts to approach—attack—each piece of musical adventure are primal and pure, so I cannot really adjust or hold back in any way. It is this demand to flow freely on each song that brought me to the ultimate application of this six string carpet-bombing approach as defined by the trio setup. Though Derek is amazingly gifted and soulful, a good friend and extremely gratifying to jam, perform and collaborate with, clearly this grease-some threesome power trio is ultimately where I belong."

But sadly, this chat with Ted corresponded with the recent shocking suicide of drummer and producer during the golden era of Ted's career, Cliff

Davies. Cliff remained bitter about what had gone down within the group, but it is said ultimately that despondence over medical issues and the lack of insurance coverage to pay for them felled the musical genius.

"Cliff was a world class virtuoso, consummate professional and fine gentleman," expressed Ted. "We are all still in shock at his untimely demise. There is no question that he played a huge role in guiding all of Derek's vocal performances on those Nugent classics. He really put his heart and soul into milking the maximum emotion from Derek's already enormous talents and Motown Funk-brother touch. That Cliff, from a lifetime of mostly jazz/rock bands, so flawlessly performed my very demanding R&B-flavoured songs with such authority and soul is a testament to his amazing musicality. In the wind, he is still alive."

"It was a lot more than that," counters long ago Ted Nugent band manager Lew Futterman, when I asked him about Cliff's self-inflicted gunshot death only four months after I had interviewed Davies. "It's the subject of what would be a very interesting book. Now you gotta remember I was not intimately involved with Cliff during his last few years. We stayed in contact; I'd speak to Cliff every three, four, five, six months. I hadn't actually seen him for about three years prior to his suicide. Things were not going well for him financially. Cliff always had a lot of psychological baggage and a lot of guilt. He came from a very, very tough life. A mother who the husband walked out, poor, real British on the dole type of people, in Aldershot, the famous British army town. You know, *Gunga Din*, the line about Aldershot in that; we all learned that as kids before we knew colonialism was racist. He had a brother that ended up in a mental institution; he had a sister who got pregnant when she was 15. Problems… mother had boyfriend after boyfriend after the father walked out, who used to beat her and so on until Cliff got to be a teenager and studied martial arts and then kicked the shit out of one of her boyfriends."

"But he was motivated and despite being dyslexic, managed to get through music college," continues Lew. "He was a very talented guy who played several instruments and actually was quite a good composer himself and he made money with Ted. Whether he made the money he was supposed to make with Ted or not, I don't know because I wasn't part of those discussions. I was not privy to Cliff's deal with Ted and I don't want to make comments on something I wasn't privy to, but then he met this girl who herself had a troubled life. Lori, was that her name? With everything that went down, with his prior life and his sort of guilt, being the only one to sort of pull himself out of that morass that he came from—and he was very good to his family. He helped them a lot. He met this girl who had some physical problems, emanating, if I remember correctly, from a car accident that she never got fully compensated on, if I remember the story correctly. She had a lot of psychological issues herself and put a lot of pressure on Cliff and just the whole thing. The fact that his post-Ted Nugent career didn't go where he thought it should go. He had a lot of bills he was having trouble paying. He had all these guilts that I mentioned."

Was he himself sick?

"Well, when I spoke to Cliff literally a month before, he did not mention to me his own... that he was really in bad shape health-wise. He said he had some health problems, but that they were pretty much past history and he was dealing with the bills and so on. He actually called me asking my opinion on what I thought about how far he could go on promoting a Ted Nugent tribute band-type of thing and going out on the road with that. Some local guys... he asked me what I thought. How much he could use the Ted Nugent name and this and that. I gave him whatever thoughts I had within the framework of my limited knowledge of copyright law and trademark and so on. Then the next thing I heard, a few weeks later or a month later, was that Cliff had killed himself. He did not give me in that last conversation any indication that it was that bad. But of course people don't. People, very often, they hide things and then one day boom."

You never know, but Cliff's death may have been a factor in Ted getting back together once again with his old nemesis Derek St. Holmes. "It's great," confided Derek, talking to Jeb Wright. "Last year was a riot. Ted is as sweet as he can be and it is just a wonderful thing, to be honest with you. It is so much fun being back. Ted is nicer than he has ever been and he is really being gracious. I guess we get older and we get kinder and gentler. Ted is really a riot to be around. Sometimes it is embarrassing how much he praises me over the microphone. Ted is at a place in his life where he is really happy. Ted called me up a few weeks after the tour was over and he said, 'Derek, I just wanted to call you and tell you how great it is to have you back in the band. I am really going to enjoy growing old together.'"

"People want to hear the songs the way they sounded on the original recordings," continues St. Holmes. "When we play, it really sounds like the real deal. We are going out with REO and Styx and we are opening up. I have to say that somebody should bring some flowers for those guys because we are a band on fire and we are going to play as hard as we can. We are just so glad to get back out there again. I am looking forward to maybe getting a chance to record some stuff. It has been a long time since we recorded together. He is into it but he is really wrapped up in doing the hunting shows and he has a new pilot he is shooting called *Welcome To The Nugent Family*, or something like that. But I have started writing music that sounds like the first Ted Nugent album. I say we go retro and we go back to the big licks and we hit it fast and hard like we used to and take no prisoners. He is thinking the same thing and I've heard some of the music he has been writing and it is awesome. I have been writing the same kind of things like we did back then. I try to add to things and give him ideas, like we used to. I have three things that are only half done because I want him to finish them. When he touches them they are going to turn into the Ted Nugent magic."

"I didn't think it was going to happen," muses Derek, about he and Ted re-joining forces. "I knew we would always play and sit in with each other, now and then. I never thought he would ask me to come back to the band. I think it is a great thing for both of us as we both get a chance to come back in the band and do what we do best. The first couple of nights we played together I saw that he could spread his wings and fly. He didn't need to be anchored to the ground like he had in the past. He didn't have to be a singer and a guitar player and an entertainer. I think it was wearing him out. Don't get me wrong, that boy can do it but why not call your buddy and make it easy? But Ted's manager called me and it took him about five minutes to tell me that Ted wanted me back in the band. When he got done I said, 'I'm in. Let's see what we can do.' So, it took all of five minutes. The first time we rehearsed, I remember that it was just like the old days. I think I am singing better today than I have ever sung in my life. I've sat around for 15 years and listened to people moan and groan about how they can't sing anymore and all I want to do is sing. I'm lucky. I pace myself through the show but that is really all I do. By the time I hit the stage I am ready to rock because I have been waiting for that moment all day."

But it's not just singing. Derek is almost incredulous at the fact that Ted is supporting him as a guitarist as well. "I have to tell you that Ted has started doing just that. He says, 'This is Derek St. Holmes from the Motor City and he knows how to play guitar. Come on Derek, play some guitar; show them how you can play that guitar.' I start wailing away and then he comes over and says, 'How about I join in with you?' We start going back and forth and we are smoking. I was at my little house out in the country with my half stack of Marshalls totally cranked up. I was going through a couple of chord changes that I'm going to bring to Ted when I see him in a couple of days. The music was so powerful that the flock of turkeys that were in my front yard took off."

"I have been through a lot of hardships that a lot of people don't even know about it," reflects Derek. "People ask me all the time, 'Derek, where have you been?' I just tell them that life just happens to you. Sometimes kids happen as well. I took a few years to take care of the kids and keep them on the straight and narrow. Now, they are all out on their own and they actually told me, 'Dad, it's time for you to go back and play music.' I think the last time you and I talked, I was standing in my driveway in Georgia and I was married to someone else and that ended up bad and it ended not too long after you and I had that conversation. I have met a girl and we are going to get married in August. She is a wonderful woman. I wanted to get married in Vegas but she has two daughters and they want to be involved and I think my kids want to be there so we are going to do it in August."

"Last year, we did about ten weeks on the road and I got tired of being on the bus so Ted told me that I could jump on the plane with him and come back to his house. He told me that I could come with him every night. I didn't want to intrude but as it turned out, a lot of the times we would show up and nobody else was home, as Ted has a few other homes and everybody was out and about. The next morning, we get up and we're sitting on the couch and we're convalescing, as we are tired. Ted looks at me and goes, 'What the heck were we thinking about back then? What did we even argue about that led to us not playing together anymore?' I said, 'I think what probably happened is that they worked us so much that we were just together so much–familiarity breeds contempt–they never let us breath or take a vacation, and it just got to the point that we exploded.' If you take three kids and put them in the back seat of a car they will do okay for a while but if you keep them there too long then they will start going, 'Mom, tell him to stop breathing on me.' I think that is what happened to us. We just exploded, inside out."

"One night we were getting ready to go on stage and Ted recites the entire night of our fight that broke us up. I thought that he didn't remember it but he remembered everything about it, exactly the way it happened. We just looked at each other and said, 'We were dumb asses.' We are so far removed from that now that it is like talking about something that happened to other people. We have different priorities now. Our families come first and then we want to get together and play music. All I want to do is to back his ass up against the wall. I know exactly when to back him up and when to let him breath, or when to stop playing and when to be there for him–no one knows that better than me."

"Ted is much more aware of the people around him and of other people's feelings," offers Derek in closing. "Sometimes I go, 'Okay, who stole Ted?' (laughs). In all sincerity, we've all travelled a really long road and some of us are not here anymore. I think all of that kind of stuff has taken a toll on us, I know it has taken a toll on me. We want to use the time we have left to make a lot of good music and to make a lot of friends and look after each other."

Not just Derek. Good ol' Charlie Huhn too. "We just did a date with Ted last year," chuckles Roger Earl, who's in Charlie's band now and that would be Foghat, of course. "He was as funny as ever. Charlie used to sing with Ted, '78 through the early '80s. *Weekend Warriors*, is that what it was called? I like to give credit where credit was due (laughs). It was the Ted Nugent band. Nobody needs to know who the name of the singer was or the drummer or the bass player (laughs). He was on a couple of key records, but Ted didn't like to let on. Though we love him. I remember one show we did this last summer out in Montana, big festival, Ted was headlining and we were second on the bill. After we got off, Ted comes into the dressing room and I don't think Charlie had seen him in a number of years. But he was really good. He sat down and had a glass of wine with us and he was just telling stories. I don't think I can repeat them. I'll let Ted repeat them. He'll be much better at telling his own stories. But he's a fun guy, really funny too. Then he gets up onstage to do his set and after about three or four songs he says to the audience, 'How 'bout those Foghats?' The audience all cheers and goes wild. He goes, 'Yeah, I love that shit too.' (laughs). It was very cool."

As we come full circle, Ted's raps on the magic of playing live, right up to the here and now... well they haven't changed. "When I'm onstage I am absolutely inebriated by my inexhaustible quest to satisfy my musical cravings. In order to play the kind of music I play, it is so intense, it is so volatile, it is so animal and outrageous, that how can you not manifest that in physical gyrations? How can you play the solo of *Wang Dang Sweet Poontang* and not hit the dust? How can you not fall back against those amps when I'm going for those feedback notes? You can't get the feedback note over there. You've gotta haul ass over here and find it in front of those speakers and you're probably going to smash into the speakers. While people went, oh my God, that guy's charging his amps and he's smashing into his speakers, yeah! But I wasn't doing it for them, I was trying to find the fucking note. You know what I mean? When James Brown went into those dances, I guarantee he didn't consult with a choreographer. It is as raw and primal. I give you ZZ Top during *Fandango!*, I give you the Cheap Trickers, I give you Green Day, I give you the Chili Peppers, I give you Jack White, I give you Kid Rock. All of us, we just... we exude what it is we're feeling up there and that's entertaining as hell when you put your heart and soul into it."

"There is no more first times. So like right now, I gotta tell you... you know, am I selling out Cal Jams today? No. Am I doing 50,000 people at a ribfest? Yes. Am I doing 30,000 people at a River's Day on the Mississippi river? Yes. Am I playing a 2,000 seat club in Fort Wayne? Yes. It's all perfect. Here's the ultimate defining statement about Ted Nugent's career. I started playing at the state fair in Michigan in 1958, and in 2011 I'm going on tour and I've already got the entire summer booked; some of the dates are as good as sold out as we're sitting here and we're talking about a 50-year career. My greatest tour in my life, 2010. Bar none. Not even close. The only thing close to it was 2009, with Mick Brown on drums and Greg Smith on bass—these guys are delivering that primal scream indecency of the original Amboy Duke music velocity. So it's all about... I think it's about longevity. I think it's about, can you still execute, celebrate and deliver your juicy, delicious apple, year after year after year? I gotta tell you, I'm a lucky motherfucker because if you looked into my audience in 2010, you see people, that much like myself, are drunk on the music. We love this shit. Mine is literally dog-paddling in the whirlpool eye of the storm. I live this stuff. I'm living this stuff more intense, more understanding and more defiant today than when I did when I was 15, 25, 35 or 45. Or 55. God help us all."

"I'm still volatile and outrageous and defiant because I'm not strangled by the music—the music is strangled by me," posits Ted further. "Because I can escape it and go hunting and fishing, spend time with special needs children that remind me of how lucky health is, how lucky life as a gift is. I spend time with heroes of the US military with their skin burned off and their legs and arms and eyeballs blown away and it humbles me to such a degree that when I pick up the guitar, I thank God I can stand and dance and breathe and scream and live this healthy lifestyle. It comes out in music outrage that celebrates that intense, sincere appreciation for every day of my quality of life. That musical influence will never, ever be compromised."

As our tale winds down, it's back to some choice bon mots from my own best chat with the Motor City Madman, beginning with a few additional loud reveries on the topic of aging gracelessly. So yeah, how was Ted treating his temple? (which, at the time of this particular pow-wow, he was 59).

"You know, I get stiff after I dance like an idiot every night on stage. I feel like I should be wearing some kind of brace. But I've got to tell you, compared to all the other buddies that I know that are 59, I ain't going to complain. Because I'm still athletic, energized... the footwork, the athleticism, is just stupid. It's because I take good care of myself."

Do any of your doctors tell you, 'Man your knees are a mess; your back is a mess.'?

"No they haven't, even though my knees are a mess, because of jumping off the amps all those years. I mean, some mornings I'll get up and I have to take a few minutes and slowly flex my legs because of all the years of jumping off those amps. But I've got to tell you, for 59, I can run with the best of them. I'm a lucky man. I'm doing the sign of the cross right now while I tell you that (laughs). But again, it's about healthy living and an intelligent diet. Not enough can be said about the venison that I eat. It is rocket fuel. The discipline of eating organic fruits and vegetables and good water and quality dairy products. No processed foods and minimal red meat. I say minimal compared to the average glutton out there who eats fucking 12 ounce and 16 ounce steaks. That's a Nugent dinner for four! I mean, my backstraps are maybe six to eight ounces—maybe! I eat fish three or four times a week. I'm a healthy motherfucker. Yeah, I weigh 210 pounds now and when I graduated from high school I was 175. But I'm not fat, and I remain buoyant and lively for an old fuck."

Now, at the risk of veering off topic further (but what the hell, we're almost at the end of our journey and it's been almost all music until now, as promised, hasn't it?), we're going to close out our time together this way. Namely, I'm gonna present to you most of the rest of this stimulating chat with our lead actor, 'cos, as you will see, it's pretty darned funny and it's perhaps representative of a final thought to leave you with: the idea that there is a whole lot more to Ted beyond guitaring. That industrial-sized can of worms is best left to another book and maybe another writer, although who knows? Maybe me someday. Anyway, consider this the casual jaw session after we've taken care of business...

"You're right," reciprocates Ted, after I agree with him, saying how big the portions are that you get hauled over to your table in restaurants these days—just enough of a prompt to set him off and away we go. "And you know what, Martin, I don't know how you can convey this—I'm sure you will do it with some sincerity and aplomb—but I watched the Van Halen press conference on the Internet. I just have nothing but glowing admiration for Alex, just a superlative virtuoso and Eddie, maybe one of the top two or three musical geniuses who ever lived. David is just the quintessential showman, clever guy, great vocalist, true soulful rocker. But there's Eddie's son—is he only like what, 17?! And he's got blubber?! The kid is fat?! I'll tell you why. The same abandonment—which is the number one crime against your soul— the abandonment of discipline that allows Eddie to rationalize smoking cigarettes, or all those years of the drugs and the alcohol. It's the same abandonment of parental discipline that allows his own child to become unhealthy and blubberous. I find that just damnable. If I was his dad, I would put that motherfucker on a treadmill and I would watch what Mr. Hand is bringing up to Mr. Fat Face."

When you see it starting at five or six years old, that kid's going to end up tormented for the rest of his life, fighting this battle... "Oh, for God sakes! It's about discipline. Now, you check out my four children. Fucking decathlon masters. Firm, athletic, muscular, bright. They have a good posture. They stand up straight. They carry themselves with dignity. You know, if this offends anybody, fuck you! If you're offended by my words, that would be guilt. Look in the mirror and get the fuck going and upgrade. I'm 59 and I still stand erect—come on! I'm in the airport every day and some of the fucking beached sperm whales I see walking around, it's an embarrassment. It's like saying, 'Hey God, thanks for the gift of life. Fuck you, I think I'll poison it.' I find it just delirious."

Sixty-five percent of people in North America are now overweight and half of those are classed as obese... "Dear God! Dear God in heaven! Inexcusable! By the way, nobody likes to eat more than I do (laughs). I can eat a fuckin' pallet of chocolate cake and stuff like that. But I don't! Because I give a shit! Instead I'm eating organic raspberries, strawberries, blueberries, and peaches from Oregon right now. That's my meal today. I had some fresh halibut earlier today, but at the restaurant, 'Would you like dessert?' I go, 'No, I'm going to be eating strawberries later.' 'Well, we've got some great chocolate, chocolate, chocolate, chocolate cake.' I went, 'That's great. Give it to that fat fucker over there.' I'm telling you, Martin, people who are offended by me are guilty. I mean, I had one of those little bite-sized Three Musketeers yesterday. There's nothing wrong about that. But kind of think intelligent—spirit management. I'm deep into spirit management, baby. You may have noticed that about me."

With Ted living in Texas by this point, nonetheless, he still grieves for Detroit. I asked him what he thought might ever have a chance of fixing the continued decay of the once rocking and rolling Motor City.

"Well, I don't think anything. I'll tell you the facts. Number one, I'm heartbroken. I'm heartbroken that liberal Democrats actually believe that the terms pimp, whore and welfare brat are legitimate job descriptions. I am appalled at the sub-chimpanzee mindset of an entire subculture of Americans and most outrageously common Detroiters who claim they can take all they can eat. They're all fatter than shit. They've all got bling bling. They have the audacity to claim they can't make ends meet, but they can afford cigarettes, drugs, alcohol and massive amounts of deadly anti-food. None of this is conjecture. None of this is opinion. These are the ugly fucking facts. That the bloodsuckers who are able-bodied otherwise, who insist on raping and pillaging the paychecks of the most productive hard-working Americans, the Michiganiacs, is the worst... is one of the worst crimes against humankind in the history of this experiment in self-government. I find myself on a hillside crying like an Indian at the white man's defamation of an otherwise pristine wilderness. The wilderness is our soul and the guilty bloodsuckers of Detroit and elsewhere are sinners of the worst kind unto themselves! The fix is the 'd' word. Discipline. But as soon as you bring up the word discipline you will be called a racist or a homophobe. Independence is about taking care of yourself, not laying around like a fat pig expecting someone to clean up after you. That has been the rewarded slovenly-ness that is most manifest in Detroit. They should be ashamed of themselves. They're soulless, they're anti-black, they're anti-human and anti-decency and anti-goodwill. I spit on their fucking stain. Because that's all they are, a stain on mankind. I abhor that."

And you're living in Texas now?

"Yeah, Texas is good (laughs). Just the machine guns alone..."

And Texas politics? Are you happy with the way the state is run?

"Well, I'm close with governors and senators. I spent many campfires with the good Governor Perry, without question, the finest governor in America today. Texas is certainly one of the finest places to really be a free man. Places like South Dakota and Idaho... Texas is right up there with them. Even though I still maintain Michigan citizenry. My tax bill will clarify that; the obscenity of my tax bill will clarify that. But I spend a lot of time in Texas now and I'm awfully tempted to change my citizenship, my residence. Even though I'm residing in Texas, I still maintain a Michigan residency. I am extremely tempted to change to Texas because there is more justice, there is more fair play, there is more celebration of real independence instead of dependence."

Life in Tedland, well, it's become defined over the midlife years as this bi-valve existence between hunting and "dancing like and idiot," half an immersion completely in nature, half about as man-made and un-natural as you can get, a smothering of the physical—if not the soul, done right, done Ted's way—in frenzied sheets of electricity amidst high, thick walls of concrete holding up hockey barns.

"Oh geez, I'm touring like an idiot. I think we're going to ramp up 75 shows on the third of September. I've already got the entire hunting season mapped out. Mostly with open time to spend with Shemane and my children. But I've also got a lot of hunts that I have sold out to book and guide and outfit, hunters from around the world, on my Michigan and Texas properties and I'm just going to have the greatest hunting season of my life. I can't believe it. I'm going to have the most spiritual campfires. I'm going to get more venison that any single man... any single living killing machine has accomplished (laughs). The wildlife is flourishing, certainly not just on the Nugent property but all across this great land. It's a great time to celebrate conservation lifestyle."

"The music will continue to flow. I have a guitar in every room. I cannot stop myself from grabbing it and end up using it on an hourly basis. I will lick my poor abused rock 'n' roll dance legs for at least six months. I will be filming a movie with Toby Keith, in a starring role with him, a movie that he has written and produced, that we will do this winter. I will be doing numerous speaking engagements this winter."

"But mostly it is the spiritual rejuvenating time of my sacred hunting season," continues this man of many sentences. "It is extremely inspiring and motivating and what is the word, re-creation—it re-creates me. So that when I come out of the woods next February, I'm going to come up with some more guitar sex god masterpieces to make the white folk dance. This saga continues. I'm a happy, happy, full, driven man, who sees no limit to the music and the nature cleansing of my American dream. I hope to spend more time in Canada. I've got some great friends in New Brunswick, Ontario, Québec, Saskatchewan, British Columbia and the Yukon. Magnificent. It creates uppity guitar licks in my soul (laughs). I tell you, if I was any happier, I'd squirt through the phone and get you all wet. With this band, it proves God loves me. They are so dedicated. Mick is great every night, Martin; he's the guitar player's dream. The only frustration I have is how to whittle down this arsenal of masterpieces into a two-hour show."

Backing up his words of praise toward his recent man-eating music through delirious deed, Ted indicates that, "Right now we're playing *Love Grenade* every night, *Girl Scout Cookies*, *Geronimo & Me*, *Lay With Me* and *Still Raising Hell*. We are doing those every night. I can't help myself. I just love it so much."

At this point, well, the musical chairs were to continue. With Tommy Clufetos off to whack for even bigger legends, Ted's new band—and band to this day—was to consist of himself plus the aforementioned journeyman bassist Greg Smith and drummer from all those golden Dokken years, one Wild Mick Brown.

"Yeah, wait 'til you hear them. You won't be able to see us for a while because we're out here in the West. We're doing Detroit. You ought to come down here to DTE. I'm sure Linda can get you tickets and passes. *Weekend Warriors, Journey To The Center Of The Mind, Rawdogs & Warhogs*, just ferocious. I swear to God, just ferocious. The spirit of James Brown dances across the stage with us every night. I mean, just think about it, our rhythm section. I mean, who is better than Marco Mendoza and Tommy Aldridge? I'll blow your mind by telling you: Greg Smith and Mick Brown. They lock in. They are locked in like animals right now. Have you ever seen two dogs that are fucking? They are just ass-to-ass and you can't separate them. That's how we are on stage (laughs)."

And the voice is good? No problem singing?

"Unbelievable. It's unbelievable because I scream like a fucking banshee every night. *Weekend Warriors*, I get that melody right every night. *Free For All* has a new funk to it; songs like *Love Grenade* are very melodic, I think. And *Girl Scout Cookies* is just so grinding and stupid. But yeah man, I've got it down. It just has a life of its own."

To closet this chapter, it was autumn when we spoke, and it's autumn as I write this...

"It re-creates," says Uncle Ted, talking about this very Ted-headed time of year. "There's a healing power in nature that you can hear in my music. It invigorates. It stimulates, gets the blood flowing. You've got to get out there though. You've got to walk to slow down and turn up the stealth. You know, my music, the intensity of my music is a direct result of my understanding of this sensuality of a higher level of awareness that is bowhunting. You just don't get protein with a sharp stick unless you have a supreme love of awareness. If you comply, as I have, with that higher level of awareness, to be a good neighbour, to be a good generous human being, a caring family neighbour, a participant, a guitar player for my guys, a reverential guitar player for the song, a dedicated performer for the audience and looking them in the eye. Laughing and smiling and getting that little teasing thing going on, real genuine heart and soul communication. A higher level of awareness will serve mankind as well as it has served me. It comes from the healing power of nature. It's as cool as it gets, man. I look forward to seeing you again. God bless."

Epic-logue 3: New Frontiers

As if to prove that the author's assessment of his latest twin-turboed studio albums was not in error, Ted followed up these (and yes, more live albums) with another smoking live record called *Ultralive Ballisticrock*, issued 22nd October 2103 for his new label, Frontiers Music.

As Ted most poetically told *Classic Rock Revisited*, "I'm up, the band is up, the attitude is up, the spirit is up and the middle finger is up. I am telling you it ain't right. You ain't right, we ain't right, it ain't right; we all deserve each other. Every night is a musical orgy. The guys are playing so good. I think we captured it well on the new *Ultralive Ballisticrock*. The most energized musical jihad of my life is going on right now. What Mick, Greg and Derek put into this is like a chronology of attitude, piss and vinegar. The energy level that we are ascending to this year really defies gravity. If Ted Nugent of 25 years ago showed up, we would kick his ass and I was pretty damn energetic then! The fun factor and the attitude are there. This band put their heart and soul into what they do. We appreciate the audience. The reciprocity is unstoppable and we captured this on this new album."

When Jeb Wright points out that as part of Ted's classic patter all over this record he says that every song is the most important song, Ted responds that, "As I was wrestling with trying to figure out what songs to play in our two hours, as there are some songs that would be a felony not to play... it would be a crime not to play *Free For All*. If I don't play *Wango Tango* then we're all going to jail. I realized that I really love these songs and that every song is really the most important song. I realized that every concert is the most important concert. Every lick and every sound is the most important of our life. We really put our heart and soul into every sound we make in this band. I learned that from the early days of Mitch Ryder, the Detroit Wheels and all of the Motown Funk Brothers. They never did a bad show. Little

Richard never did a bad show. James Brown never did a band show. You can't let yourself be anything but the maximum best every night. With Derek, Mick and Greg, I am the luckiest guitar player on the face of the earth because they are 100% every time, 100% all of the time."

Of note there is that Derek St. Holmes is back with Ted, always on and off, but when he hits the stage and sings *Hey Baby*, well, he's always on. "That is why we had to record this stuff, because I knew we were on fire. Derek has been back the last few years and he has brought back that great voice to those Nugent classics. We are fans way before we are musicians. We love the inspiration of those black gods that inspired us to play music in the first place. We learned how the Rolling Stones took that American black music and brought it back and turned it into what they did. We were on that wave and we love it more today than ever and we wanted to capture that intensity."

Wright makes sure to thank Ted for all the charitable work he does behind the scenes, his love of people that is often shouted down by the aggressive politicking he does from the stage or at speaking podiums. "When you go through life as gregarious as I do, I hang with a lot of people. You will never find a backstage area roped off, as we have the band and crew and their families and my friends and family are there. There is a real openness and a sense of gathering. This means outside families too. This goes all the way back to the 1960s, as I was very gregarious way back then. I emphasize the genuine connection because there have always been my hunting buddies. That is a passionate lifestyle and there is a strong bond when you kill and eat your own food and you monitor the quality of the air, soil and water. All of this that I tell you now proves that I really, really care. When you really care, you are always driven, instinctively, to give back. I have families whose dying little boy or girl wants to go hunt with Ted Nugent before they pass away. I'm a pretty creative guy, but I can't think of anything more emotional than that. I feel blessed and humbled that they would even think of me in their traumatic and painful times. When it comes to charities, there is not a children's charity on the planet that we don't donate to, or raise funds for, or donate things for auctions to raise money for them. We are also touched very deeply by military charities because those are the ones that touch me the deepest, so we give to them the deepest."

Looking down the road to the creation of a new studio album, Ted let's his positive shield down a bit and laments what is happening to artist now that music is essentially free. "I have so much new stuff, it is unnatural. I have some cranking sons of bitches ready to go. I will have a brand new record out next summer. It is about logistics, and here is the painful, ugly, and what I believe is a criminal reality: you invest your life savings to go in and hire producers, engineers, go into a studio and buy equipment, and get the band hotels and lodging and travel and salary... you invest your life savings into a product that people get for free when you distribute it. Are you kidding me? Where is the incentive there? In the last couple of days, I have been on the phone with Billy Gibbons, Kid Rock, Steven Tyler and Sammy Hagar and we are all saying the same thing. I don't know if you saw the episode of Guitar Sessions with Joe Walsh, but he nailed it: 'The digital monster ate the music.' It's a tragedy. Thank God for those of us who were there at the explosion of it. We are all still out here cranking it up because we still have it, we still love it and we still believe in it. Real music lovers that feel and understand that soulfulness of those inspirations will always show up. I've got to believe that Kid Rock will come up with something, or maybe Jack White. I don't know maybe Green Day's next record will have some throttle left in it. I know mine will, but I have to hope that the industry is alive enough to embrace it."

There was definitely some throttle left in Uncle Ted as he delivered what he was promising there, a new studio album, called *Shut Up & Jam!*, issued 8th July 2014. With that came another one of those happy hellos from the Whackmaster that I look forward to every time the man has got some music to jaw over. "How can I not celebrate the next musical adventure?" roars Nugent. "I mean, what are you gonna do, be mute on it? I'm so fuckin' excited I might squirt through the phone on ya. I'm having so much fun. Have you heard any of this yet, Martin?"

Indeed I had, and once more, it was so deep an' damn inspiring that Ted had not lost any of the fire burning red hot from the last two records. And yet *Shut Up & Jam!* was more of a homey and organic collection of songs and sounds, a little more retro and even Southern than the metal might exhibited on the last two, but every bit as well-written.

"You know, I gotta tell you, I predicted that assessment. Because I have a feeling there's a bunch of us still around—and I mean a bunch, a huge swath of humanity, hundreds of millions of us—that like rock, that like that honest, spontaneous garage band spirit, but after a lot of practice (laughs). I've read all the reviews of *Love Grenade* and especially *Craveman*. *Crave* might be the greatest song I ever wrote—until some of these. I mean, I think *Fear Itself* and *Shut Up & Jam!* and *Everything Matters...* are you kidding me? These fucking songs are ridiculous! If I wasn't me, I'd buy ten copies of this motherfucker. You don't need me to apologize because you love this shit. I know you love this shit! Some of us still love this shit."

But there's that difference, an analogue warmth here and I wondered if Ted saw it without me suggesting it to him... "It was so eruptive. By that... you and I have known each other a long time, so I don't really have to explain this in detail like I will a lot of interviewers, but I've lived such an escaped lifestyle. I mean, I literally just came in from running dogs. I mean we ran a rabbit, a big jackrabbit; didn't shoot him, because I don't shoot 'em this time of year. But my fucking dogs are completely dilapidated. I mean, they're so happy, their tongues are draggin', they just went in the pond and cooled off, because it's already hot here. My point is, every day of my life, I go back to year one. I go back to a primal scream as clearly as some Swahili in South Africa might. You know, yeah, I just slept in an air-conditioned house, so I'm not claiming to be as tough as they are, but I do run with the dogs. Even though my legs are worthless and I'm not running at all. I'm barely hobbling. In fact, one squirrel I couldn't shoot this morning because my legs literally wouldn't take me through the maze of the woods."

With that, Ted was referring to the double knee replacement that had him doing a bunch of his guitar work and vocals on *Shut Up & Jam!* sitting down and on painkillers.

"And it's worse right now than it's ever been, even in the 14 weeks since the surgery. But my point being is this music came directly from the cave. You know, typically all my songs are written—no, not all, but a lot of my songs—either on the road in the whirlwind of musicality, or in extensive rehearsals with the band. So there's a lot of music and a lot of jamming. A lot of old blues and a lot of inspiration from the spontaneous jam sessions that erupt. But all these came from coming in from these primal scream daily manoeuvres, grabbed a guitar and it happened. The licks happened! It's like a kid experimenting on a guitar the first time he gets a loud amp. But I can actually play. You know, I'm not fumbling."

"It's from sheer years of relationships with every one of those guys," continues Ted, referring to the extended band family on here, collaborating with old and new friends alike. "I could cry on the phone for you, Martin, because I love these guys so much. They love the same music I love and they really love me. They really love the passion and the excitability for an old fuck. Because in their lives, they don't know anybody even half my age or even a quarter my age that loves this stuff, gets more excited and silly and giddy and irreverent and just goofy with the music—and they thinks it's so cute (laughs). I mean, Johnny Badanjek has been around forever, but listen to his drumming on *I Still Believe* and *She's Gone*. This guy is almost 70 years old. I've known him for 60 years! He's been there, and he called me a dozen times since the recording, 'Yo, Ted, I can't believe this music. I don't know where you get this stuff. But I'm singing these songs. I can't get 'em out of my head. You have the best record of your life here.' That's an unsolicited testimonial from a guy that should be jaded. He shouldn't care, but he came in on take one. There was such an uppityness, such a positive... and I'm not talking about the bullshit uppityness because we all smoke the same reefer. Because that's just the opposite of what I'm talking about. We all came in and had a flood of mocha and jammed these songs and got high on the songs and each other's musical communication."

"Here at 60 fucking five and a half, I think it's more youthful, more garage band, more spontaneous. I literally called the guys and go, 'I'm gonna send you this riff I made on my iPhone. Listen to this riff! We're gonna record this. It's a song. It's a song called *I Still Believe*!' (laughs). So they couldn't have come from a more honest, guttural, spontaneous... I'll give you this as an example. I don't think anybody loves Eddie Van Halen more than you and I do, because of what his music has done. I can pick on a thousand artists, but I'll pick on Eddie right now. He never gets out of the fuckin' studio! He never put down the fuckin' guitar. So how can a pair of Labradors howling at a tree... and a lot of people go, 'What does that have to do with anything,

Ted?' Well, if you don't understand it, I'm not going to try to explain it. But I think you do understand it. That takes me so far from the music that I am so horny to play the music that these kind of songs happen! The Ramones wish they coulda wrote a fuckin' song like this! Am I close to your overview of this?

Heh heh, indeed, that pretty much explains it and if it all ends now—as our book must—Uncle Ted has nothing left to explain. But given how irrepressible The Nuge is, we'll let him get the last word in and explain it to us (well, this time, actually my best bud Jeb, but by extension, me and you too) just one more time...

"What stimulates us and what makes us want to dance and what makes us smile can be categorized as uppity, defiant, fun, tight, authoritative garage-band irreverent kick-ass rock 'n' roll. Who else could have written a song called *Shut Up & Jam* but me? I am an organic guy. I don't over-think anything. I respect and work on my intellect as much as possible so that I make proper and clever and positive decisions in life. When it comes to music, however, I can just turn the brain off. My guitar is plugged into my balls—and my spirit. I know that anything that comes blowing up off my guitar is so me. We've talked about this before, I don't think the music loving public—I was going to say that they don't understand the spontaneity of my career and my musical statements and visions. Now, however, with Facebook, if you want to have the time of your life, mostly good, but unfortunately in this time of good, bad and ugly, there is also bad and ugly, there are people that want to kill me because I eat venison. That is how sick some people can be. But, the positive, celebratory spirit of the millions of people that I communicate with on Facebook every day is a great thing.

What a relief that there are open-minded, educated, intellectual real rock 'n' roll lovers, real soul music lovers and real rhythm and blues aficionados out there. They don't ask any questions about where it comes from or how it happens. They know that the first Amboy Dukes album was a 17-year-old kid that just let it rip. They know that *Hibernation* and *Migration* and that every record I ever made was just how I felt. They know it is just a natural thing and that it is just spontaneous and honest as you'd ever want your music to be. I think the vast majority of the people who pay attention to my music get that completely."

"In my 66 year life, I have found that you migrate towards people who are honest and friendly and good and positive. In my music world, those attributes manifest themselves. You only go through life once and you end up migrating towards and attracting like-minded good, confident, intelligent, caring, positive, friendly, generous and fun people. In all of those categories I just mentioned are attributes of really good people. This band I have has those attributes and we all have that in the music. We all love and it is very diverse and far reaching. I think the tightness, soulfulness and that the band cares to play well and communicate with each other to communicate the emotion and passion of the song...I think that attracts real music lovers everywhere."

"My work ethic makes this easy," says Ted in closing, but, hopefully far from done. "I am sitting here with two tired Labradors from a squirrel hunt this morning. I played some licks on my guitar that are going to become monstrous new songs. I'm getting ready to go on a monstrous tour with the greatest musicians who love the music like we do. Why would anybody put a halt to that?"

Discography

I'm keeping this tight and disciplined folks. This discography being designed to be a handy, dandy guide you might flip back to and reference as you read along and ponder the albums, a quick checklist for you to see which songs hail from where. I've not put song titles in italics, the rule used elsewhere in this book, 'cos it would mean too many italics here. I've kept compilations and live albums just down to the necessary ones and have included timings, again, only on key releases to lessen redundancies.

When it comes to the Amboy Dukes, given that, that band is a short layer back from the focus of the book, I've left out compilations completely. One thing I figured mattered is a pointing out of band personnel because it changed so much record to record.

As I usually do in my books, I've also added a notes section to point out anything else I figured was important enough to make known. Additionally, I was on the edge with this one, but I figured I'd include the Damn Yankees because if you think about it, that was the most high exposure use of Ted's time within the realm of the music business post 1981 to this day 35 plus years later.

The Amboy Dukes

The Amboy Dukes (Mainstream, November '67)

Side 1: 1. Baby Please Don't Go (5:35) 2. I Feel Free (3:42) 3. Young Love (2:45)
4. Psalms Of Aftermath (3:19) 5. Colors (3:20)
Side 2: 1. Let's Go Get Stoned (4:24) 2. Down On Philips Escalator (3:00)
3. The Lovely Lady (2:58) 4. Night Time (3:11) 5. It's Not True (2:42) 6. Gimme Love (2:43)
Personnel: Ted Nugent: guitar; John Drake: vocals; Steve Farmer: guitar; Rick Lober: piano,

organ; Bill White: bass; Dave Palmer: drums

Notes: CD bonus tracks: J.B. Special (2:33) and Sobbin' In My Mug Of Beer (2:22); another version included only J.B. Special.

Journey To The Center Of The Mind (Mainstream, April '68)

Side 1: 1. Mississippi Murderer (5:12) 2. Surrender To Your Kings (2:52)

3. Flight Of The Byrd (2:50) 4. Scottish Tea (4:01) 5. Dr. Slingshot (3:09)

Side 2: 1. Journey To The Center Of The Mind (3:33) 2. Ivory Castles (3:21) 3. Why Is A Carrot More Orange Than An Orange (2:26) 4. Missionary Mary (2:35) 5. Death Is Life (2:08) 6. Saint Philips Friend (3:33) 7. I'll Prove I'm Right (1:38) 8. Conclusion (1:57)

Personnel: Ted Nugent: guitar; John Drake: vocals; Steve Farmer: guitar; Andy Solomon: organ, piano, vocals; Greg Arama: bass; Dave Palmer: drums

Notes: CD bonus track: You Talk Sunshine, I Breathe Fire (2:44) .

Migration (Mainstream, '69)

Side 1: Migration (6:06) 2. Prodigal Man (5:48) 3. For His Namesake (4:26)

Side 2: 1. I'm Not A Juvenile Delinquent (1:53) 2. Good Natured Emma (4:37) 3. Inside The Outside (3:22) 4. Shades Of Green And Grey (3:05) 5. Curb Your Elephant (3:49) 6. Loaded For Bear (3:05)

Personnel: Ted Nugent: lead guitar, percussion; Rusty Day: lead vocals, percussion; Steve Farmer: rhythm guitar, vocals, strings; Andy Solomon: keyboards, vocals, horns, percussion, strings; Greg Arama: bass, bass vocals, percussion; Dave Palmer: drums, percussion.

Notes: CD bonus tracks (same as for the debut): J.B. Special (2:32) and Sobbin' In My Mug Of Beer (2:21). Also issued, covering the Mainstream years, were three compilation: The Best Of The Original Amboy Dukes ('69), Dr. Slingshot ('74) and Ted Nugent And The Amboy Dukes ('76).

Marriage On The Rocks/Rock Bottom (Polydor, March '70)

Side 1: 1. Marriage: Part 1: Man, Part 2: Woman, Part 3: Music (9:02) 2. Breast-Fed Gator (Bait) (2:52) 3. Get Yer Guns (4:23) 4. Non-Conformist Wilderbeastman (1:25) 5. Today's Lesson (Ladies & Gentlemen) (5:30)

Side 2: 1. Children Of The Woods (8:27) 2. Brain Games Of Yesteryear (3:42) 3. The Inexhaustible Quest For The Cosmic Cabbage: Part 1, Part 2, Includes Excerpts From Bartok: Second String Quartet, Beginning Second Movement (10:05)

Personnel: Ted Nugent: guitar; Andy Solomon: keyboards, vocals; Greg Arama: bass; Dave Palmer: drums.

Ted Nugent And The Amboy Dukes

Survival Of The Fittest Live (Polydor, April '71)

Side 1: Survival Of The Fittest (6:17) 2. Rattle My Snake (3:00)
3. Mr. Jones' Hanging Party (4:55) 4. Papa's Will (9:00)
Side 2: 1. Slidin' On (3:03) 2. Prodigal Man (21:20)
Personnel: Ted Nugent: guitar, vocals; Andy Solomon: keyboards, saxophone, vocals: Rob
Ruzga: bass; K.J. Knight: drums, vocals
Notes: Band name as Ted Nugent And The Amboy Dukes.

Call Of The Wild (DiscReet, July '73)

Side 1. Call Of The Wild (4:51) 2. Sweet Revenge (4:06) 3. Pony Express (5:21)
4. Ain't It The Truth (4:57)
Side 2: 1. Renegade (3:33) 2. Rot Gut (2:45) 3. Below The Belt (7:03) 4. Cannon Balls (5:43)
Personnel: Ted Nugent: guitar, vocals, percussion; Rob Grange: bass, vocals; Vic Mastrianni:
drums.
Notes: band name as Ted Nugent & The Amboy Dukes. Additional personnel: Gabe Magno:
keyboards, flute; Andy Jezowski: vocals.

Tooth, Fang & Claw (DiscReet, July '74)

Side 1: 1. Lady Luck (5:57) 2. Living In The Woods (3:54) 3. Hibernation (9:19)
Side 2: 1. Free Flight (4:03) 2. Maybelline (3:28) 3. The Great White Buffalo (4:57)
4. Sasha (3:06) 5. No Holds Barred (4:48)
Personnel: Ted Nugent: guitar, vocals, bass, percussion; Rob Grange: bass; Vic Mastrianni:
drums, percussion
Notes: Band name as Ted Nugent's The Amboy Dukes. Additional personnel: Andy Jezowski:
backing vocals; Rev. Atrocious Theodoeius: guitar, backing vocals.

Ted Nugent (studio albums)

Ted Nugent (Epic, September '75)

Side 1: Stranglehold (8:22) 2. Stormtroopin' (3:07) 3. Hey Baby (4:00) 4. Just What The
Doctor Ordered (3:43)
Side 2. 1. Snakeskin Cowboys (4:38) 2. Motor City Madhouse (4:30) 3. Where Have You Been
All My Life (4:04) 4. You Make Me Feel Right At Home (2:54) 5. Queen Of The Forest (3:34)
Personnel; Ted Nugent: lead and rhythm guitar, vocals, bass, percussion, arrangements; Derek
St. Holmes: vocals, rhythm guitar, arrangements; Rob Grange: bass; Cliff Davies: drums,

vibraphone, backing vocals

Notes: CD reissue bonus tracks: live versions of Stormtroopin' (6:36), Just What The Doctor
Ordered (4:52) and Motor City Madhouse (8:38) plus Magic Party (studio outtake) (2:55);
Additional musicians: Steve McRay: keyboards; Brian Staffeld: percussion; Tom Werman:
percussion.

Free For All (Epic, October '76)

Side 1: 1. Free For All (3:20) 2. Dog Eat Dog (4:04) 3. Writing On The Wall (7:08)
4. Turn It Up (3:36)
Side 2: 1. Street Rats (3:36) 2. Together (5:52) 3. Light My Way (3:00) 4. Hammerdown (4:07)
5. I Love You So I Told You A Lie (3:47)

Personnel : Ted Nugent: lead and rhythm guitar, vocals, bass, percussion; Derek St. Holmes:
rhythm guitar, lead vocals; Rob Grange: bass, guitar; Cliff Davies: drums, percussion,
background vocals.

Notes: CD reissue bonus tracks: live versions of Free For All (5:13) and Dog Eat Dog (6:21)
plus an alternate version of Street Rats (4:14) featuring Derek St. Holmes on vocals; Additional
musicians: Meat Loaf: vocals, Steve McRay: keyboards, background vocals; Tom Werman:
percussion.

Cat Scratch Fever (Epic, May '77)

Side 1: 1. Cat Scratch Fever (3:41) 2. Wang Dang Sweet Poontang (3:17)
3. Death By Misadventure (3:31) 4. Live It Up (4:02) 5. Home Bound (4:43)
Side 2: 1. Workin' Hard, Playin' Hard (5:44) 2. Sweet Sally (2:34) 3. A Thousand Knives
(4:48) 4. Fist Fightin' Son Of A Gun (2:51) 5. Out Of Control (3:27)

Personnel: Ted Nugent: lead and rhythm guitar, vocals, bass, percussion; Derek St. Holmes:
rhythm guitar, lead and background vocals: Rob Grange: bass; Cliff Davies: drums,
background vocals, producer

Notes: CD reissue bonus tracks: live versions of Cat Scratch Fever (4:52) and Wang Dang
Sweet Poontang (5:44); Additional musicians: Alan Spenner, Boz Burrell, Rory Dodd:
background vocals; Montego Joe: percussion; Tom Werman: percussion, background vocals.

Weekend Warriors (Epic, September '78)

Side 1: 1. Need You Bad (4:19) 2. One Woman (4:04) 3. I Got The Feelin' (3:05)
4. Tight Spots (2:55) 5. Venom Soup (5:47)
Side 2: 1. Smokescreen (4:15) 2. Weekend Warriors (3:09) 3. Cruisin' (3:26)
4. Good Friends And A Bottle Of Wine (4:00) 5. Name Your Poison (4:30)

Personnel: Ted Nugent: lead and rhythm guitars, lead vocals, bass on track 10, percussion;
Charlie Huhn: lead and backing vocals, rhythm guitar on track 2; John Sauter: bass; Cliff
Davies: drums, electronic drums, backing vocals

Notes: Additional musicians: David Hull: bass on tracks 2, 5, 6, 8.

State Of Shock (Epic, May '79)

Side 1: 1. Paralyzed (4:09) 2. Take It Or Leave It (4:07) 3. Alone (5:20)

4. It Don't Matter (3:08) 5. State Of Shock (3:22)

Side 2. 1. I Want To Tell You (4:52) 2. Satisfied (5:49) 3. Bite Down Hard (3:21)

4. Snake Charmer (3:19) 5. Saddle Sore (3:16)

Personnel: Ted Nugent: lead and rhythm guitars, lead vocals, percussion; Charlie Huhn: lead and backing vocals, rhythm guitar; Walt Monaghan: bass; Cliff Davies: drums, backing vocals

Notes: Additional musician: Leah Kilburn: backing vocals on track 3.

Scream Dream (Epic, June '80)

Side 1: 1. Wango Tango (4:50) 2. Scream Dream (3:18) 3. Hard As Nails (3:39)

4. I Gotta Move (2:18) 5. Violent Love (2:54)

Side 2: 1. Flesh And Blood (4:44) 2. Spit It Out (3:53) 3. Come And Get It (3:18)

4. Terminus El Dorado (4:13) 5. Don't Cry (I'll Be Back Before You Know It Baby) (2:21)

Personnel: Ted Nugent: lead vocals, lead and rhythm guitar; Charlie Huhn: lead vocals on tracks 4 and 10, backing vocals, rhythm guitar; Dave Kiswiney: bass, backing vocals; Cliff Davies; drums, lead vocals on track 8

Notes: Additional musicians: The Immaculate Wangettes: backing vocals on track 1.

Nugent (Atlantic, August '82)

Side 1: 1. No, No, No (3:39) 2. Bound And Gagged (4:34) 3. Habitual Offender (3:09)

4. Fightin' Words (3:59) 5. Good And Ready (4:19)

Side 2: 1. Ebony (4:26) 2. Don't Push Me (2:34) 3. Can't Stop Me Now (2:35)

4. We're Gonna Rock Tonight (3:21) 5. Tailgunner (7:03)

Personnel: Ted Nugent: guitars, 6 string bass, lead vocals; Derek St. Holmes: lead vocals; Dave Kiswiney: bass, backing vocals; Carmine Appice: drums, backing vocals

Notes: Additional musicians: Donnie Backus: piano on track 8; Randy Bishop, Bart Bishop, D.C. Hawks, Mark Gerhardt, Verne Wagner, Jude Cole, Shawn Murphy, Rick Wagoner, Kurt Wagoner: background vocals.

Penetrator (Atlantic, January '84)

Side 1: 1. Tied Up In Love (4:23) 2. (Where Do You) Draw The Line (3:25) 3. Knockin' At Your Door (3:53) 4. Don't You Want My Love (3:30) 5. Go Down Fighting (4:42)

Side 2: 1. Thunder Thighs (4:07) 2. No Man's Land (3:24) 3. Blame It On The Night (4:13)

4. Lean Mean R & R Machine (3:56) 5. Take Me Home (5:06)

Personnel: Ted Nugent: guitars, six-string bass, vocals; Brian Howe: lead vocals; Alan St. Jon: keyboards; Doug Lubahn: bass; Bobby Chouinard: drums

Notes: Additional musicians: Peter Wolf: percussion, sequencing; Cynthia Shiloh, Kevin Russell, Rahni Raines, Tod Howarth, Zoe Fox: background vocals.

Little Miss Dangerous (Atlantic, March '86)

Side 1: 1. High Heels In Motion (3:35) 2. Strangers (3:53) 3. Little Miss Dangerous (4:50)
4. Savage Dancer (3:55) 5. Crazy Ladies (3:43)
Side 2: 1. When Your Body Talks (3:16) 2. Little Red Book (3:06) 3. Take Me Away (3:14)
4. Angry Young Man (3:57) 5. Painkiller (6:02)
Personnel: Ted Nugent: guitars, bass, 6-string bass, percussion, lead and backing vocals; Dave
Amato: rhythm guitar, guitar synthesizer, synthesizer, lead and backing vocals
Notes: Additional musicians: Patrick Leonard, David "Hawk" Wolinski, Lawrence Dermer:
keyboards and synthesizers; Ricky Phillips: bass, background vocals; Jay Ferguson: bass;
Michael Mason: drums and percussion, background vocals; Joe Galdo, Duane Hitchings: drums
and percussion; Rick Baron, Tommy Thayer, Sandy Slavin, Bobby Columby, Robby Weaver,
Jaime St. James, Carmine Appice: background vocals.

If You Can't Lick 'Em... Lick 'Em (Atlantic, February '88)

Side 1: 1. Can't Live With 'Em (4:19) 2. She Drives Me Crazy (2:45) 3. If You Can't Lick
'Em... Lick 'Em (6:10) 4. Skintight (3:10) 5. Funlover (4:45)
Side 2: 1. Spread Your Wings (5:59) 2. The Harder They Come (The Harder I Get) (3:39)
3. Separate The Men From The Boys, Please (3:55) 4. Bite The Hand (2:58) 5. That's The
Story Of Love (3:01)
Personnel: Ted Nugent: lead and backing vocals, lead guitar, bass; Dave Amato: rhythm guitar,
backing vocals; Jai Winding: Hammond B3 organ; John Purdell: keyboards, producer on tracks
2, 3, 8-10; Chuck Wright: bass; Pat Torpey: drums, backing vocals; Tom Werman: percussion.

Spirit Of The Wild (Atlantic, May '95)

1. Thighraceous (3:48) 2. Wrong Side Of Town (5:15) 3. I Shoot Back (3:50)
4. Tooth, Fang & Claw (6:49) 5. Lovejacker (4:32) 6. Fred Bear (7:41) 7. Primitive Man (5:56)
8. Hot Or Cold (4:31) 9. Kiss My Ass (3:20) 10. Heart & Soul (4:44)
11. Spirit Of The Wild (4:22) 12. Just Do It Like This (6:08)
Personnel: Ted Nugent: guitar, vocals, lyrics, attitude, backstraps and security; Derek St.
Holmes: vocals; Dough Banker: piano, background vocals; Michael Lutz: bass, keyboards,
vocals; Benny Rappa: drums, background vocals; Denny Carmassi, Gunner Ross: drums; Larry
Fratangelo: percussion.

Craveman (September 24, '02)

1. Klstrphnky (3:55) 2. Crave (6:19) 3. Rawdogs & Warhogs (3:37) 4. Damned If Ya Do (4:21)
5. At Home There (3:49) 6. Cum N Gitya Sum-O-This (2:37) 7. Change My Sex (3:03)
8. I Won't Go Away (5:32) 9. Pussywhipped (3:00) 10. Goin' Down Hard (4:13)
11. Wang Dang Doodle (2:58) 12. My Baby Likes My Butter On Her Gritz (3:52)
13. Sexpot (3:11) 14. Earthtones (5:39)
Personnel: Ted Nugent: guitars, lead vocals; Marco Mendoza: bass guitar, percussion, backing
vocals; Tommy Clufetos: drums, percussion, backing vocals.

Love Grenade (Eagle, September 4, '07)

1. Love Grenade (5:03) 2. Still Raising Hell (3:21) 3. Funk U (4:00) 4. Girl Scout Cookies (4:03) 5. Journey To The Center Of The Mind (4:21) 6. Geronimo & Me (4:44) 7. EagleBrother (4:38) 8. Spirit Of The Buffalo (7:29) 9. Aborigine (3:22) 10. Stand (2:43) 11. Broadside (3:36) 12. Bridge Over Troubled Daughters (3:36) 13. Lay With Me (6:23)

Personnel: Ted Nugent: lead guitar, vocals; Barry Sparks: bass guitar (except Love Grenade, Spirit Of The Buffalo and Lay With Me); Tommy Clufetos: drums; Jack Blades: bass guitar on Love Grenade, Spirit Of The Buffalo and Lay With Me, background vocals; Eric Martin, Will Evankovich, April Grisman, Amber Morris, Tommy Shaw: background vocals.

Shut Up & Jam! (Frontiers, July 8, '14)

1. Shut Up & Jam! (2:54) 2. Fear Itself (4:40) 3. Everything Matters (3:20) 4. She's Gone (2:59) 5. Never Stop Believing (6:11) 6. I Still Believe (3:44) 7. I Love My BBQ (2:52) 8. Throttledown (2:53) 9. Do-Rags And A .45 (2:13) 10. Screaming Eagles (2:52) 11. Semper Fi (2:37) 12. Trample The Weak Hurdle The Dead (3:28) 13. Never Stop Believing (Blues) (6:15)

Personnel: Ted Nugent: lead guitar, Fender Bass VI, vocals; Derek St. Holmes: rhythm guitar, backing vocals, lead vocals on Everything Matters; Greg Smith: bass; Mick Brown: drums on Screaming Eagles; Johnny "Bee" Badanjek: drums on She's Gone and I Still Believe; Jonathan Kutz: drums on Shut Up & Jam!, Fear Itself, Throttledown, Trample The Weak Hurdle The Dead, Semper Fi, Do-Rags And A .45, Everything Matters, I Love My BBQ, Never Stop Believing, Never Stop Believing (Blues); Sammy Hagar: vocals on She's Gone.

Ted Nugent (live albums)

Double Live Gonzo! (Epic, January '78)

Side 1: 1. Just What The Doctor Ordered (5:26) 2. Yank Me, Crank Me (4:29) 3. Gonzo (4:00) 4. Baby Please Don't Go (5:55)

Side 2: 1. Great White Buffalo (6:21) 2. Hibernation (16:55)

Side 3: 1. Stormtroopin' (8:43) 2. Stranglehold (11:11)

Side 4: 1. Wang Dang Sweet Poontang (6:19) 2. Cat Scratch Fever (4:50) 3. Motor City Madhouse (10:35)

Personnel: Ted Nugent: lead and rhythm guitars, lead and backing vocals, arrangements; Derek St. Holmes: rhythm guitar, lead and backing vocals; Rob Grange: bass; Cliff Davies: drums, backing vocals.

Intensities In 10 Cities (Epic, March 1 '81)

Side 1: 1. Put Up Or Shut Up (3:21) 2. Spontaneous Combustion (3:53) 3. My Love Is Like A Tire Iron (5:48) 4. Jailbait (5:15) 5. I Am A Predator (3:16)

Side 2: 1. Heads Will Roll (4:07) 2. The Flying Lip Lock (4:07) 3. Land Of A Thousand Dances (4:39) 4. The TNT Overture (4:31) 5. I Take No Prisoners (3:30)

Personnel: Ted Nugent: lead vocals, lead and rhythm guitars; Charlie Huhn: lead and backing vocals, rhythm guitars; Dave Kiswiney: bass, backing vocals; Cliff Davies: drums, percussion, backing vocals.

Live At Hammersmith '79 (Epic/Legacy, March 11 '97)

1. Stormtroopin' (5:57) 2. Just What The Doctor Ordered (4:57) 3. Free For All (8:17)
4. Dog Eat Dog (5:52) 5. Cat Scratch Fever (4:08) 6. Need You Bad (5:17) 7. Paralyzed (5:03)
8. It Don't Matter (3:19) 9. Wang Dang Sweet Poontang (8:05)
10. Stranglehold//Smokescreen (10:29) 11. Motor City Madhouse (10:10) 12. Gonzo (3:57)

Personnel: Ted Nugent: guitar, percussion, vocals; Charlie Huhn: guitar, vocals; Steve McRay: keyboards; Dave Kiswiney: bass; Cliff Davies: drums, background vocals; Tom Werman: percussion.

Full Bluntal Nugity (Spitfire, June 5 '01)

1. Klstrphk (3:59) 2. Paralyzed (4:27) 3. Snakeskin Cowboys (5:58) 4. Wang Dang Sweet Poontang (6:43) 5. Free For All (4:10) 6. Yank Me, Crank Me (2:43) 7. Hey Baby (4:12)
8. Fred Bear (8:11) 9. Cat Scratch Fever (5:26) 10. Stranglehold (9:47)
11. Great White Buffalo (5:20) 12. Motor City Madhouse (6:58)

Personnel: Ted Nugent: guitars, vocals; Marco Mendoza: bass; Tommy Aldridge: drums

Sweden Rocks (Eagle, May 13 '08)

1. Stormtroopin' (3:39) 2. Wango Tango (5:50) 3. Snakeskin Cowboys (6:14) 4. Free For All (3:55) 5. Wang Dang Sweet Poontang (8:15) 6. Rawdogs & Warhogs (3:53) 7. Soul Man (1:22)
8. Hey Baby (4:29) 9. Dog Eat Dog (4:30) 10. Still Raising Hell (3:20)
11. Cat Scratch Fever (4:37) 12. Stranglehold (9:55) 13. Great White Buffalo (8:26)

Personnel: Ted Nugent: guitars, vocals; Barry Sparks: bass, backing vocals; Mick Brown: drums

Notes: also available on DVD with additional track Klstrphnky plus the following bonus material: Live 2007: Journey To The Center Of The Mind, Weekend Warriors, Love Grenade; Interview with Barry Sparks and Tommy Clufetos, Bow Hunting with Ted
Ted on the Gun Range.

Motor City Mayhem (Eagle, June 30 '09)

CD1: 1. Ted Nugent Intro (0:57) 2. Star Spangled Banner (2:33)
3. Motor City Madhouse (5:17) 4. Wango Tango (7:53) 5. Free For All (4:28) 6. Stormtroopin' (3:26) 7. Dog Eat Dog (4:13) 8. Need You Bad (4:20) 9. Weekend Warriors (3:22) 10. Love Grenade (4:20) 11. Honky Tonk (2:17)
CD2: 1. Wang Dang Sweet Poontang (5:34) 2. Bo Diddley/Lay With Me (6:08) 3. Baby Please Don't Go (4:01) 4. Geronimo & Me (2:47) 5. Jenny Take A Ride (3:45) 6. Soul Man (1:30)

7. Hey Baby (4:30) 8. Cat Scratch Fever (4:30) 9. Stranglehold (10:43)
10. Great White Buffalo (9:43) 11. Fred Bear (10:00) 12. Outtro (0:58)
Personnel: Ted Nugent: guitar and vocals; Barry Sparks: bass; Mick Brown: drums
Notes: Also issued on Armoury Records as a single CD with 14 tracks. Eagle version also
issued as DVD and blu-ray; guest musicians include Derek St. Holmes, Joe Podorsek, Mitch
Ryder and Johnny "Bee" Badanjek.

Ultralive Ballisticrock (October 22 '13)
CD1: 1. Free For All (5:28) 2. Stormtroopin' (4:45) 3. Wango Tango (8:44) 4. Just What The
Doctor Ordered (5:40) 5. Wang Dang Sweet Poontang (7:55) 6. Need You Bad (7:23) 7. Turn
It Up (6:46) 8. Raw Dogs & Wart Hogs (7:43) 9. Dog Eat Dog (4:30)
CD2: 1. Hey Baby (6:32) 2. Fred Bear (10:26) 3. I Still Believe (4:40) 4. Motor City Madhouse
(7:01) 5. Cat Scratch Fever (4:30) 6. Stranglehold (10:35) 7. Great White Buffalo (9:22)
Personnel: Ted Nugent: lead guitar and vocals; Derek St Holmes: rhythm guitar and vocals;
Greg Smith: bass and vocals; Mick Brown: drums.

Ted Nugent (key compilations)

Great Gonzos! The Best Of Ted Nugent (Epic, November '81)
Side 1: Cat Scratch Fever 2. Just What The Doctor Ordered 3. Free For All 4. Dog Eat Dog
5. Motor City Madhouse 6. Paralyzed
Side 2: 1. Stranglehold 2. Baby Please Don't Go 3. Wango Tango 4. Wang Dang Sweet
Poontang
Notes: 1999 CD reissue includes Yank Me, Crank Me (live), Home Bound and new song Give
Me Just A Little.

Out Of Control (Epic/Legacy, June 22, '93)
CD1: 1. Baby Please Don't Go 2. Journey To The Center Of The Mind 3. You Talk Sunshine, I
Breathe Fire 4. Gloria 5. Call Of The Wild 6. Great White Buffalo 7. Stranglehold
8. Stormtroopin' 9. Hey Baby 10. Motor City Madhouse 11. Free For All 12. Dog Eat Dog
13. Turn It Up 14. Street Rats (alternate version) 15. Magic Party 16. Hammerdown
CD2: 1. Cat Scratch Fever 2. Wang Dang Sweet Poontang 3. Live It Up 4. Home Bound 5. Out
Of Control 6. Carol (live) 7. Just What The Doctor Ordered 8. Yank Me, Crank Me 9. Walking
Tall 10. Need You Bad 11. Weekend Warriors 12. Paralyzed 13. State Of Shock 14. Wango
Tango 15. Scream Dream 16. Terminus Eldorado 17. Jailbait 18. Little Miss Dangerous
Notes: Out Of Control is a tall format box set, featuring extensive liner notes by Ted. Rarities
include Gloria, Carol, Magic Party, Street Rats (alternate version with Derek St. Holmes on
vocals) and Walking Tall.

The Ultimate (Epic/Legacy, March 26 '02)

CD1: 1. Stranglehold 2. Stormtroopin' 3. Hey Baby 4. Just What The Doctor Ordered 5. Snakeskin Cowboys 6. Motor City Madhouse 7. Where Have You Been All My Life 8. Free For All 9. Dog Eat Dog 10. Writing On The Wall 11. Turn It Up 12. Street Rats 13. Hammerdown 14. Cat Scratch Fever 15. Wang Dang Sweet Poontang 16. Death By Misadventure
CD2: 1. Out Of Control 2. Live It Up 3. Home Bound 4. Need You Bad 5. Weekend Warriors 6. Smokescreen 7. Paralyzed 8. Take It Or Leave It 9. State Of Shock 10. Snake Charmer 11. Wango Tango 12. Scream Dream 13. Jailbait 14. Yank Me, Crank Me 15. The Flying Lip Lock 16. Baby Please Don't Go.

Hunt Music (Broadhead Music, June 1 '04)

CD1. 1. Spirit Of The Wild (4.26) 2. Fred Bear Jam – Live (10:46) 3. Sunrize Instrumental (4:57) 4. Tooth, Fang & Claw (6:52) 5. Fred Bear – The Original (7:42) 6. Earthtones (5:39) 7. I Just Wanna Go Hunting (7:40) 8. Sunrize Narrated (5:21) 9. Klstrbk (2:50) 10. My Bow & Arrow (5:14) 11. Great White Buffalo (8:10)
CD2 1. Physics Of Spirituality Part One (28:14) 2. Physics Of Spirituality Part Two (30:06) 3. Hibernation (16:54)
Notes: limited issue; a mix of previous issued music, rarities and spoken word.

Damn Yankees

Damn Yankees (Warner Bros., February 22, '90)

1. Coming Of Age (4:21) 2. Bad Reputation (4:29) 3. Runaway (4:02) 4. High Enough (4:43) 5. Damn Yankees (4:37) 6. Come Again (5:38) 7. Mystified (4:14) Rock City (4:28) 8. Tell Me How You Want It (4:32) 9. Piledriver (4:18)
Personnel: Ted Nugent: guitars and vocals; Tommy Shaw: guitars and vocals; Jack Blades: bass guitar and vocals; Michael Cartellone: drums

Don't Tread (Warner Bros., '92)

1. Don't Tread On Me (5:08) 2. Fifteen Minutes Of Fame (4:50) 3. Where You Goin' Now (4:40) 4. Dirty Dog (4:53) 5. Mister Please (4:19) 6. Silence Is Broken (5:03) 7. Firefly (4:57) 8. Someone To Believe (4:57) 9. This Side Of Hell (4:00) 10. Double Coyote (4:44) 11. Uprising (5:31)
Personnel: Ted Nugent: guitars and vocals; Tommy Shaw: guitars and vocals; Jack Blades: bass guitar and vocals; Michael Cartellone: drums

Credits

Interviews With The Author:

Appice, Carmine. October 23, 2002.
Appice, Carmine. 2010.
Blades, Jack. January 30, 2007.
Blades, Jack. March 8, 2012.
Branker, Don. 2010.
Bogert, Tim. 2010.
Brewer, Don. 2010.
Cummins, Jim. 2011.
Davies, Cliff. January 9, 2008.
Drake, John. 2010.
Driscoll, Kenny. January 8, 2008.
Futterman, Lew. 2010.
Gibb, Russ. 2010.
Grange, Rob. January 4, 2008.
Huhn, Charlie. 2003.
Knight, KJ. 2010.
Krebs, David. 2010.
Lyman, Steve. 2010.
McCarty, Jim. July 26, 2006.
Mendoza, Marco, May 1, 2012.
Nugent, Ted. May 4, 2001.
Nugent, Ted. August 16, 2007.
Nugent, Ted. May 14, 2008.
Nugent, Ted. June 2, 2014.
Shaw, Tommy. March 15, 2003.
Sinclair, John. 2010.
Steinbicker, Earl. 2011.
St. Holmes, Derek. January 3, 2008.

St. Holmes, Derek. 2015.
St. Holmes, Derek. May 28, 2016.
Uhelski, Jaan. 2010.
Wagner, Dick, 2010.
Werman, Tom. 2003.
Werman, Tom. 2010.
Whitford, Brad. May 11, 2016.

Additional Citations

Note: Some of these citations are incomplete with respect to date etc. If informed or corrected, I would be pleased to expand or amend any and all credits in future editions.

Back Door Man. Ted Nugent "Always Tomorrow's Licks",
Thom Gardner. June/July '76.
Circus. Tough Nugies: Ted Tells Tales Of Sin & Salvation
by Robert Duncan. 1976.
Circus. The House That Nugent Built. 1976.
Circus. Mister Mayhem, Ted Nugent by Drew Abrams. 1976.
Circus: Stalking The Elusive Rock Crown by Jim Farber. 1977.
Circus. Nugent's Cat Scratch Fever Spreading Fast by Stan Mild.
Issue 163, Sept 1977.
Circus. Double Live Gonzo! record review by John Swenson. 1978.
Circus. Is There Life After 'Double Live Gonzo'? by Scott Cohen. 1978.
Circus. A gallery of guitar heroes: Ted Nugent by Shel Kagan. January 2, 1979.
Classic Rock Revisited. Interviews with Ted Nugent and Derek St. Holmes
by Jeb Wright.
Creem. Ted Nugent: The Night They Drove Old Gonzo Down
by Kat Gisi. January 1979.
Day, The. Ted Nugent is awesome – just ask him
by Carol Brown. New London, Connecticut. September 23, 1980.
Detroit News, The. Dr. Decibel and Mr. Clean
by Jim McFarlin. October 19, 1980.
Dunn, Sam. Interview with Don Branker, 2011.
Dunn, Sam. Interview with David Krebs. 2011.
Dunn, Sam. Interview with Ted Nugent. 2011.
Dunn, Sam. Interview with Tom Werman. 2011.

Fuse. Interview with Derek St. Holmes.

Goldmine. Saints and sinners by Michael B. Smith. No.511. February 25, 2000.

Guitar World. Pride Of The Yankees by Mordechai Kleidermacher. June 1990.

Hard Rock. Ted Nugent: The Mad, Bad-Ass of Rock and Roll!!
Vincent Ford. June 1978.

Hit Parader. Ted Nugent Down And Dirty by Charley Crespo. January 1981.

Hit Parader. Ted Nugent rock and roll machine
by Hank Thompson. September 1984.

Hit Parader. Motor City Madman Roars Back With Little Miss Dangerous
by Andy Secher. 1986.

Kerrang!. 100% Proof by Laura Canyon. 1982.

Kerrang!. Ted Nugent On The Penetration Trail
by Dave Dickson. No. 61. Feb 9-22, 1984.

Kerrang!. A Byrd in the hand... by David Sinclair. 1984.

Kerrang!. Howe Now by Malcolm Dome. 1984.

Kerrang!. The Mouthtrap by Howard Johnson. 1986.

Kerrang!. Lick 'Em And Smile by Sal Treppiedi. 1988.

Melody Maker. Call Of The Wild record review
by Michael Oldfield. August 24, 1974.

Melody Maker. Cat Scratch Fever record review
by Michael Oldfield. June 18, 1977.

Melody Maker The Scream Dream by Steve Gett. June 14, 1980.

Music Express. Ted Nugent – 'Workin Hard, Playin Hard'
by Shelby. September 1977.

NME. Ted Nugent record review by Max Bell. June 19, 1976.

Record Mirror. Scream Dream record review by Malcolm Dome. June 7, 1980.

Rolling Stone. Call Of The Wild record review
by Alan Niester. Issue 159. April 25, 1974.

Rolling Stone. Ted Nugent Unleashes His Little Ball of Fire
Tom Vickers. Issue 210. April 8, 1976.

Rolling Stone. Nugent Raves On: Free For All record review
by Billy Altman. Issue No.226. November 18, 1976.

Rolling Stone. The Ted Offensive by Fred Schruers. Issue No.286. March 8, 1979.

Rolling Stone. Weekend Warriors record review
by Mitchell Schneider. Issue No.282. Jan 11, 1979.

Rolling Stone. Ted Nugent gets intense by James Henke. March 19, 1981.

Sounds. Pure power for numb people by Sylvie Simmons. April 8, 1978.

Sounds. Nuge is a monster: Scream Dream record review by Phil Sutcliffe. 1980.

Ted Nugent Special. Ted Nugent: It's More Than Cat Scratch Fever
by Jymm Parrett. Sept 1979.

Ted Nugent Special. Ted Nugent: Going 'Gonzo' With The Man-Beast.
September 1979.

Toronto Star. I'll be a good father now
by Malcolm Balfour. September 23, 1979.

Tour Book. 1977.

About The Author

At approximately 7900 (with over 7000 appearing in his books), Martin has unofficially written more record reviews than anybody in the history of music writing across all genres. Additionally, Martin has penned 50 books on hard rock, heavy metal, classic rock and record collecting. He was Editor In Chief of the now retired Brave Words & Bloody Knuckles, Canada's foremost metal publication for 14 years, and has also contributed to Revolver, Guitar World, Goldmine, Record Collector, bravewords.com, lollipop.com and hardradio.com, with many record label band bios and liner notes to his credit as well. Additionally, Martin has been a regular contractor to Banger Films, having worked for two years as researcher on the award-wining documentary *Rush: Beyond The Lighted Stage*, on the writing and research team for the 11-episode *Metal Evolution* and on the 10-episode *Rock Icons*, both for VH1 Classic. Additionally, Martin is the writer of the original metal genre chart used in *Metal: A Headbanger's Journey* and throughout the *Metal Evolution* episodes. Martin currently resides in Toronto and can be reached through martinp@inforamp.net or www.martinpopoff.com.

Martin Popoff
A Complete Bibliography

Motor City Madhouse: Going Gonzo With Ted Nugent (2017)

From Dublin to Jailbreak: Thin Lizzy 1969-76 (2016)

Wind of Change: The Scorpions Story (2016)

Agents of Fortune: The Blue Öyster Cult Story (2016)

Metal Heart: Aiming High with Accept (2016)

Ramones at 40 (2016)

Time and a Word: The Yes Story (2016)

This Means War: The Sunset Years of the NWOBHM (2015)

Wheels of Steel: The Explosive Early Years of the NWOBHM (2015)

Swords And Tequila: Riot's Classic First Decade (2015)

Who Invented Heavy Metal? (2015)

Sail Away: Whitesnake's Fantastic Voyage (2015)

Live Magnetic Air: The Unlikely Saga Of The Superlative Max Webster (2014)

Steal Away The Night: An Ozzy Osbourne Day-By-Day (2014)

The Big Book Of Hair Metal (2014)

Sweating Bullets: The Deth And Rebirth Of Megadeth (2014)

Smokin' Valves: A Headbanger's Guide to 900 NWOBHM Records (2014)

The Art Of Metal (co-edit with Malcolm Dome; 2013)

2 Minutes To Midnight: An Iron Maiden Day-By-Day (2013)

Metallica: The Complete Illustrated History (2013)

Rush: The Illustrated History (2013)

Ye Olde Metal: 1979 (2013)

Scorpions: Top Of The Bill (2013)

Epic Ted Nugent (2012)

Fade To Black: Hard Rock Cover Art Of The Vinyl Age (2012)

It's Getting Dangerous: Thin Lizzy 81-12 (2012)

We Will Be Strong: Thin Lizzy 76-81 (2012)

Fighting My Way Back: Thin Lizzy 69-76 (2011)

The Deep Purple Royal Family: Chain Of Events '80 – '11 (2011)

The Deep Purple Royal Family: Chain Of Events Through '79 (2011)

Black Sabbath FAQ (2011)

The Collector's Guide To Heavy Metal: Volume 4: The '00s (2011; with David Perri)

Goldmine Standard Catalog Of American Records 1948 – 1991, 7th Edition (2010)

Goldmine Record Album Price Guide, 6th Edition (2009)

Goldmine 45 RPM Price Guide, 7th Edition (2009)

A Castle Full Of Rascals: Deep Purple '83 – '09 (2009)

Worlds Away: Voivod And The Art Of Michel Langevin (2009)

Ye Olde Metal: 1978 (2009)

Gettin' Tighter: Deep Purple '68 – '76 (2008)

All Access: The Art Of The Backstage Pass (2008)

Ye Olde Metal: 1977 (2008)

Ye Olde Metal: 1976 (2008)

Judas Priest: Heavy Metal Painkillers (2007)

Ye Olde Metal: 1973 To 1975 (2007)

The Collector's Guide To Heavy Metal: Volume 3: The Nineties (2007)

Ye Olde Metal: 1968 To 1972 (2007)

Run For Cover: The Art Of Derek Riggs (2006)

Black Sabbath: Doom Let Loose (2006)

Dio: Light Beyond The Black (2006)

The Collector's Guide To Heavy Metal: Volume 2: The Eighties (2005)

Rainbow: English Castle Magic (2005)

UFO: Shoot Out The Lights (2005)

The New Wave Of British Heavy Metal Singles (2005)

Blue Öyster Cult: Secrets Revealed! (2004)

Contents Under Pressure: 30 Years Of Rush At Home & Away (2004)

The Top 500 Heavy Metal Albums Of All Time (2004)

The Collector's Guide To Heavy Metal: Volume 1: The Seventies (2003)

The Top 500 Heavy Metal Songs Of All Time (2003)

Southern Rock Review (2001)

Heavy Metal: 20th Century Rock And Roll (2000)

The Goldmine Price Guide To Heavy Metal Records (2000)

The Collector's Guide To Heavy Metal (1997)

Riff Kills Man! 25 Years Of Recorded Hard Rock & Heavy Metal (1993)

See martinpopoff.com for complete details and ordering information.

Other Martin Popoff titles available from Wymer

The Deep Purple Family:
Year by Year Vol 1 (- 1979)
Martin Popoff

ISBN: 978-1-908724-42-7
Paperback: 234 x 153 mm, 256pp. Illustrated
throughout.
RRP: £14.99
Publication date: June 2016

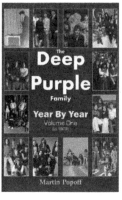

An exhaustive and detailed timeline of Deep Purple milestones - often to the day -
looks at the band's influences, cultural milieu, tours, recording sessions, charts,
singles, certification news, break-ups, personal stuff, trivia, mixed with lots of artist
quotes to add to the entries, turning the book into a quasi-oral history but loaded
with factual matter.

But this book is not just about Deep Purple but the whole family of bands that
surrounds it. Weaved in and out of the story are the dastardly diaries of Rainbow,
Whitesnake, Ian Gillan Band, Gillan, Paice Ashton Lord, all the solo projects, guest
slots, even Captain Beyond, Warhorse, Jerusalem, Jesus Christ Superstar,
Bedlam, Elf, Episode Six, The Outlaws, and Trapeze.

The book also touches on a whole host of other artists including the likes of
Uriah Heep, Black Sabbath, Led Zeppelin, Nazareth, Moxy, Silverhead, Hard Stuff,
Lord Sutch, Warpig, Vanilla Fudge, Brian Auger, Judas Priest, James Gang, Angel
and Legs Diamond - but always with contextual explanation that make this book
such a fascinating read and an absolute smorgasbord of facts surrounding one of
the greatest rock bands' of all time.

Agents Of Fortune
The Blue Öyster Cult Story
Martin Popoff

ISBN: 978-1-908724-41-0
Paperback: 234 x 153 mm, 256pp,
1 x 8 b/w plate section
RRP: £14.99
Publication date: May 2016

Forty years in the business... six gold & platinum U.S. albums... classic songs like (Don't Fear) The Reaper, Godzilla, Burnin' For You, Astronomy and E.T.I. Donald "Buck Dharma" Roeser, Eric Bloom, Allen Lanier, Albert Bouchard & Joe Bouchard comprised one of the great stadium acts of the '70s & '80s. BOC were heavy enough to duke it out with Kiss, Rush, Aerosmith, Ted Nugent & Black Sabbath, yet smart, funny, ironic & jaded enough to please the tough New York critics.

Agents of Fortune examines the complicated early days of the band, graphically demonstrating the showbiz sweat that goes into making a successful act. The book is centred around the peerless intellectual quality of the songs - made entertaining by the band's psychotropic & ghoulish humour; its interest in all manner of conspiracy theories, cults, monsters, vampires, UFOs, foul play, arcane spiritualism, alchemy, love lost & love buried, science fiction & friction.

Popoff draws on his personal interviews with Roeser, Bloom, Albert & Joe Bouchard, along with drummer Bobby Rondinelli, legendary band producer Murray Krugman & BOC expert Bolle Gregmar. For insight into the band's fantastic lyrical world, Popoff went right to the source, the writers of the BOC classics highlighting their creativity through the author's countless interviews with Sandy Pearlman (manager during the golden years), Richard Meltzer, John Shirley, cover artists Greg Scott and Ioannis, as well as the late Helen Wheels and David Roter. An essential read for Blue Öyster Cult devotees.

Wind Of Change
The Scorpions Story
Martin Popoff

ISBN: 978-1-908724-40-3
Paperback: 234 x 153 mm, 256pp,
1 x 8 b/w plate section
RRP: £14.99
Publication date: May 2016

No question Scorpions, Germany's loudest and proudest rock band ever, have been one of that country's most successful musical exports. *Wind of Change* documents the band's career with analysis of every song on every album the Teutonic tone-masters ever crafted.

Beginning with *Lonesome Crow* back in '72 through to the triumphant "retirement" album *Sting In The Tail*, and beyond into *Comeblack* - the stories of their making are all here.

Wind of Change draws on the authors interviews with all of the principals and beyond, including Klaus Meine, Uli Jon Roth, Herman Rarebell, Rudolf Schenker and Matthias Jabs, along with the likes of legendary manager David Krebs, Ralph Rieckermann and Francis Buchholz.

From Dublin To Jailbreak
Thin Lizzy 1969-76
Martin Popoff

ISBN: 978-1-908724-39-7
Hardback: 234 x 153 mm, 256pp,
1 x 8 b/w plate section
RRP: £19.99
Publication date: April 2016

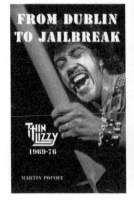

Dublin's Thin Lizzy have become one of the most revered cult acts of all time. Studious and discerning fans of hard rock the world over revelling in the storytelling acumen of the legendary Phil Lynott and the craft and class of his band.

Through numerous new interviews with most of the principles involved and a mountain of painstaking research, *From Dublin To Jailbreak: Thin Lizzy 69 - 76* examines the band's career up to 1976 culminating in the superlative and sparkling *Jailbreak*, home of such hits as 'Cowboy Song', 'Emerald', 'Jailbreak' and 'The Boys Are Back In Town' and *Johnny The Fox* that included the hit single 'Don't Believe A Word'.

Along the way, alcohol and drugs wreaked havoc between band members, producers and managers, but despite line-up changes and a mostly grinding, rock scrabble existence, Ireland's favourite sons persevered, finally achieving the smash hit record they'd deserved for so long.

Popoff's celebrated record-by-record methodology highlights a new appreciation of the deep album tracks hiding within this singular band's often forgotten early years. The book also reveals Phil Lynott in all his dastardly guises, making *From Dublin To Jailbreak: Thin Lizzy 69 - 76*, an essential read for the devoted fans.

All titles also available on Kindle